SOCIO-LEGAL INTEGRATION

Cultural Diversity and Law

Series Editor:
Prakash Shah, School of Law, Queen Mary, University of London, UK

Around the world, most states are faced with difficult issues arising out of cultural diversity in their territories. Within the legal field, such issues span across matters of private law through to public and constitutional law. At international level too there is now considerable jurisprudence regarding ethnic, religious and cultural diversity. In addition, there are several layers of legal control – from communal and religious regulation to state and international regulation. This multiplicity of norm setting has been variously termed legal pluralism, inter-legality or inter-normativity and provides a fascinating lens for academic analysis that links up to cultural diversity in new and interesting ways. The umbrella of cultural diversity encompasses various population groups throughout the world ranging from national, ethnic, religious or indigenous groupings. This series particularly welcomes work that is of comparative interest, concerning various state jurisdictions as well as different population groups.

Also in the series

Law, Religious Freedoms and Education in Europe
Edited by Myriam Hunter-Henin
ISBN 978-1-4094-2730-8

Islamic Law in Europe?
Legal Pluralism and its Limits in European Family Laws
Andrea Büchler
ISBN 978-1-4094-2849-7

The Challenges of Justice in Diverse Societies
Constitutionalism and Pluralism
Meena K. Bhamra
ISBN 978-1-4094-1928-0

Law and Religion in the 21st Century
Relations between States and Religious Communities
Edited by Silvio Ferrari and Rinaldo Cristofori
ISBN 978-1-4094-1143-7

Socio-Legal Integration

Polish Post-2004 EU Enlargement Migrants in the United Kingdom

AGNIESZKA KUBAL
International Migration Institute, University of Oxford, UK

Routledge
Taylor & Francis Group
LONDON AND NEW YORK

First published 2012 by Ashgate Publishing

Published 2016 by Routledge
2 Park Square, Milton Park, Abingdon, Oxfordshire OX14 4RN
711 Third Avenue, New York, NY 10017, USA

First issued in paperback 2016

Routledge is an imprint of the Taylor & Francis Group, an informa business

British Library Cataloguing in Publication Data
Kubal, Agnieszka, 1983–
Socio-legal integration : Polish post-2004 EU enlargement migrants in the United Kingdom.–(Cultural diversity and law)
1. European Union–Membership. 2. Culture and law. 3. Emigration and immigration law–Great Britain. 4. Immigrants–Great Britain –Attitudes. 5. Polish people –Great Britain–Attitudes. 6. Polish people–Cultural assimilation–Great Britain–History –20th century. 7. Foreign workers, Polish–Legal status, laws, etc.–Great Britain. 8. Ethnological jurisprudence –European Union countries. 9. Legal polycentricity–European Union countries. 10. Conflict of laws–Agency–European Union countries.
I. Title II. Series
340.1'15'089185'041-dc23

Library of Congress Cataloging-in-Publication Data
Kubal, Agnieszka, 1983–
Socio-legal integration : Polish post-2004 EU enlargement migrants in the United Kingdom / by Agnieszka Kubal.
p. cm.
Includes index.
ISBN 978-1-4094-3699-7 (hardback : alk. paper)
1. Emigration and immigration law–Great Britain. 2. Polish people–Great Britain. 3. Immigrants–Great Britain. 4. Emigration and immigration law–European Union countries. 5. Immigrants–European Union countries. 6. Sociological jurisprudence. I. Title.
KD4139.P65K83 2012
342.4108'2 –dc23

2011047350

ISBN 13: 978-1-138-27161-6 (pbk)
ISBN 13: 978-1-4094-3699-7 (hbk)

In loving memory of Stefan Adam Kalinowski, M.D.

Contents

List of Figures and Tables

Figures

Tables

Preface and Acknowledgments

My greatest intellectual debt is to Dr Marina Kurkchiyan, my mentor at the Centre for Socio-Legal Studies at the University of Oxford. I would like to thank her for the patient, thorough and many readings of the earlier drafts of this book, and her sharp, eye-opening, inspiring, sometimes painful, yet always extremely helpful comments. Remarking on the last four years, I feel extremely privileged to have been able to work with her and draw on her research experience and analytical thinking during the numerous meetings, discussions and conferences, dinners in Oxford and London, and ad hoc lunches at Wolfson and The Trout Inn.

I would like to express my deepest gratitude to the researchers: Dr Marina Kurkchiyan, Dr William L. Miller and Dr Åse Berit Grødeland, partners on the *Legal Cultures in Transition – The Impact of EU Integration* project, for allowing me to consult the data and use them in my DPhil thesis and this book. I would like to show my deep gratitude to the *Europaeum* Foundation for awarding me the Jenkins Memorial Scholarship for the years 2007–2008, which made it possible to commence my DPhil at the University of Oxford, and – during the crucial, initial years of the project – focus solely on the research work.

I am grateful to Dr Fernanda Pirie, Director of the Centre for Socio-Legal Studies and Professor Reza Banakar from the University of Westminster for their constructive and very useful suggestions regarding the future development of my work. I would like to thank Dr Prakash Shah, the editor of the 'Cultural Diversity and Law' series at Ashgate, for the inspiring debates on legal culture and legal pluralism, and his extremely helpful comments and cooperation whilst preparing the manuscript. I am also grateful to Professor Robin Cohen, Dr Oliver Bakewell and Dr Hein de Haas for their gentle and considerate questions, and for allowing me to take time off work and responsibilities at the International Migration Institute to polish the final draft of this book. I would like to thank Professor Hieronim Kubiak, Dr Jacek Nowak and Dr Arkadiusz Baron for instigating my research interests and supervising my development. I am grateful to the editors at Ashgate: Lianne Sherlock, Jon Lloyd, Fiona Dunford, Sarah Horsley and Alison Kirk for their support and thoughtful collaboration.

I would like to thank all my interviewees for sharing with me their life stories and the ups and downs of their migration experiences. Special thanks to Agnieszka, Aleksandra, Anna, Magdalena, Marian, Małgorzata, Piotr and Szymon. Without you it would not have been possible to complete this book! That said, any mistakes and omissions in this book are solely my responsibility.

I would like to thank my *Mama i Tato*, Anna and Kazimierz Kubal, for their love and understanding. I am very grateful that the alternatives they suggested to pursuing my DPhil were never tempting enough. I would like to thank my siblings Magdalena, Szymon and Marta for their support and encouragement (and generally for putting up with me). My special thanks are to *Babcia Danusia* for always believing in me, and to my late *Dziadek Stefan* – to whose memory I dedicate this book – who taught me that *Audaces Fortuna Iuvat!* (Virgil, *Aeneid*, X: 284). I would like to thank my dear friends Susan, Marc, Tatiana, Anna, Avanti, Ambika, Priscilla, Gunvor and the fantastic IMI team, as the times off work we spent together were always energizing, head clearing and totally worth it! My special thanks to Rebecca and Dominic for allowing me to draft the conclusions in the inspiring surroundings of their play room.

Aur anth mein, most special thanks to my husband, Ashish Thandavan, for always being there for me, just like he promised – for better or for worse.

Chapter 1
Introduction

Migration has grown in recent years to be an all-important social phenomenon. More people than ever are considered to be 'on the move', transcending various state, local and legal borders.

Globalization has additionally altered the context for migration. The growth of new technologies of communication and transport allow the frequent and multi-directional flows of people, ideas and cultural symbols. The erosion of nation-state sovereignty and autonomy weakened systems of border control and migrant assimilation (Castles 2002).

This happened in parallel with the growing 'super-diversity' of migrant populations (Vertovec 2007). Many host countries, like the United Kingdom, which traditionally attracted stable flows of populations from Commonwealth or formerly colonial territories, are now characterized by 'an increased number of new, small and scattered, multiple-origin, transnationally connected, socio-economically differentiated and legally stratified immigrants who have arrived over the last decade' (Vertovec 2007).

As a result, various studies examined these new forms of migratory processes and migrants' incorporations, particularly the emergence of transnational communities (Glick Schiller et al. 1995), various forms of identities and citizenship (Portes 1996).

However, with the exception of the legal pluralism scholarship (Ballard 1994, 2006, 2007; Grillo et al. 2009; Menski 1993, 2006, 2008; Shah 2007, 2008, 2009, 2011), not much has been said about how migrants build their relationship with law in the host country, about the nature of their legal adaptations. But it is primarily the South Asian immigrant communities (Bangladeshis, Sikhs, Gujaratis and Pakistanis) arriving in the UK since the 1940s–1950s which have constituted the main focus of the legal pluralists' analysis.

I argue that it is important to re-think our understanding of new forms of migrants' legal incorporations and adaptations, their multiple legal identities and multi-layered citizenship. Given this super-diversity of contemporary migrants, it is rather naïve to assume that one analytical lens will do justice to their various characteristics and relationships with law. Not all migrants arriving in the host country will carry their own 'legal baggage' in the form of alternative (to the state law) unofficial laws or customary practices of social ordering based on indigenous, religious or private laws (Chiba 1998).

If we are to understand immigrants' legal adaptations today, immigrants stemming from diverse and heterogeneous parts of the world, with different yet at the same time not so distant legal traditions (e.g. civil law), we need to examine how the perception of law is produced and consumed and then draw out its social implications, such as what meaning people attach to law, what expectations they have and how they behave towards it in everyday life (cf. Kurkchiyan 2010). This book looks at how contemporary migrants build their relationship with law in the host country, how this relationship is being formed – and transformed – and which factors this is influenced by.

Since 2004 Eastern European migrants (hailing from the 'A8' – EU Accession States)[1] have become an inseparable part of the British ethnic mosaic. Using the case study of Polish post-2004 EU enlargement migrants, this study focuses on the legal behaviour of migrants in the UK, that is, the strategies and tactics they employ in order to follow, comply with, avoid or manoeuvre around the law and their choices of 'semi-legal' over legal status. The study is also concerned with migrants' values and attitudes to the rules that govern their work and residence in the UK (and to the legal system in general) and the interpretations of legality that they result in, especially in terms of how they affect the choices migrants make while dealing with the body of law (subsequent legalization strategies).

Therefore, contrary to the traditional approach to socio-legal research representing the 'law-first' perspective (Cowan 2004), where the primary concern is the study of law per se and its effects in society (Currie 2008b), this book makes a case for a 'proper' recognition of migrants' agency and their legal culture – their values, attitudes and accustomed patterns of legal behaviour – in the study of their socio-legal integration.

As a result, although the Polish post-2004 EU enlargement migrants in the UK provide the case study of this book, the analysis presented has far broader consequences. It suggests a framework for the future approaches of researching migrants in the new socio-legal environment.

Factors of Socio-Legal Integration

Drawing on the legal and migration literature, I propose a combination of several factors with which to investigate migrants' relationship with law.

Legal Environment

Assimilation, acculturation and integration were the distinctive theoretical approaches – characteristic of the earlier historical periods between the 1900s and the 1960s – which considered migrants' compliance with the law in civic and legal matters[2] as unquestionable and fairly unproblematic. It was the 'minimum'

1 'A8' Accession State nationals hail from the Czech Republic, Estonia, Hungary, Latvia, Lithuania, Poland, Slovakia and Slovenia .

2 Although I appreciate that civic also encompasses legal matters, this terminology has been taken from migration studies literature (Cronin 1970).

migrants were expected to conform to and – as the research evidence and migration literature records – these changes and adjustments, at least in the behavioural sphere, were quite rapid and profound (Cronin 1970; Gordon 1964; Hein and Beger 2001b; Kallin 2003).

These research accounts of smooth and somewhat unproblematic changes of migrants forming their new relationship with the law in the receiving country could be explained in a twofold way. Firstly, they mark the early stage of migration research, the stage of accumulating the knowledge and constructing the methodological premises of the field. Secondly, migrants' rapid assimilation in the civic and legal spheres was undoubtedly aided by the sole focus on the legal framework and legal institutions of the host society. Migrants' compliance with the law was taken for granted.

These early research frameworks particularly concentrated on the host country's legislation of that time, which 'encouraged' migrants to come, work (e.g. programmes targeted at migrant workers after the Second World War in the USA, Canada and Western Europe) and subsequently, yet perhaps unintentionally, to settle.

With the change in migration patterns, as long settlement plans were replaced by a proliferation of cross-border flows, the globalization of trade and the reduction of the old boundaries and borders, the role of host states' immigration policies and legal frameworks changed from accommodative to exclusionary practices aimed at securing and controlling the borders of nation states. Many jurisdictions, which in *de jure* terms considered themselves to be homogeneous nation states with legal systems firmly grounded in Austinian principle, became confronted with the *de facto* reality of significant plurality of their own populations throughout the twentieth century. The official political views on illegal immigration transformed dramatically as economic conditions worsened, unemployment increased and anti-immigrant political movements began to attract support in the 1970s and 1980s. Several scenarios – state responses to the increasing diversity of their populations – have taken effect. On the one end of the spectrum, there was the French model – that any formal recognition of ethnic plurality would undermine the homogeneity and hence the integrity of the Republic. On the other end, there was the newly emerged South African model, which – at least according to its constitutional principles – emphasized the nation's intrinsic condition of ethnic plurality and consequently introduced it into all legislation under its jurisdiction. Western Europe and the USA – traditionally immigration countries – have now been moving closer to the former end of the spectrum, tightening their admission policies and reconceptualizing their citizenship models. As a result of these developments, a substantial shift in the studies of migrants' responses to the host country's legal environment arose from the 'problem' of undocumented immigrants crossing borders escaping from civil wars, political persecution or in search of better economic conditions.

Within the framework of transnationalism (Portes 1996; Glick Schiller et al. 1995; Vertovec 2007), the growing legalization literature focused on the complex set of structural factors stemming from the legal system of the host country itself – via immigration policies and nationality laws – which legally constructed immigrants' 'otherness' through the reproduction of contingent illegality (Calavita 2005). 'Illegal' migration therefore became, by definition, a product of the laws made to control migration (Castles and Miller 1998). Legalization programmes and amnesty measures designed by the host state became the increasingly present tools of immigration policy. These restrictive and erratic inflections that can be seen in many parts of the law, combined with changes in the nationality legislation, produced a dyke against a full integration or foreign residents in many states of the North. These structural factors were deemed responsible for the shift in migrants' responses to the legal system of the host country, when the traditional responses (i.e. compliance and assimilation) ceased to be straightforward, as migrants, labelled 'illegal aliens' at entry itself, confined themselves to the liminal sphere of law (Coutin 2000; Hagan 1994; Mahler 1995; Menjivar 2000, 2006).

The general typology of the elements that give rise to a particular legal environment could be put forward as follows:

1. The admission policies of host countries, e.g. the immigration laws enacted by government in state legislation.[3]
2. The international legal obligations to which the host country is a signatory (human rights).
3. The rationale behind these rules reflecting the dominant political discourse on immigration.
4. Migrants rights upon admission (Ruhs 2011), e.g.:
    a. The employment (workplace) regulations that migrants face in the host country,
    b. The social security (welfare) legislations.
5. How these rules and regulations are enforced and executed by the host state – 'law in action' (Pound 1910), particularly in the niche of the low-wage, low-skilled echelons of the host state's labour market, where majority of contemporary migrants find employment (cf. dual labour market theory (Reich et al. 1973), segmented assimilation (Alba and Nee 2003)).

Agency: Migrants as Actors

One cannot help but notice that the sole focus on the host state's legal frameworks in addressing the issues of legal adaptations portrays migrants as

3 This broad definition encompasses immigration laws and policies aimed at voluntary migrants and asylum laws directed towards involuntary migrants. However, I would like to acknowledge that the clear-cut division between voluntary and involuntary migrants (or migrants and refugees and asylum-seekers) is a problematic one and perhaps it obscures more than it clarifies. How we know whether a movement is 'forced' or 'voluntary', or why we should assume that this is significant, is rarely considered.

passive recipients of the opportunity structures consisting of immigration laws and state integration policies as expressed in the works of legal institutions. In the case of 'illegal' migrants, it is the 'procedural delays and release pending removals [that] enable them to gain most of what they migrated for in the first place' (Schuck 2007: 195). Any indications of migrants as active and responsive agents are limited to those 'few who do manage to beat the system and elicit criticism of the immigration agency' (Schuck 2007) – immigrants as villains or victims (Anderson 2008).

From the review of migration literature, it became apparent that people, by making their decision to migrate or deciding to lead transnational lives between the home and host countries, exercise a certain degree of agency and choice (Glick Schiller et al. 1995).

However, the dominant way in which the problem of agency has been addressed in migration studies is unsatisfactory. Many studies suggest that we must take account of people's agency, but then give a predominantly structuralist account or claim that the context is important while the analysis is based simply on the aggregation of individual responses to questionnaires. Those who attempt to find the balance have tended to draw on Giddens' theory of structuration (Giddens 1984). However, migration scholars have rarely paid enough attention either to important critiques of Giddens (Archer 1982; Sewell 1992) or more recent debates about approaches to post-positivist social science, in particular those drawing on critical realist perspectives (Cruickshank 2011).

As a result, the very nature of agency constitutes an important question in itself. Can agency be identified with the behaviour of individuals (actors)? In sociology and anthropology, the actor-oriented approach was popular in the 1960s and early 1970s, and ranged from transactional and decision-making models to symbolic interactionism and phenomenological analysis (Long 2001). However, it is important to point out that in attempts to combat simple culturalist and structuralist views of change, some of the 'actor-oriented' studies concentrated on the behaviour of individuals, stressing the voluntaristic view of the decision-making process. They therefore failed to examine how individual choices are actually shaped by larger frames of meaning and action, such as cultural dispositions, or what Bourdieu calls 'habitus' or 'embodied history' (Bourdieu 1981).

Therefore, should agency be viewed as an irreducible collective attribute? As Carter and Charles (2010), observed, agents are collectivities sharing the same life chances and therefore, the term 'agency' is always and only employed in the plural (cf. Archer 1996). As collectivities, agents are contrasted to 'actors', who are always singular (Carter and Charles 2010). The (always) plural understanding of agency, as a property of collectives sharing similar life chances, precludes that everyone is necessarily an agent since everyone occupies a position in society's distribution of scarce resources (cf. Bruno Latour's Actor–network theory (Latour 2005)). However, this might lead to a controversial proposition that one's agentic position may be conceived as involuntary – 'we are born into a certain place at a certain moment and, because these distributions predate our arrival, they do not require our consent or complicity' (Carter and Charles 2010: 237).

For the purposes of the analysis, human agency has been conceptualized after Emirbayer and Mische (1998: 970) as 'temporary embedded engagement by actors of different structural environments through the interplay of habit, imagination, and judgement which both reproduces and transforms those structures in interactive response to the problems posed by changing situations'. To be an agent means to be capable of exerting some degree of control over the social relations in which one is enmeshed, which, in turn, implies the ability to transform those social relations to some degree (Sewell 1992).

Introducing the Legal Culture Perspective

Socio-legal integration provides a framework in which the agency of migrants could be meaningfully examined to understand its relationship with the law. Upon arrival, the lives of migrants are intertwined with the works of the law in multiple webs of allegiances and connections. As a result, different groups of migrants possess different degrees of choice about their actions (and legalization strategies) upon arrival. This depends of course on the degrees of restrictiveness of the immigration laws and the level of their enforcement (e.g. fear of deportation (De Genova and Peutz 2010), but also on individual strategies of coping with the legal frameworks, efforts to legalize one's status, priorities, values and attitudes associated with law and legality.

This study therefore argues that structural factors stemming from the legal system of the host country and its immigration policies are not sufficient to fully account for migrants' responses (agency) to the legal environment of the host country – whether they comply with the laws, remain within the 'illegal' sphere or 'in-between'.

This research is a systematic attempt to bring the culture of migrants and, specifically, their legal culture – that is, a particular configuration of values, attitudes and behaviour concerning law which migrants internalized prior to their migratory experience – into the picture. The culture of migrants has already been widely recognized as a factor that heavily influences and conditions their social and cultural integration in the host society (Bhattacharya 2008; Foner 1996; Hondagneu-Sotelo 1994; Kibria 1993; Lim and Wieling 2004; Read 2004; van Niekierk 2004; Wakil et al. 1981; Yanagisako 1985b).

Legal culture is an established term in the scholarship of socio-legal studies (Blanke and Bruinsma 1994; Blankenburg 1998; Cotterrell 1997, 2001; Friedman 1975, 1990, 2001; Gibson and Caldeira 1996; Kurkchiyan 2005, 2010; Legrand 1999; Nelken 1995a, 1995b, 2004a, 2004b, 2007; Nelken and Feest 2001). At the same time, legal culture is one of the most general and ubiquitous concepts in the study of law and society. Various scholars argue that the concept, being all-inclusive, is theoretically incoherent, as it explains too much and tends to lean toward a self-contained 'super-organic' reality: 'the concept of legal culture seems to cover too many things, seems to explain everything that happens or fails to happen within the legal system' (Cotterrell 1997: 20).

Formal definitions of legal culture vary across disciplines and scholars (Gibson and Caldeira 1996) and are often intertwined with alternative concepts such as legal tradition (Glenn 2000, 2004), legal ideology (Cotterrell 1997) or legal consciousness (Merry 1990). Even Lawrence M. Friedman, the 'father' and the greatest advocate of the concept of legal culture, agrees that it serves more of an artistic than a scientific function as it allows an impression of general tendencies to be sketched (Friedman 1975: 12). The following sections examine the most contentious theoretical intricacies of the term – its interpretations, unit, internal dynamics and change.

There are many interpretations of legal culture. In Lawrence Friedman's early and most extensive theoretical discussion on legal culture, he offers a variety of characterizations of the concept. Legal culture refers to 'public knowledge, attitudes and behaviour patterns toward the legal system' (Friedman 1975: 193). Legal cultures may also encompass 'bodies of custom organically related to the culture as a whole' (Friedman 1975: 194). Legal culture, as part of general culture, relates to 'those parts of general culture – customs, opinion, and ways of doing and thinking – that bend social forces toward or away from the law in particular ways' (Friedman 1975: 15).

Other approaches to legal culture seem to put the analytical stress equally on ideas, attitudes and behavioural patterns. Roger Cotterrell, in his critique of the notion of legal culture, observes that in Friedman's later formulations, legal culture appears only as ideational, while the behavioural elements seem to have been discarded (Cotterrell 1997: 15). Friedman's 1977 work *Law and Society* portrays legal culture as attitudes, values and opinions held in society with regard to law, the legal system and its various parts (Friedman 1977: 76); in *Republic of Choice* (1990), legal culture consists of ideas, attitudes, expectation and opinions about law held by people in a given society (Friedman 1990: 213). While acknowledging the definitional inconsistencies, this approach remains faithful to the original conceptualization, stressing the importance of the cognitive (values, attitudes and interpretations) and behavioural (legal behaviour) aspects of people's relationship with law in a particular society.

The notion of legal culture employed here encompasses a specific configuration of values to, attitudes to and behaviour with respect to law – how they are intertwined, what they produce and the complex interplay between them. The stress on 'configuration', on how the values, attitudes and behaviour transcend individuals and are aligned to create a distinguishable pattern is particularly important (as a different 'configuration' would inevitably produce a different outcome in the form of a different legal culture).

In this study, the concept of legal culture will be employed heuristically as an umbrella concept – a useful way of lining up a range of phenomena into one very general category – where behaviours and attitudes (as well as institutions and processes) could be intelligibly – that is, thickly – described (Geertz 1975: 3). However, there is no doubt that legal culture is a much more multi-faceted concept than that.[4]

Looking into the relationship between culture and law, Saguy and Stuart (2008), in their review of contemporary socio-legal scholarship, distinguished a strong and promising strand of research that made successful use of the notion of culture conceptualized as 'vocabularies', 'repertoires' or 'toolkits' (Swidler 1986). Reviewing the various scholarships on the relationship between law and culture (cf. Ewick and Silbey 1998; Mezey 2001) they broaden the traditional notion of 'legal actor' to include ordinary individuals (as well as businesses, associations and institutions) (Saguy and Stuart 2008: 158) in order to shift the attention away from the opinions and decisions of formal legal bodies and decision makers onto everyday life, social movements (Kostiner 2003), and workplace culture.

This perspective of employing culture into socio-legal research is an exciting development that builds on cultural sociological concepts of cultural repertoires or toolkits, interpretive frameworks through which individuals come to understand their lives (Saguy and Stuart 2008: 158). This employment of culture in socio-legal research focuses on peoples' own perceptions, values, attitudes and experiences (of law) through their agency as an intermediary. The social actors are therefore viewed as knowledgeable actors, and the usual social scientific term for 'what people know' is culture (Sewell 1992: 7).

Culture can therefore also be viewed as a method of empowerment, as agency arises from an actor's knowledge of schemas, toolkits and repertoires, and the ability to apply them in new contexts (Sewell 1992: 20). As a result, this approach to culture is reflexively sensitive to peoples' expectations regarding what the law should be in specific circumstances (Saguy and Stuart 2008: 159). These expectations often problematize – and even run counter to – official legal narratives that enjoy the legitimacy of the state.

This study, drawing from the rich socio-legal, sociological and anthropological scholarship in this field, focuses on legal culture as a crucial factor in shaping migrants' relationship to law in the new socio-legal environment. Migrants' values, attitudes to law and specific, entrenched behavioural patterns and established, accustomed practices – which could best be summed up as 'legal culture' – are treated as 'luggage' that migrants brought with them from home, their 'legal background' of repertoires and toolkits vis- à-vis law (cf. the discussion on the plural conception of legal culture in Banakar 2008). Although the above thesis has no intention of supporting bold claims of cultural determinism, it nevertheless demonstrates that the particular quality of migrants' responses to the host country's laws and institutions brings about the reflexive relationship between the factors of the host country's legal environment and the 'soft' cultural factors.

4 For discussions on legal culture, its unit(s), theory and analytical usefulness, see Friedman 1975, 1990, 2001; Kurkchiyan 2003; Nelken 1995, 1997, 2001, 2004.

The varieties of conceptual approaches to legal culture raise the question of the unit of legal culture. They range from a position that 'each nation has a legal culture' (Friedman 1975: 15) to 'there are no two legal cultures exactly alike' (Friedman 1975: 199). Other scholars, when discussing the unit of legal culture, distinguish between micro-, mezzo- and macro-levels. As Nelken puts it: 'At the sub-national level the appropriate unit of legal culture may be the local court, the prosecutor's office, or the lawyer's consulting room ... At the macro level, historical membership of the continental or common law world transcends the frontiers of the nation state' (Nelken 2004b: 3).

Other micro level approaches can be found in the works of legal anthropologists, in their insights into 'local legal cultures' (Nader 1990; Pirie 2006; Yngvesson 1993). Further examples of the macro-level are illustrated in Friedman's later work (1990), when he talks of the legal culture of modernity – or modern legal culture – which is a characteristic feature of many contemporary societies (Cotterrell 1997: 16). The relevant question for this research is whether the national (mezzo-) level can be treated as a unit of analysis.

The nation state was originally built on the idea of an identifiable culture and, in spite of the growing importance of sub-cultures and of external cultural influences, it can, in most cases, still be treated as a cultural unit (Gessner 1994). Nelken observes that 'there is *more* in common in legal culture across the country than in many other aspects of national culture' (Nelken 2004b: 3, emphasis in original). Therefore, in the case study for this book, the unit of legal culture will continue to be identified with the nation state in question – Poland or the UK (Bell 2001; Blanke and Bruinsma 1994; Feldman 2001; Johnson 2002).

Although it is the Polish legal culture that constitutes the main unit of analysis, I am far from assuming that all Polish migrants in the UK share the same legal culture. While modern nation states, being relatively stable, defined and powerful, are the most obvious mechanisms capable of sustaining the conditions necessary for normative orientations to emerge and be maintained through socialization within such institutions as the family, the educational system, the legal order, etc., other formal and informal organizations with such capacities can be noted (including national and ethnic groups, local communities, social occupations and classes, religious groups, etc.) (Whitefield 2005). The methodological approach to culture adopted here acknowledges not only the diversity within the group itself but also the plurality of culture – a repertoire of various habits, attitudes, values and behaviours (Swidler 1986) – rather than a determinist force. However, this research is underpinned by a general assumption that (while acknowledging the existence of sub-groups and sub-cultures) there are some common tendencies, patterns of behaviour and attitudes to law at the national level which can be distinguished. Certain repertoires are chosen more often than others and certain 'cultural tools' are more popular than others.

Legal culture, like all culture, is the product of the contingencies of history. The past very often contributes to a better understanding of the present. In shaping their identity and understandings of the present, people learn from the past, look towards the past or re-invent the past. The collective past experiences have their impact on individual beliefs, popular myths, group identity and memory as well as, to a certain extent condition contemporary individual and collective behaviour. This is particularly observable in the case of Polish post-2004 EU enlargement migrants in the UK. At the nation-state level, Polish migrants coming to the UK have, for generations, lived under the influence of (common to their collective experiences, yet changing) state institutions – political, social and legal – and their complex interplay. It is reasonable to suggest that the conditions created by the state institutions intertwined with the legal tradition in the historical perspective resulted in a largely shared pattern of accustomed behaviour, attitudes to and experiences of law (Starr and Collier 1989). Although the past was much more striated, some of these patterns are sharper and more visible than others.

Finally, legal culture – like all culture – is always undergoing change (Nelken 1995a). The changes had (and have) different origins and source. They were induced by factors ranging from internal forces – developments within a society – such as the historical interplay between various institutions within a country and planned or unplanned processes of differentiation. They could have been a consequence of changes stimulated or imposed by another society – external forces including colonialism or conquest, resulting in transfers of legal institutions and borrowed systems of laws (Cotterrell 2001; Harding 2001; Legrand 2001; Nelken 2001).[5]

This book looks into those aspects of legal adaptation and legal culture when it is the people who are migrating, not the laws, and who are experiencing and encountering new legal frameworks and new ways of interpreting and understanding the law. Therefore, it also responds to Cotterrell's call for changing terrain for the sociology of law towards legal transnationalism, where the nation states and other legal actors have to respond to migration as one of the 'cultural and political pressures taking shape outside their borders, and to that extent beyond their control' (Cotterrell 2009: 1) (cf. earlier discussions on transnationalism in legal anthropology (Merry 1992)).

In exploring the relationship between the Polish post-2004 EU enlargement migrants and the law in the UK, the factors influencing the character of these relations and the consequences of certain preferences that migrants have, the category of legal culture leaves scope for a certain predictability regarding a

5 In the context of changes in legal culture, many legal scholars have been interested in the sociology of legal adaptation (Harding 2001; Jettinghoff 2001; Legrand 2001). Nelken and Feest in their seminal book *Adapting Legal Cultures* (2001) set off to clarify what was meant by legal adaptation and legal culture, and how best to analyse current developments in legal and social change. However, the rich debate – both theoretically and empirically – on legal culture adaptation has been almost entirely dominated by legal transplants, how they have been inspired by current globalizing developments and how far legal adaptation could be engineered.

society's response to socio-economic change and its compliance or non-compliance with newly introduced institutions.

Polish migrants fashioning their responses towards the legal environment of the UK are motivated by certain salient, pre-migratory values and attitudes to law. While there is rarely a one-to-one match in what an one prefers and sees (attitudes) and what one is actually able to do (behavioural response) (Berry 2002: 21), the changes in behaviour could result from various social constraints (e.g. norms and discrimination) which do not have to be correlated with the primary changes in attitudes.

Usually, however, once people act in a certain fashion, their behaviour becomes part of their everyday experiences upon which they can reflect (Hill 1981); equally, after engaging in certain actions, people may experience greater awareness of their relevant attitudes. The fact that Polish migrants are given a choice in terms of the pace and character of their legalization in the UK makes them engage in a process of active self-persuasion to find attitudinal support for the action they have already decided to take (Kelman 1974: 319).

Of course, people do not change overnight. The change is observable, but it is not as rapid as the change of structural conditions for action, as customs, attitudes and behaviours are much more impervious to deliberate policies. This points to a certain inertia within the legal culture – a tendency to resist immediate change in favour of a gradual adaptation to the conditions and structures provided. Migrants continue to draw, in the new environment from the toolkit of pre-migration strategies, cultural codes and practices. Thus, cultural stabilization – the repetition of behaviours, attributions and evaluations – leads to the building of social structures (cf. process of structuration (Giddens 1984)).

As a result, immigrants' pre-migration conceptions and practices with regard to the law do not continue unchanged. They are restructured, redefined and renegotiated in the new setting. The investigation of the consequences of Polish migrants' preference for certain relations with law over others, and the reasoning behind this, therefore invites a wider theoretical inquiry into the change of legal culture.

Away from Cultural Determinism

Legal culture, although an established and theoretically rich concept within socio-legal studies, presents the risk of trapping any research as 'culturally deterministic'. The concept, in a similar vein to more traditional cultural approaches, neither recognizes nor give enough attention to the 'hard' structural factors stemming from the legal system of a given country, its laws, legal enforcement and respective policies, which also prove indicative in investigating peoples' responses to the legal environment.

The classic definition of legal culture sees it as a 'way of doing and thinking … that bends social forces toward or away from the law' (Friedman 1975: 15).

Assuming that 'the bending force' has solely cultural origins leaves no space for other factors that can also 'bend social forces toward or away from the law', as the growing scholarship of legalization literature suggests (Calavita 2005; Coutin 2000; Mahler 1995; Menjivar 2006).

Therefore, in order to overcome these conceptual shortcomings in analysing the responses of Polish migrants towards British law, an approach based on the reflexive analysis of the legal environment and the cultural predispositions is adopted to distinguish between the social institutions of law – actors and organizations that make and apply the law – from the social actions constituted by interpretive schema and migrants' understandings and attitudes (Ewick and Silbey 1998: 150). Yet, moving away from cultural or legal determinism (where law is viewed as dependent on culture or culture as dependent on law, respectively), this approach assumes a less static and homogeneous role than is implied by these cause-and-effect models.

This book therefore intends to bring into the fields of socio-legal and migration studies a combined focus on the structural factors (law, rules and regulations, and their enforcement in the host country) and soft cultural factors (the legal culture), nevertheless recognizing migrants' agency in navigating and negotiating their relationship to law in the complex process of socio-legal integration. It also aims to offer an understanding of how people in their daily interactions gradually change their behaviour, views and attitudes when engaging in the complex interplay between the new environment, their needs and their cultural background.

This methodological approach was introduced and successfully employed by Patricia Ewick and Susan Silbey in their analysis of legality (Ewick and Silbey 1998), where actions and interpretations given by individuals to their world – and law and legal institutions as part of the lived world – become repeated, patterned and stabilized, and these stabilized patterns become part of the meaning system deployed by, as well as constraining, the individual (Ewick and Silbey 2002: 150). Ewick and Silbey's approach attempts to integrate human agency and structural constraints by showing how individual understandings and social interactions aggregate to partly shape institutions while institutions and larger social structures provide the foundations for and constraints on individual understanding and social interaction (Mezey 2001: 151).

The reason for the reflexive analysis, integrating both the legal environment and peoples' culturally mediated responses towards it is that neither a structurally determinist nor an idealist perspective by itself would sufficiently serve to explain the puzzle. By employing the structuralist account, one risks neglecting the actual work people do in choosing a particular strategy to deal with the body of law and erases the subjects from the field of analysis, giving priority to structural determination over actions and choices. On the other hand, the idealist perspective, focusing on legal culture as a set of preferences and potential behaviours, fails to take into account the different options available to people within the legal environment (where they operate in fashioning their interpretations and behaviours).

The exploration of the relationship between the factors stemming from host country's legal environment and migrants' behavioural choices (their agency and legal culture) contributes to the more comprehensive picture of migrants' socio-legal integration and should be of great importance not only to the area of socio-legal studies dealing with sociological approaches to law but also to the fields of migration studies, legal anthropology and migration policy.

Structure of the Book

This introductory chapter is followed by Chapter 2, 'Theoretical Approaches to Understanding Migrants in the New Socio-Legal Environment', which places the research at the intersection of migration and legal studies.

This chapter reviews traditional (assimilation, acculturation and integration) and more recent (transnationalism) approaches to immigrant incorporation from the perspective of migration studies. These approaches are mapped against the legal perspectives on migrants' incorporation. They range from traditional concepts of legal assimilation to the more complex responses of various legalization strategies and the confinement of immigrants to the sphere of liminal law.

The aim of this chapter is to identify a general typology of factors – stemming from migration and legal studies, respectively – affecting the formation of migrants' relationship with the law of the host country. According to the traditional approach to integration, migrants' responses have been predominantly attributed to the institutional, legal factors stemming from the host country's immigration laws and policy. While recognizing the importance of the factors related to the legal environment, the chapter nevertheless argues that something else must also be at stake. The culture of migrants, their 'cultural luggage' has been widely acknowledged in the research on immigrants' social integration and incorporation. This chapter therefore makes a case for a 'proper' recognition of legal culture in the study of migrants and their socio-legal integration.

Chapter 3, 'Polish Post-2004 EU Enlargement Migrants in the UK: Case Study', presents the case study group on which the analysis focuses. Who are the migrants and what general statistical picture do we have of them? Why did they arrive? How do they manage in the British labour market? The chapter also places this group of Polish migrants in the larger context of Polish migratory movements, reviewing the literature on Polish migration and incorporation experience in the twentieth and early twenty-first centuries. Finally, the chapter also presents a note on empirical data gathered for the book.

The subsequent chapters appropriate the analytical tools with which to study socio-legal integration (as put forward in Chapter 2) on the example of Polish post-2004 EU enlargement migrants in the UK.

Chapter 4, 'The British Legal Environment in the Context of the 2004 EU Enlargement Free Movement Regime', takes a closer look at the *law* and the legal frameworks of the UK into which the Polish post-2004 EU enlargement migrants arrive. Analysing the nature and character of the British legal environment towards the post-2004 EU enlargement migrant workers from Poland and their families (and migrants from other A8 countries) substantively, this chapter firstly traces its origins in the primary and secondary European legislation on free movement. Secondly, it outlines in detail the transitory provisions regarding the free movement of persons between the 'old' EU Member States and the accession states as specified in the Treaty of Accession 2003.

Thirdly, this chapter investigates the final shape of the transitory provisions as revealed in the British Accession Regulations 2004. Due to the fact that Polish migrants mainly come to the UK as workers, the chapter also reviews the workplace regulations that migrants encounter and must respond to upon arrival. It analyses the rationale behind and the character of British immigration law and workplace regulations, and their enforcement within a particular legal niche of a deregulated and flexible labour market embracing working and living conditions common to workers within the low-skilled, low-wage sectors.

The chapter concludes that the complicated, confusing and inconsistently applied laws produce a rather unstable legal environment which might not necessarily command compliance.

Chapter 5, 'Polish Migrants in the British Legal Environment: the Question of Semi-Legality', focuses on the *agency* aspect of the theoretical framework. It is a systematic attempt to empirically address the sub-areas of the research question – to investigate how Polish post-2004 EU enlargement migrants relate themselves to the 2004 immigration and workplace regulations in the UK and to explore their behavioural strategies as well as reasons for and significance of their interpretations of legality employed during this process.

From migrants' initial responses to the 2004 Accession Regulations, the problem of semi-legality and semi-compliance (Anderson and Ruhs 2010) with immigration and workplace regulations emerges. Semi-legality is then subsequently analysed and contextualized.

The chapter concludes by stating that although the multiple 'hard' structural factors of the legal environment present a good explanation of the semi-legality phenomenon among the Polish post-2004 EU enlargement migrants, their socio-legal integration cannot be studied solely in relation to them. Migrants are not passive recipients of the opportunity structures available to them upon arrival, but are engaged in the negotiation of their responses to the new socio-legal environment. An approach combining the institutional factors with migrants' agency and cultural interpretations of law is likely to reveal a more comprehensive picture of their socio-legal integration.

Therefore, Chapter 6, 'The Polish Socio-Legal Tradition', is an attempt to bring to the picture and comprehensively analyze the role of *legal culture*. By starting with the socio-legal tradition of Poland, this chapter looks at the historical formations of legal institutions in Poland and how they were intertwined with the values, attitudes, myths and interpretations of law, as well as specific patterns of legal behaviour. The historical accounts very often contribute to the better understanding of the present. Polish people shape their self-image of the group with reference to historical symbols and past traditions, which figure as one of the sources of their identity.

The chapter concludes that although the past can shed much light on the understanding of the present, it nevertheless does not explain it.

For that reason, Chapter 7, 'Polish Contemporary Legal Culture in Comparative Perspective', looks at the present, legal-cultural factors and their role in migrants' responses to the new legal environment. It is an attempt to analyse the current, popularly held values and attitudes towards law, and how they are behaviourally expressed towards the legal institutions and the Polish state. The chapter compares these with the dominant values, attitudes and behaviour towards the law prevalent within British society.

The chapter concludes by stating that the choice between legality and semi-legality is a long-standing one in Polish legal experience and seeks the origins of this phenomenon in the normative gap between peoples' expectations, images, associations of the law and their daily experiences of it.

Chapter 8, 'Gradual Legality: Changing Behaviour, Changing Attitudes', focuses on the consequences of the specific shape of Polish migrants' responses to law in the UK. The chapter reveals that the initial semi-legality is not static and ascribed but fluid and changing. Over time, migrants comply with the rules designed to govern their work and residence in the UK. These peculiar legalization strategies are gradual, as migrants prioritize certain rules which benefit them immediately over others which do not. Migrants interpret legality in a gradual manner as they cognitively place themselves on different stages between two poles of legality and illegality. By focusing on interpretations and understandings of legality in their interplay with changes of legal behaviour, this chapter makes a case for the meaningful employment of culture in socio-legal integration research.

Chapter 2
Theoretical Approaches to Understanding Migrants in a New Socio-Legal Environment

Assimilation, Acculturation, Integration

The well-established frameworks of assimilation (Alba and Nee 1997; Gordon 1964; Park and Burgess 1921; Portes and Bach 1985), acculturation (Berry 1980, 1997, 2002, 2005, 2008; Redfield et al. 1936; Ward and Kennedy 1994) and integration (Hansen 2000; Joppke and Morawska 2003; Lucassen et al. 2006; Portes and Rumbaut 1990; Tubergen 2006) have traditionally been used to account for migrants' incorporation and their responses to the new environments of the host society.

The analysis of the historical and current literature points to the USA as the main source of research in the subject of understanding migrants in the new environment. The history of the USA as 'the immigrant country' could serve as a partial explanation of this observation. It figures prominently, although not solely, on the map in the current *Age of Migration*, as framed by Castles and Miller in their seminal book of the same name (Castles and Miller 1998). The twentieth century saw increasing migration movements and subsequently research on immigrants in the host countries, not only in the USA but also Canada, Australia, the UK and continental Europe (France and Germany) that was very often related to their colonial past (Castles and Miller 1998). The end of the Cold War and the dissolution of the Soviet Bloc added a new dimension to the picture – intensified East-West migration, from previously isolated Eastern European countries entering global migratory flows.

Various scholars have examined migrants' responses to the host environment by reference to one of the three dominant models of assimilation proposed by Milton M. Gordon in his classic study on *Assimilation in American Life* (1964). The theories of assimilation introduced by Gordon encompassed the 'Anglo-conformity', the 'melting pot' and 'cultural pluralism' (Portes and Bach 1985: 20–26; Gordon 1964) and were originally constructed with reference to the American experience of immigration. The first definition of assimilation by Robert E. Park and Ernest W. Burgess (1921) conceptualized it as 'a process of interpretation and fusion in which persons and groups acquire the memories, sentiments, and attitudes of other persons or groups, and by sharing their experience and history, are incorporated with them in a common cultural life' (Park and Burgess 1921).

Penninx, analysing the legal dimension of assimilation, referred to the basic question of whether (or at what stage) immigrants could be regarded as fully-fledged members of the political community (Penninx 2005: 139). In practice it encompassed immigrants' secure residence rights and the scope of their political rights and duties (and whether these differ from those of natives) (Penninx 2005: 139). Many other definitions followed (for the review of definitions, see Portes and Bach 1985), bringing about eclecticism of the term and the necessity of choosing from various available interpretations.

Assimilation theory sees a gradual adaptation of immigrants not only socio-economically but also culturally. Gradually immigrants do away with the cultural baggage transported from their country of emigration. Feist argues that as immigrants continue to embark upon the various memberships of the receiving country, the logical end-point is single nation-state citizenship, characterized by a dominant and unitary political cultural core (Feist 2000: 204).

Most recently, the theory of assimilation recognizes that the actions of immigrants are shaped by the host society institutions and the social capital and networks of immigrant groups, where the boundaries between immigrants and the mainstream are not fixed (as the traditional assimilation model suggested), but change over time as boundaries might become more blurred or shift entirely (Alba and Nee 2003: 38). While Alba and Nee argue that assimilation remains a viable and often unexpected and unplanned outcome for many immigrants, by adding the adjective *segmented* and focusing specifically on the second generation, assimilation has also returned in a different and decidedly more pessimistic guise (Alba and Nee 1997).

The second framework focusing on migrants' responses towards the host society's culture and institutions is acculturation. Redfield et al. (1936) in their early account of acculturation defined it as one aspect of the broader process of culture change (the latter was treated more holistically as a change in the whole cultural system: 'acculturation comprehends those phenomena which result when groups of individuals having different cultures come into continuous first-hand contact, with subsequent changes in the original culture patterns of either or both groups … under this definition, acculturation is to be distinguished from culture change, of which it is but one aspect' (Redfield et al. 1936: 149–52).

In social psychology literature on acculturation, these initial 'changes', resulting from first-hand contacts, are referred to as 'adjustments' – 'behavioural shifts' by Berry (1997), 'culture learning' (Brislin et al. 1983) and 'social skills acquisition' (Furnham and Bochner 1986). Psychological adaptations to acculturation are considered to be a matter of learning a new behavioural repertoire that is appropriate for the new cultural context. This also requires some 'culture shedding' (Berry 1997) to occur (the unlearning of aspects of one's previous repertoire that are no longer appropriate).

Berry distinguished acculturation from assimilation (of which the former may at times be a phase) (Berry 2002: 18). Along the same lines, Gordon sees acculturation as only one, initial stage of assimilation. It is characterized by the sub-processes of change in cultural patterns towards those of the host society (Gordon 1964: 71). Acculturation is argued to be a phase of assimilation and does not necessarily result in complete assimilation (Gordon 1964: 71). According to Portes and Bach, 'greater knowledge of the language and culture by new immigrants and greater familiarity with members of the dominant group do not necessarily lead to more positive attitudes and more rapid assimilation' (Portes and Bach 1985: 23–4).

Yet another framework for analysing the responses of the immigrant population towards the receiving environment focused on integration. 'To say that integration is a happier and more exact term than others to describe the successful inclusion of a new group into an existing society is not idle pedantry', argued W. D. Borrie et al. in a survey based upon the papers and proceedings of the UNESCO Conference held in Havana as early as 1956.

The early conceptualization of integration proposed by Borrie originated with the dissatisfaction with assimilation, due to its misleading biological connotations and its implication of a one-way street in group relations. Critics of assimilation suggested that the framework divested the newcomer of his or her old culture completely and virtually re-moulded everything from clothes to ideology (Borrie 1959: 93). According to the proponents of the paradigm shift from assimilation to integration, the former 'denied or ignored the many gifts brought by the immigrant to his new home, and the impact of his ideas, talents and hopes upon the community that has admitted him' (Borrie 1959: 93).

'Integration' was to capture the fact that each element of the society has been changed by association with the other, without a complete loss of its cultural identity and with a change in the resultant cultural amalgam that was vital, vigorous and an advance compared to its previous level (Borrie 1959).[1] It was to refer to the inclusion of individuals in a system and the creation of relationships among groups (and individuals) as a result of their conscious and motivated interaction and cooperation (Lockwood 1964). Joppke and Morawska (2003) observe that integration 'assumed a society composed of domestic individuals and groups (as the antipode to "immigrants") which were integrated normatively by a consensus and organizationally by a state' (Joppke and Morawska 2003: 3). Integration in some cases replaced the notion of assimilation, seeing adaptation as a more gradual process.

Whilst assimilation and acculturation dominated the migration discourse in the USA, integration gained more popularity in Europe (Schneider and Crul 2010). Broadly following the unfolding of the developments outlined above, research on migration and integration in Europe has expanded greatly in recent years. From the 1960s and 1970s onwards, researchers focused on one particular flow of migrants or immigrant group, or on the specific nature of the immigration, such as the 'guestworker' type. In the 1980s and 1990s migration and integration research was strongly embedded within national contexts, both in terms of its framing of

---

1 Needless to say, this definition of integration was very similar (if not identical) to the definition of assimilation in the conditions of a multicultural society as introduced by Gordon (1964).

the questions and the selection of what issues should be addressed. Topics and priorities related primarily to destination countries and their policy preoccupations (Penninx 2005: 6). This is due to the fact that the term 'integration' (more explicitly than assimilation) in the European context includes structural aspects of incorporation into society, especially with regard to legal status, educational achievements and access to the labour market (Schneider and Crul 2010: 1145).

The three frameworks of assimilation, acculturation and integration, although theoretically established and fruitful, have certain considerable shortcomings. For instance, they do not account for the diversity of migrants' pre-migration experiences and they paint a rather monolithic picture of the host society. With reference to the immigrant population, it is impossible to do justice to all its varied characteristics and to its complex internal and external relationships (Price 1969: 232).

Berry distinguishes a variety of general factors which reflect the complexity of a society, such as demographic factors (age, gender and education), economic performance, motivation and cultural distance, as well as personal factors (Berry 1997: 21–3), to indicate the heterogeneity of pre-migration experiences. It results from the fact that each person, over the course of his or her personal history, is a member of a unique combination of social categories; therefore, the set of social identities making up that person's self-concept is unique (Tajfel 1981).

The host society is also not unitary. Its citizens display certain general orientations towards immigration and pluralism. Some have been built by immigration over the centuries and this process may be a continuing one, guided by a deliberate immigration policy (Berry 1997: 17). The historical conditions and attitudes faced by migrants in the society of settlement are important issues, which, in turn, influence the responses of migrants. Other researchers, like Suarez-Orozco and Suarez-Orozco (2002), point out the flaws in the assumption of homogeneity of cultures in the host society in the American context.

However, there are certain parallels with the British case: 'to assume that immigrants today are joining the homogeneous society dominated by the white middle-class European/American protestant ethos … may no longer be useful' (Suarez-Orozco and Suarez-Orozco 2002: 27). Rather, today's immigrants come as representatives of a far more diverse set of cultures than did earlier generations, and they arrive in a society that is itself far more diverse.

As a consequence, the immigrant experience seems to many observers to be much more heterogeneous than ever before (Deux 2006: 135). The relationships between immigrants and others (the receiving society, its minorities and settled migrants) can vary along several axes other than acceptance of the host society and its roles. The immigrant is not just moving from one culture to another, but is striving to find an alternative to both.

Castles and Davidson (2000) argue that minorities can no longer be assimilated due to the speed and volume of migration, the continual nature of population mobility, the cultural and social diversity of the migrants, the ease with which they can remain in contact with the society of origin and the process of rapid economic and cultural change (Castles and Davidson 2000: 154).[2] The assimilation theorists have also not envisaged the necessity of considering the implications of transnational ties beyond the first generation, with exceptions pertaining mainly to folkloric expressions (Feist 2000: 204). This indicates the complexity of actual responsiveness of migrants to the new social, cultural and legal environments.

Transnationalism as a Response to the Changing Profile of Migration

To respond to the theoretical dilemmas and shortcomings of the classical analytical frameworks, a new framework of transnationalism was developed to reflect the greater complexity of migration in the contemporary globalized world. Although the theoretical framework of transnationalism does not resolve all the confusion relating to contemporary migrations and migrant incorporation, it definitely provides tools to address at least some of these issues. Research and scholarly literature reflect the changes in migration patterns, the greater complexity of the issues concerning immigrant integration, assimilation and acculturation, as well as the changes in the receiving country's legislation. With the framework of transnationalism, the new reality was followed by an academic response.[3]

Firstly, transnationalism acknowledges the diversity of pre-migration experiences as well as the heterogeneity of the host society, and, as a result, draws attention to the new and complex forms of culture and identity that the immigrants negotiate for themselves, together with the various sub-groups of the host population (Castles and Davidson 2000).

Secondly, the framework of transnationalism contradicts or, at least, very much blurs 'the clean break' between the home country and the receiving society. Although, as Foner (1996) has argued, the link between old and new was never actually drawn sharply (and thus the clean break may never have existed in a pure form anyway), the assumption that a person definitively leaves the country of origin and takes up residence, citizenship and identity in the new country has

---

2 Alba and Nee (1997) have called for the resurrection of the assimilation model, properly modified. Others have detected evidence of 'a return to assimilation' in Western democracies (Brubaker 2001). This contentious intellectual history indicates that discussions of incorporation are never neutral and the line between description and prescription is exceptionally thin (Freeman 2006: 123).

3 There has been a long-standing debate over transnational migrations. One dominant view claims that transnationalism is indeed a new phenomenon resulting from the social, political, technological and communicational transformations of the twentieth century. Some researchers, however, trace transnational practices to the times of *The Polish Peasant in Europe and America* by Thomas and Znaniecki focusing on the analysis of the letters and 'human documents' of early Polish migrants to the USA (Liao and Halas 2007; Morawska 2011; Smith and Guarnizo 1998). This book acknowledges these various views, yet the discussion on how 'old' (or 'new') the transnational phenomena really are lies beyond the scope of this research and does not affect its conclusions.

never been challenged so strongly as by the recent international migration (Deux 2006; Foner 1996).

Contemporary migrants, through the use of technology, travel and financial mechanisms, are more intensely engaged than ever before in a there-and-back movement on a massive scale. Contrary to the perspective presented in the traditional approaches to migrants' incorporation, contemporary immigrants cannot be characterized as 'uprooted', as those who leave behind their homes and countries, and face the painful process of incorporation into a different society (Glick Schiller et al. 1995: 48). Although residing in the host country, they sustain regular or situationally mobilized involvement in the economic, political, social and cultural (symbolic and material) affairs of their home or other countries at different national or local levels (households, informal communities and institutions) (Morawska 2004). They do not display serious settlement plans (or they are forbidden from doing so due to the immigration laws of the host country), they do not leave their origins and past behind but take them with them, and by maintaining their networks and lives in-between the country of origin and the migration destination, they begin to act as conduits between the two or more nations where they have connections.

Glick Schiller et al. (1995) in their seminal article on transnationalism distinguished various sets of factors that motivate migrants to lead transnational lives. From the perspective of the legal integration debate, one of them becomes particularly important, namely the strong political loyalties of transmigrants to each nation-state in which they maintain their social ties (Glick Schiller et al. 1995: 50).[4] Glick Schiller et al.'s observation concerning the strong political ties and loyalties that contemporary migrants display towards both the host and the sending state seem to be confirmed and illustrated by the insights into the actual number of applications for British citizenship among those migrants granted indefinite leave to remain (ILR).

The most recent figures reveal that although the grants of settlement rose by 19 per cent from 124,855 in 2007 to 148,740 in 2008 (Danzelman 2009: 13), the number of applications for British citizenship in 2008 was 156,015 – a fall of one per cent compared to the previous year, when 157,055 applications were received (Danzelman 2009: 5). This data suggests that – at least in the British example – although migrants might indeed display proactive responses aimed at securing their leave to remain, not that many of those who have actually settled are prepared to 'go all the way' and denounce their political loyalties to their country of origin (cf. Schuck 1998). This enables us to see migrants as being incorporated into the host country economy and institutions but, at the same time, maintaining

4 The other two being: (1) global restructuring of capital based on changing forms of capital, which led to deteriorating social and economic conditions in the labour markets of both the sending and receiving countries; (2) racism in both the USA and Europe that contributes to the economic and political insecurity of the newcomers (Glick Schiller et al. 1995: 50).

connections, building institutions, conducting transactions and influencing local and national events in the countries from which they have emigrated (Glick Schiller et al. 1995: 48).

Culture as a Factor in Understanding Migrants in the New Environment

The transnational approach has led to the change of our understanding of immigrants' incorporations that were focused on their settlement and assimilation. It complicated the picture of benign changes and adaptations with the growing research evidence of migrants living transnational lives.

In migration literature there is also another substantive type of scholarship – cultural scholarship – which focuses on the understanding of migrants in the new environment from the perspective of their attachments to pre-migration experiences and drawing on familiar cultural frameworks in negotiating their presence and new lives.

'Culture' is one of the most ambiguous and multiply defined terms in the social sciences. At the same time, it is a term that 'burst upon the intellectual landscape with a tremendous force', gave rise to the discipline of anthropology and 'seemed to promise to resolve all fundamental problems and clarify obscure issues' (Geertz 1975: 3–4).

Culture's success as a new paradigm was attributed to its unprecedented ability to attract an enduring group of adherents away from competing modes of scientific activity and to have sufficient open-endedness to leave all sorts of problems for the group of practitioners (and their students) to resolve (Kuhn 1962: 10). Using Geertz's language, 'all sensitive and active minds turned to culture to exploit it' (Geertz 1975: 3).

As a result, the first broad definitions of culture – E. B. Tylor's 'most complex whole' – came into being. However, the excessive popularity of the term 'culture' at some stage led to its saturation. In turn, the discipline that the popularity of 'culture' gave rise to – anthropology – struggled to balance its actual uses: how to limit, specify, focus and contain the concept to make it more narrowed, specialized and theoretically more powerful (Geertz 1975: 4).

Drawing on the idea that even though the nature of culture prevents it from being measured in a direct way, researchers are not prevented from drawing inferences about it indirectly from empirical observations that they actually can make (Friedman 1975), various studies focused on the empirically observed 'qualities' of culture – behaviour, values and attitudes. It is not an easy task to discover the catalogue of these measurable subcategories empirically. Attitudes and values are never particularly easy to measure and some are especially hard; behaviour is hard to measure, yet nobody would argue that these attitudes and behaviours are just not there or that they are not measurable in principle (Friedman 1975: 35).

However, it is important to stress that culture is not a unified system that pushes action in a consistent direction. Culture shapes the web of cognitive, affective and bodily schemas through which actors come to know how to act in particular social worlds (Emirbayer and Mische 1998). Not as a determinist or instrumentalist force, culture is more like a 'toolkit' or repertoire (Hannerz 1969: 186–8) from which actors select differing pieces for constructing 'strategies of action'. Swidler (1986) speaks of a cultural toolbox of practical competences that predispose actors to feel a fit within some actions and not others. Both individuals and groups know how to do different kinds of things in different circumstances (cf., for example, Gilbert and Mulkay 1984). People may have in them the readiness of cultural capacities that they nevertheless rarely employ, as all people know more culture than they use (if only in the sense that they ignore much that they hear) (Swidler 1986: 277).

This interpretation of culture leaves scope for the operation of agency of individual actors. In the new environment, while certain sets of actors might resist change and hold tightly to past routines in an attempt to ward off uncertainty, others may be more likely to engage in projective activity (as conceptualized by Swidler in *ideologies* and *utopias* (1986)) as they seek to imagine alternative futures for a problematic present. As a counter-effect, the strong future orientations provoked by historical change might inhibit actors' responsiveness to situational complexity and practical exigencies. As Emirbayer and Mische put it, 'actors engaged in emergent events find themselves positioned between the old and the new and are thus forced to develop new ways of integrating past and future perspectives' and new ways of responding to changing situations (Emirbayer and Mische 1998: 1006). As a result, relatively enduring cultural repertoires and scripts may emerge out of previous collective experiences and influence subsequent individual and group behaviours.

Several studies have pointed out ways in which pre-migration cultural conceptions and social practices continued to have a force in the destination country of immigrants (Bhattacharya 2008; Foner 1996; Hondagneu-Sotelo 1994; Kibria 1993; Lim and Wieling 2004; Read 2004; van Niekierk 2004; Wakil et al. 1981; Yanagisako 1985a). The empirical research demonstrates that the cultural 'luggage' provides some sort of a lens or an algorithm through which to interpret the 'unfamiliar' and to make sense of the new experiences. Certain cultural meanings became imprinted in the understanding of the new environment. Although the migrants do not exactly reproduce the cultural understandings, meanings and symbols brought with them from their home, their choices of lines of action continue to be influenced by values and norms as well as actual patterns of behaviour that they had internalized at home.

This culture-favouring argument is supported by extensive research on immigrant families in the USA. Offering an interpretative synthesis, the research stresses the role of pre-migratory cultural legacies in migrants' responses to the new environment (Foner 1996; Hondagneu-Sotelo 1994; Kibria 1993). For instance, it reveals how family and kinship patterns among different ethnic groups in the USA diverge in many ways, at least in part because of the cultural background of each group (Foner 1996). South Asian immigrant families continue the practice of formally arranged marriages and, as a result, one-half of American-born or American-raised people of South Asian origin agree to formally arranged marriages (Foner 1996: 965). In a similar vein, among Vietnamese immigrant families, the Vietnamese ideology of family collectivism promotes cooperative kin-based economic practices that help families cope and survive in the immigrant setting (Foner 1996: 974).

Attention to the role of immigrants' cultural legacies in shaping new family patterns enables Foner 'to capture the way these patterns differ from one group to another – despite *common structural conditions* they face' (Foner 1997: 962, emphasis added). This reveals that immigrants continue to draw on pre-migration family experiences, norms and cultural frameworks as they carve out new lives for themselves in the USA (Foner 1997: 963; Hondagneu-Sotelo 1994).

The cultures from which immigrants come are themselves the product of change, so that it is misleading to assume a timeless past of family tradition there. Although there is no such thing as a timeless tradition, immigrants may nevertheless come to think of life in their home society in these terms. As Foner puts it, they may construct their own versions of tradition as they re-conceptualize the past to make sense of their current experience and to speak of current dilemmas and issues. These 'invented traditions' can have a life of their own, in that immigrants may interpret and act upon the present in light of their models of the past (Foner 1997: 963; Yanagisako 1985b: 247). However, faced with new circumstances in the USA, many beliefs, values and cultural symbols as well as behaviour patterns undergo change. Foner attributes one of the factors that influences the change to the legal environment in the USA, which makes certain pre-migration customs and practices illegal or gives legal support to challenge these practices. As a result, Vietnamese immigrants in the USA 'are less likely to beat their wives in the USA than in Vietnam' as they become conscious that such behavior is 'illegal' (Foner 1997: 971). Foner concludes that new immigrant family patterns are shaped by the cultural meanings and social practices that immigrants bring with them from their home countries as well as social, economic and cultural forces in the USA.

These conclusions seem to be supported studies on the socialization of immigrants into the new social and cultural environments of Canada and the USA. Wakil et al. (1981) examined the values and ideals emphasized by parents in upbringing their second-generation Canadian children and the children's reaction to these values. Their findings indicate that although the immigrant families have willingly accepted changes in more pragmatic aspects of life, they have strongly resisted alterations in their core values (Wakil et al. 1981: 929). Although the predominant themes that emerged from the research were the contradictions and ambiguities experienced in the struggle to be both adaptive and culturally appropriate in the new context, it became prominent that organizing principles and values of family life remained largely unchanged over the two generations (Lim and Wieling 2004: 148).

Pre-migratory cultural legacies also play a role outside the family sphere and could be drawn on as helpful in explaining the different patterns of economic activity of immigrants. Bhattacharya examined Indian immigrants in New York City and his study found that India's hierarchical social class system was present in the City's Indian immigrant community, despite the widespread stereotype in the USA of its Asian Indian population as being uniformly composed of affluent professionals (Bhattacharya 2008: 65). Likewise, conclusions could be drawn from studying immigrant women's participation in the labour force of the USA. Read (2004), using data from the US Census and a national mail survey, examined the employment rates of Arab immigrant women, which rank among the lowest of any immigrant group and contrast sharply with the rates of native-born Arab-American women, which resemble those of US-born white women. He concluded that, contrary to findings for other immigrant groups, differences among Arab-American women cannot be explained by their human capital characteristics or family resources, but are almost entirely due to traditional cultural norms that prioritize women's family obligations over their economic activity and to ethnic and religious social networks that encourage the maintenance of traditional gender roles (Read 2004: 52). Read's research clearly underscores the impact of culture on immigrant women's employment.

Cultural characteristics also proved crucial in explaining the patterns of social mobility of Afro-Surinamese and Indo-Surinamese immigrants in the Netherlands (van Niekerk 2004). Van Niekerk observed that social mobility depended not just on the opportunity structure of the receiving society but, more importantly, on the past experiences and the socio-cultural repertoires that immigrants bring with them on arrival (van Niekerk 2004: 158). While both groups left Surinam at the same time and settled into very similar conditions in the Netherlands, their pre-migration histories differed considerably. These different pre-migration cultural legacies seem crucial to van Niekierk in order to understand the current differences in the economic and educational performance of these immigrants and their offspring upon arrival in the Netherlands (van Niekerk 2004: 158).[5]

Culture as a factor affecting the quality and intensity of migrants' relationships with the new environment was also stressed in the research on Mexican-immigrant welfare behaviours in the USA, which focused on the importance of employment-related cultural repertoires that migrants were socialized towards prior to their arrival (Van Hook and Bean 2009). Van Hook's and Bean's research suggests that strong pro-employment cultural orientations characterize Mexican immigrants and discourage reliance on welfare, except when participation is necessary for transitional financial support between jobs. Cultural resources may be exerting their own independent influence on behaviours and outcomes, even though the strength of such tendencies may fluctuate across situational contexts (Van Hook

5 For a parallel analysis of how differences in the cultural and historical conditions experienced by Mexicanos and Chicanos result in their different strategies of adaptation in the USA, see Hurtado et al. 1994.

and Bean 2009: 427). Van Hook and Bean conclude that family and employment-related imperatives for migration among Mexican immigrants, together with strong working-class expectations about the importance and necessity of holding a job, may operate not only to reduce public assistance recipiency among Mexican immigrants by shortening the duration of periods spent on welfare but also to increase the likelihood of such periods ending in employment (Van Hook and Bean 2009: 428).

The above literature review reveals that the question of cultural, pre-migratory legacies is very important and impacts on the way in which immigrants respond to the various environments of the host country. However, in this research, culture was not employed in a deterministic way, but its importance arises from looking at it in interplay with other factors – structural elements of the host country's environment and migrants' agency – in making choices and guiding the actions of migrants.

The knowledge accumulated in the above research enables us to conclude that culture is a widely recognized factor that assists in the understanding of immigrants in the new environment, as well as their different patterns and intensity of integration. Although the review was confined to the contexts of family, private life and economic activity of immigrants, where cultural legacies were prominent and therefore studied more closely, culture surely must also play a role in shaping migrants' relationships with the law and the legal system of the host country.

Socio-Legal Perspectives on Researching Migrants in the Host Country

Legal Assimilation

In the body of literature on assimilation, acculturation and integration, the law of the host country and its legal environment, especially immigration rules, have so far been considered as the minimum that migrants should comply with upon arrival in the new country. Many scholars of migrant adaptations portray the complinace as 'a habit change' – e.g. Cronin on Sicilian migrants in Australia (Cronin 1970: 14) – a change of behaviour resulting from migrants' experiences with the state.

The comparative review of early immigration policies emphasized the demands from the state of conformity at certain levels. These were usually associated with legal and civic matters:

> Whatever the ultimate extent of the voluntary acculturation … immigration today demands – and quite clearly will demand in the foreseeable future – it is the conformity in civic and legal matters from the time of first contact. This is the minimum which will inevitably be required by any national government. (Borrie 1959: 94)

The classic studies on migrants' assimilation and acculturation regarded compliance with the legal sphere – including the body of immigration laws – as the common denominator; the immigrant had to conform to the political and legal framework of the land and, after a period of apprenticeship during which he or she showed they were prepared to obey the rules of the game, they could generally (if so wished) become full participating members at these levels through the act of naturalization (Borrie 1959; Cronin 1970; Kallin 2003).

In other words, the sphere of law was included into those broad areas of life which fall in the public sector (as opposed to those areas of life which fall in the private sector – family patterns, friendships, membership in associations, home language, etc.) and were therefore controlled to some extent by the legal and moral sanctions of the country. Public sphere was reserved for all those activities which the immigrant was coerced to conform to, like societal rules and regulations, and where deviancy was punished. Thus, adherence to the laws of the new country was considered to be affected quickly and easily by conditions of change:

> In the workplace, he [immigrant] must obey the rules of the company in his tasks and the rules of the society in his interaction with fellow workers. If he … turns to a life of crime, then he has transgressed several societal and legal norms and will be imprisoned. (Cronin 1970: 14)

Empirically, migrants' legal assimilation – as the behavioural response to the legal environment of the host country – was studied by Jeremy Hein and Randall R. Beger (2001b). Their research focused on how international migrants litigate civil matters and therefore use the host society's legal system to seek redress for grievances during the resettlement process. Legal adaptation was defined as the process of change (adjustment) which enabled international migrants to proactively participate in the host society's legal system. The core indicator of legal adaptation was the increasing number of immigrant plaintiffs in civil litigation.

Immigrant plaintiffs provided the most direct indicator of legal adaptation because civil litigation occurs on terms that are entirely dictated by the host society. As such, Vietnamese migrants, in order to become plaintiffs, had to acquire legal competence – knowledge, social contacts and material resources – to participate effectively in American institutions and complete what legal scholars term 'the dispute process': the complex, often incomplete chain of events leading from grievance to a claim, from a claim to a dispute and from a dispute to litigation (Hein and Beger 2001b: 420). In the research, a sample (N = 137) of state and federal civil cases with at least one Vietnamese litigant was used to analyse the temporal patterns in legal adaptation among Vietnamese refugees from 1975 to 1994.

The authors identified that the changes that occurred among Vietnamese refugees in terms of swift legal adaptation (Hein and Beger 2001b: 420) civil suits with a Vietnamese plaintiff and a native defendant tended to occur earlier than civil suits with a native plaintiff and a Vietnamese defendant. In conclusion, Hein and Beger stressed 'rapid and profound changes' in immigrants' legal behaviour, a smooth legal assimilation attributed mainly to the role of legal organization of the host country (Hein and Beger 2001b: 420).

The legal environment – the legal architecture, law enforcement and institutions of the legal system of the host society – has therefore been widely recognized in the current socio-legal literature, where it figures most prominently as a factor responsible for the quality and timescale of the legal integration of immigrants:

> law defines individuals' rights to property and economic activity, political participation, physical security, religious and cultural identity [sic!], and family relationships ... the content and configuration of these extra-immigration rights help to structure the set of opportunities that people can exploit. (Schuck 2007: 241)

It is the law that determines the formal status that migrants might enjoy and entitlements they can claim; the law contributes to the normative and cultural settings in which migrants find themselves upon arrival. It is the law that designs, disciplines and legitimizes the political institutions and legal procedures of the immigration process that migrants must pass through (Schuck 2007: 254).

Studies of migration policies 'in the making' and of their administrative actors have focused on the trajectories and developments of those policies and have highlighted the fundamental role they play at both the national and supranational levels (Boswell 2008; Lahav and Guiraudon 2000). Moreover, several authors have focused on the role of institutional actors from decision to implementation, they are the ones carrying out immigration policies, fashioning and shaping their evolution (Guiraudon 2003; Joppke and Morawska 2003).

The impact of law and state institutions on the quality and character of migrants' legal integration has also been stressed by researchers grouped around the Migration Policy Index (MIPEX). This defined legal integration purely with reference to hard, institutional factors in the competence of the state as: 'migrants' legal status, residence rights, citizenship, and access to rights, goods, services, and resources' (Huddleston 2008). Similarly, Hofinger saw the destinies of migrants' adaptations widely determined by the national legal systems of host states. He pointed to legal integration as a necessary condition for social integration as the systematic prolongation of legal differences between the citizens of the state and immigrants reinforced social discrimination against the latter (Hofinger 1997: 29).

Indeed, the law's impact on international immigrants is now claimed to be more visible than ever. With the change in character of contemporary migration movements came the changes in legislation – exclusionary practices aimed at securing the borders of nation states – especially in view of the national labour markets. There was an observable turn in the policies of almost all states 'to limit immigration and to enforce those limitations through legal and extra-legal techniques' (Schuck 2007: 241).

As Bill Jordan and Franck Duvell in their study of incorporation of irregular migrants observed:

> irregular migration occurs because states make rules about who can legally cross their borders. Under conditions of globalization, these rules promote transnational economic activity, but limit who can work and stay. (Jordan and Duvell 2002: 235)

Although the restrictions on migratory inflows imposed by governments on the basis of race, national or labour market criteria could be traced back as early as the 1880s (Castles and Miller 1998: 91), the official views on illegal immigration changed dramatically as economic conditions worsened, unemployment increased and anti-immigrant political movements began to attract support in the 1970s and 1980s.

The growing apprehension about the numbers of immigrants and the subsequent regulatory measures to tighten up controls on immigration confirmed the power of the state to distinguish between its own citizens and 'aliens' in step with the extension of its welfare functions at the national level. The state re-established its position not only in deciding who is admitted but also who is treated as a full citizen.

In the UK changes in immigration policy and legislation were implemented by the Commonwealth Immigrants Acts 1962 and 1968 and the Immigration Act 1971 (the cornerstone of UK immigration law), followed by the British Nationality Act 1981, the Immigration Acts 1987 and 1988, the Asylum and Immigration Appeals Act 1993, the Asylum and Immigration Act 1996, the Immigration and Asylum Act 1999, the Nationality, Immigration and Asylum Acts 2002 and 2004, the Immigration (European Economic Area) Regulations 2004 and 2006 (revised), the Immigration and Nationality Act 2006, the UK Borders Act 2007 and the most recent Criminal Justice and Immigration Act 2008 and the Borders, Citizenship and Immigration Act 2009. In the USA they took the shape of a large-scale 'amnesty' programme under the Immigration Reform and Control Act of 1986, only to be followed by the tightening of immigration controls in the National Immigration Act in 1990, the Personal Responsibility and Work Opportunity Reconciliation Act 1996, the Illegal Immigration Reform and Immigrant Responsibility Act 1996 and the American Competitiveness and Workforce Improvement Act 1998. In the aftermath of 9/11 a battery of new laws was introduced focusing on enforcement of previously enacted immigration policies (e.g. Enhanced Border Security and Visa Entry Reform Act 2001, REAL ID Act of 2006, Secure Fences Act of 2006), in the context of the securitization and antiterrorism measures (USA PATRIOT Act of 2001).[6]

Although these laws were passed in an effort to curb immigration by restricting access to citizenship and restricting labour markets to legal citizens,

---

6 Analogous acts and changes in legislation aimed at securing nation-state borders were passed in other traditionally receiving countries – Australia, Canada, France and Germany. The detailed presentation of data for the UK is justified by the fact that it is the main focus of this analysis. The USA was selected for the purposes of comparison.

legal permanent residents and other authorized workers (highly skilled migrant workers in particular), they also transformed legal status into an elitist and exclusive concept that was practically unattainable for many contemporary economic migrants. As a result of these legal changes, immigrants' 'otherness' has become legally constructed through the reproduction of contingent illegality (Calavita 2005: 72). In *Immigrants at the Margins* (2005), Calavita, looking at the receiving countries of Spain and Italy, argued that the genuine integration (and assimilation) framework became exhausted and this failure was linked to the immigrants' economic marginality that the law reproduced. Empirical support for Calavita's claims of the legal production of the 'illegality' of immigrants was also found in the US context. De Genova observed that while no other country has contributed to the US economy as much as Mexico in terms of supplying a labour force, the changes in US immigration laws since 1965 have created increasingly severe restrictions on 'legal' migration from Mexico (De Genova 2004: 16).

The restrictive laws and hardening of the immigration policy have curtailed the rights of both legal and illegal immigrants, shifted the orientation of immigration law from serving to policing functions and, most importantly, linked immigrants' work contracts more closely to their legal status (Calavita 2005: 41–5). The law has become critical of immigrants' strategies, in that legal status was increasingly a pre-requisite for rights and services, and that immigration law became embedded in other institutions and relationships (Coutin 1998: 901).

Although the role of the legal environment is decisive for migrants' legal adaptations, one cannot help but notice that the sole focus on the host state's legal frameworks portrays migrants as passive recipients of the (ever so limited) opportunity structures consisting of immigration laws and state policies as expressed in the works of legal institutions. In case of 'illegal' migrants, it is the 'procedural delays and release pending removals [that] enable them to gain most of what they migrated for in the first place' (Schuck 2007: 248). Any indications of migrants as active and responsive agents are limited to those 'few who do manage to beat the system and elicit criticism of the immigration agency' and therefore weaken enforcement incentives in future cases (Schuck 2007: 248) – immigrants as villains or victims.

Legal Transnationalism

The shift in focus from how immigrants are accommodated in the host state's legal systems towards migrants themselves to help explain their differentiated patterns of legal adaptations was therefore a direct response to the shortcomings and limitations of the legal assimilation, top-down perspective. As early as 1988, Menski, in the context of the presence of South Asians in the UK, argued that the sole focus on the host state's (in this case English) law remains too formal and almost completely overlooks the viewpoint 'from within' minorities (Menski 1988).

Legal transnationalism, whilst highlighting the more exclusionary nature of immigration laws as a framework of looking at migrants' relationship with the law in the host country, also provided a lens to understand why migrants' responses towards the legal environment of the host country became more complex, multi-faceted and less straightforward than anticipated by the earlier research. At first glance, migrants may lead transnational lives between two locations (their home and receiving countries), not only because that may constitute their choice but also due to the exclusionary character of the laws of the host country, which may not allow them to settle. Nevertheless, transnationalism acknowledged migrants as active agents in shaping their behavioural and attitudinal responses to the law of the host country (Abrego 2008; Coutin 2000; Hagan 1994; Mahler 1995; Menjivar 2000).

Behavioural Responses and Legalization Strategies

The nature of the changes in immigration legislation transferred legal status in the host country from being considered the required minimum, which migrants, via the initial period of 'apprenticeship', should (and actually would) obtain relatively easily by 'mastering the rules of the game' (Borrie 1959: 90–91), into a 'good' that migrants should now struggle for. The level of requirements migrants have to undergo in order to comply with the law of the host country was transformed into complicated and time-consuming immigration regulations. For those who entered the country via other routes, conforming to the political and legal framework of the land now means engaging with legalization strategies (Coutin 2000; Hagan 1994; Mahler 1995). Not surprisingly, therefore, many of the migrants, having faced a complicated bureaucracy of application requirements and renewal deadlines, frequently fall into illegality, sometimes despite their best efforts (Calavita 2005; Menjivar 2006).

Relatively few studies have so far focused on the intricacies of – especially undocumented – immigrants' behavioural responses to the legal environment of the host country via the legalization strategies they have devised to deal with the body of law (Coutin 1998, 2000; Hagan 1994; Mahler 1995). These approaches combined focus on migrants' efforts to follow and/or to challenge immigration law over the struggle for legalization and change of their legal status from illegal immigrants to residents.

Coutin (2000) in *Legalizing Moves* looked at the battle Salvadoran immigrants had fought for two decades to win legal permanent residency in the USA.Drawing on interviews with Salvadoran asylum applicants, observations from deportation hearings and fieldwork within the Salvadoran community in Los Angeles, Coutin illustrated not only the profound effects of increasingly restrictive immigration laws on the lives of undocumented immigrants in the USA but also how immigrants in their 'legalizing moves' wrangled with the system that classified them, structured and, in some cases, re-structured the law. Activists and immigrants themselves challenged and stretched the law in order to define and sometimes re-define themselves in legal categories (Coutin 1998: 907). By shifting the focus from the law's ability to control entry to immigrants' attempts to negotiate their legal status in the USA, Coutin suggested that migrants are far from being powerless and in fact actively respond to authorities' political manoeuvrings (Coutin 2000).

Similar conclusions could be drawn from various studies looking into the impact of the large-scale amnesty programme in the USA over the past two decades – the Immigration Reform and Control Act of 1986 (IRCA 1986). Hagan (1994), examining the responses of the Maya community in Houston, also portrayed immigrants as active and empowered decision makers as they subverted the legalization process in ways that challenged the assumptions of policy makers. Hagan's message is particularly visible through the title of her book: *Deciding to Be Legal* (1994). Initially, most of the immigrants assumed that they could not become legalized because they considered themselves ineligible, but as time passed they discovered that the Immigration and Naturalization Service (INS) office was interpreting the documentation requirements of the legalization programme fairly loosely. As a result, immigrants who were technically ineligible began to apply, securing the necessary documentation through their social networks. Though their goal at the time of applying was merely to obtain work authorization while their applications were pending, most were granted legal status. Despite obtaining legal status, many of these immigrants maintained that they might eventually return to Guatemala, thus countering the popular notion that US citizenship was every immigrant's dream. Hagan's research demonstrates that 'the Maya were far more than passive recipients of immigration policy: they perceived, interpreted, and ultimately acted upon the programme' (Hagan 1994: 91).

A different set of responses to the same amnesty programme in the USA could be observed among the Salvadoran and Guatemalan immigrant populations, as documented by Mahler (1995). *American Dreaming* bitterly assessed the impact of the IRCA 1986 on straining the relations between employers and employees and making many people feel illegitimate (Mahler 1995: 165). As a result, many undocumented migrants excluded by the legalization programmes were enticed into fraud by the hope of securing legal papers. The desire for legalization was therefore often achieved by the employment of illicit and illegal means. Mahler paints a portrait of a community fraught with internal tensions and ample opportunities for migrants to exploit each other. Her ethnography brings evidence of a pseudo-legal industry of offices and assistants that materialized quickly after the passage of the IRCA 1986 and undertook, on a large scale, the forging of documents, the production of bogus green cards and the filling in of invalid asylum application forms on behalf of immigrants believing that they had merely applied for work authorization (Mahler 1995: 164). These pseudo-legal practices found a good market for their illicit business among many of those immigrants who could not avail themselves of the legalization programme or could find no other means to obtain legal status other than to buy fake documents and present them to their employers (Mahler 1995: 167).

These studies of migrants' responses to law related to the behavioural changes that migrants had chosen to undergo (or were coerced into undergoing) in order to adapt; they brought to the forefrontmigrants' agency vis-à-vis the law and the legal system of the host country. Contradictions of adaptation, settlement and legalization, for women as well as men, underscore the importance of moving from a simplistic, unilinear continuum whose end-points are marked by supposedly mutual exclusive categories such as 'sojourner' and 'settler' to more multi-dimensional perspectives that recognize that many migrants live for long periods of time in a transnational context where categories may overlap and community boundaries may be fluid in time and space.

The above accounts of differentiated patterns of legalization strategies integrate human agency and structural constraint by showing how individual understandings and social interactions aggregate to partly shape institutions, while institutions and larger social structures provide the foundations for and constraints on individual understanding and social interaction. Migrants were not merely passive recipients of the institutional and legal structures designed by the host country (very often prior to their arrival), but are actively engaged themselves with the law in the pursuit of their goal – the change in their legal status. They re-defined themselves in legal categories (Coutin 1998), very often challenging the top-down divisions and strict legal definitions (Coutin 2000). Others exercised their agency by acting upon the legal system and legalization programmes with the purpose of making more or less informed decisions whether or not to legalize their status (Hagan 1994).

This revealed the complex dynamics in migrants' behavioural strategies towards the law of the host country and prompted the observation that not all migrants were oriented towards the change in their legal status. Yet, as documented by Mahler (1995), migrants' agency and engagement with the immigration laws of the host country were not benign in their consequences; they resulted in the establishment of pseudo-legal business links among the migrants, with an army of 'legal assistants' recruited from within the immigrant networks whose inadequate interpretation of the immigration regulations left many fellow applicants in direct danger of deportation. The failed applications, compromising their identity, in turn trapped many migrants in the state of 'liminal legality' (Menjivar 2006).

Attitudes towards Law

The cognitive responses of migrants towards the legal environment of the host country in terms of attitudes, values, images and interpretations of law have been given considerably less attention.

In the area of law enforcement, Song (1992) analysed qualitatively and quantitatively the attitudes of Chinese immigrants and Vietnamese refugees towards the law in the USA. The application, enforcement and interpretation of legal rules tend to be more mechanical in the USA than in China and Vietnam, where the ideas of rule and law are more flexible and more situational (Song 1992). As a result, many Asians maintained a deep distrust of formal institutions such as the police and the courts, which addressed situations that they believed should be handled privately and exposed them to public scrutiny and public decision making.

Culture, as a factor mediating migrants' responses to the legal system in the USA (Renteln 2004), has been considered with regard to a wide variety of immigrant groups: Asian-born (Ma 1995), Albanian (Brelvi 1997), Russian (Korkeakivi and Zolotukhina 1999; Ojito 1997), Chinese (Potter 1999), Middle Eastern (Hamed and Moore 1999) and Vietnamese (Ta 1999). Bauer (1999) demonstrated how prior legal experiences (e.g. fear and aversion towards the legal system) influenced a Ukrainian immigrant to refuse to accept a court-appointed lawyer to help defend him against charges of bear trapping, implying that a court-appointed attorney was part of the KGB (Bauer 1999). In the European context, Banakar (2008) showed how cultural background provided a mitigating circumstance in the criminal lawsuit against a Kurdish immigrant before a Swedish (Sandviken) lower court (Banakar 2008).

A similar argument concerning the presence of immigrants' culture in American courts has been made by Hein and Beger (2001b), who concluded that invocations of culture in litigation cases involving immigrants were far more multi-dimensional: they encompassed a variety of legal actors (not only defendants), involved far more issues than just conduct norms and consisted of more diverse legal strategies than those reported in the literature on cultural defence (Hein and Beger 2001a). Hein and Beger's research illustrated not only the defensive employment of culture (Hein and Beger 2001a: 49) but also the offensive, proactive use of culture when an immigrant's culture was used by the prosecution against an immigrant defendant (Hein and Beger 2001a: 54). The authors also revealed discretionary uses of culture by judges at the sentencing stage, where culture became employed as a proxy for deeply ingrained distrust of the government and the legal authorities (Hein and Beger 2001a: 55).

Although the influence of culture on migrants' responses to the host country's laws and institutions figures prominently in the legal literature, in these studies culture exists as a given sets of values and attitudes that are somewhat 'incompatible' with the host country's laws and norms. The research review on migrants who employed and invoked their culture in courts suggests that culture has so far been discussed and debated as a 'problem', an 'issue' in a given context of civil or criminal litigation, pointing to its static yet determining role in shaping one's behaviour. The misuse of cultural arguments in court may also result in the criminalization of culture. Kusters (2009) observed how Romani culture is envisaged in the jurisprudence as supposedly implying a certain (fixed) heritage and tradition. In *Smith v. United Kingdom (No. 2)*, just because the Roma applicant had bought a plot of land to put her caravan on, the court did not consider her a 'true' gypsy as her nomadic lifestyle was neither 'genuine' nor 'real' enough to be worthy of protection (Kusters 2009: 222).

Suffice to say that this approach added to the portrayal of migrants as passive carriers of their cultural values, leaving no space for recognizing their agency in the process of legal adaptation or even punishing them for adapting their customs. Discussing the use and abuse of cultural defence, Renteln (2009) argues that culture can be contested or may be 'dying out' in the country of origin. It is also important to stress that culture can adapt to the host country's environment and assume a different form from that in the country of origin, making any invocation of cultural argument in front of the court a very sensitive issue. In the UK a Yoruba woman was charged with assault occasioning bodily harm for making tribal markings on her son's faces on New Year's Day to ensure the maintenance of their cultural identity (*R v. Adesanya*). The judge rejected her defence that it was a 'Nigerian custom' as she did it at New Year ('which was not the custom') and that she did it when her son was much older than is 'the usual practice' (Renteln 2009: 79). Not surprisingly, a common criticism of the cultural defence is that it leads to the 'essentializing' of culture and does not leave much scope for change or adaptation.

However, recent conceptualizations have enabled more flexible interpretations of culture (Swidler 1986). Culture is not a unified system that pushes action in a consistent direction. It is employed as it shapes the web of cognitive, affective and bodily schemas through which actors come to know how to act in particular social worlds (Emirbayer and Mische 1998: 981). Neither a determinist nor a instrumentalist force, culture is more like a 'toolkit' or repertoire (Hannerz 1969: 186–8) from which actors select differing pieces in order to construct 'strategies of action' (Swidler 1986). Culture is also not static; it is dynamic and it is changing, and it influences migrants' responses to law, although not as a determinant force. An approach to culture that recognizes human agency enables us to see culture as not only shaping migrants' actions but as also being shaped by them.

Legal Pluralism

This flexible, indeterministic and non-essentialist approach to culture has been at the core of legal pluralists' writings. Within legal pluralism, there are two distinguishable lines of enquiry which investigated the relationship between migrants and the law in the British context. One looked at how migrants retained their legal practices and principles, including values and attitudes to the law, not in an unchangeable fashion but devising all manner of adaptive responses to their new environment (Ballard 2007; Menski 1993, 2007; Shah 2008). The second strand of scholarship demonstrated how the English state law adapted to accommodate the legal traditions and practices of migrants (Davies 2005; Menski 2007; Poulter 1986, 1988, 1998; Shah 2008).

Ballard's (1994) indepth examination of South Asians in Britain over the last 30 years concluded that they were continuing to deploy their own distinctive values, conventions and expectations to order their personal and domestic lives. It is the legal principle of *riwaj* – 'a convenient means of maintaining order' within the community – that the elders would routinely turn to in their efforts to achieve dispute resolution in the UK, just as they did back home in South Asia (Ballard 1994).

Nonetheless, these customary legal principles have not remained unchanged but were re-articulated and re-negotiated by users in the British context in response to various social, cultural, linguistic, moral and legal pressures stemming from the new surroundings. As a result of migrants reconstructing their lives in the

UK on their *own preferred terms* along the lines articulated by Ballard (1994), a 'new', *self-adapted* form of *riwaj* emerged. It could best be described as a form of unofficial law (Chiba 1998) suited to the conditions that South Asians encountered in the UK (Ballard 2006: 51).

In this context, Menski (1993) pondered whether uniformity in immigrants' responses to law, as an outcome of adaptation, was a truly desirable aim and urged that we should not avert our eyes from the emerging realities of legal pluralism as a result of migration processes. By recognizing migrants' agency in building their relationship with the host state's legal system, legal pluralists demonstrated how South Asians in Britain have been following English law *and* their respective traditional laws, leading to the emergence of new forms of Hindu, Muslim and Sikh laws in Britain that were different from their sub-continental prototypes (Menski 1993: 244). Rather than adjusting to English law by abandoning facets of their customary obligation systems, South Asian communities in the UK incorporated the requirements of host state law into their traditional laws, thereby constructing new forms of legal rules. Menski concluded that the transformations and adaptations of *shariat* among the Muslim immigrants and *dharma* among the Hindu immigrants (and second generation) in the UK rather resemble *angrezi shariat* (British Shariat) or *angrezi dharma* (British Dharma), respectively – law adapted to conditions encountered in the host environment (Menski 2008).

On the other side of this relationship, we have English state law and impressive research into its adaptation to accommodate the legal customs and practices of migrants. Poulter pioneered the study examining the approach adopted by English judges towards the recognition of African (Poulter 1988), Asian, Chinese and Muslim customs (Poulter 1986), either through the operation of conflicts of law principles or invoking the notions of 'public policy' and 'reasonable tolerance', avoiding the charges of ethnocentricity, or via the application of human rights principles (Poulter 1988: 216–19; Shah 2008: 7).

Critical of Poulter's approach – seeing it as too formal and completely overlooking the viewpoint of the ethnic minorities – Menski turned to how new *British-based* forms of ethnic customary laws have been juxtaposed with English law (Menski 2007). His analyses revealed how judges, in delivering their judgments, strike a balance between strong notions of justice and fairness (the principle of equity) and protecting English law from the unrelenting pressure to accept personal laws, such as those of the Muslims, as part of the new British legal framework (Ballard 2006). It led Menski to propose this normative statement:

> Unless Northern legal systems learn to restructure their rule systems in such a way that they can formally and more fully incorporate what migrants from the South and their descendants claim to be 'their' *law*, we will not achieve satisfactory integration at the legal level or a sustainable balance of official and unofficial law. (Menski 2006: 28, emphasis in original)

This suggests that pluralist approaches are more dialectic in character and are as concerned with highlighting transgressive bottom-up perspectives of ethno-religious subalterns as they are with delineating the hegemonic (and all too often exclusionary) legal frameworks.

Fresh demonstrations of these conclusions can be found in the most recent volume edited by Holden (2011), which raises the important issue of expert witnessing in cases involving migrants and ethnic minorities in different jurisdictions. It proves that work on legal transnationalism is no longer restricted to the rights of irregular migrants but also now discusses transjurisdictional engagement with different legal systems by migrants as transnational actors. Transjurisdictional practices such as marriages among members of Britain's South Asian diaspora (Shah 2011) or the adoption of children (Shah 2009) occur within a wider habitus of 'transnational social fields' and raise questions about how British officials and courts respond to the facts and decide the legal validity of such transjurisdictional practices in British private international law and immigration law.

It is however primarily the South Asian immigrant communities (Bangladeshis, Sikhs, Gujaratis and Pakistanis) arriving in the UK since the 1940s and 1950s which have constituted the main focus of the legal pluralists' analysis. Ballard nevertheless goes a step further and concludes that:

> Unless our courts of law – no less and no more than all our other major public institutions – begin to be able to take more adequate cognizance of the plural character of our society, there is a grave danger that they will all too frequently find themselves delivering injustice rather than justice when New European litigants appear before them. (Ballard 2007: 13)

While immigrants from countries with plural legal traditions (combining religious laws with strong customary or personal law orders) or legal systems significantly different from that of state law dominance have been at the core of the above analysis, I would argue that it is not justified to say that legal pluralism provides 'the lens' to observe immigrants' relationship with law in the host country.

Since the early 1990s, the UK has experienced a new immigration flow that – contrary to that of the post-war years – is mostly from non-Commonwealth countries with no prior colonial ties to it. Vertovec (2006) observed that the UK is increasingly characterized by: a sizeable migrant population from developing countries with no direct colonial link to the UK; a greater linguistic diversity (with over 300 languages spoken in London); a proliferation of 'new' immigrant groups (e.g. Brazilians, Colombians and Eastern Europeans) alongside large and long-standing 'ethnic communities'; a more fluid duration and greater variety of legal statuses; and the sustenance of greater transnational connections (social, religious, political, etc.) on the part of migrants (Vertovec 2006).

Given this super-diversity of contemporary migrants, it is rather naïve to assume that one analytical lens will do justice to their various characteristics and relationships with the law. Not all migrants arriving in the host country will carry their own 'legal baggage' in the form of alternative (to the state law) unofficial laws (Chiba 1998) or customary practices of social ordering based on indigenous, religious or private laws (Chiba 1998). While the plurality of laws, legal orders and legal traditions was an inseparable part of the history of many states, it is not safe to assume that the past determines the present. That said, equally not all cultures developed strong legal-normative orders that would 'survive' migration as the 'distance experience' (Mead 1964).

Furthermore, what about immigrants who come from countries where it is the state law that is constitutionally sanctioned by the legitimate authority of the government to have overall jurisdiction? However, the dominance of state law does not mean that migrants arrive in the host country without any 'baggage'. On the contrary – the baggage is just of a different character. It comprises different values, different attitudes to state law and different patterns of legal behaviour towards the state law and its institutions, which could be best interpreted as legal culture or collective legal consciousness (Kurkchiyan 2010).

These values and attitudes to law continue to be employed by migrants on arrival in the host country as signposts and a compass for behaviour in their following, avoiding and manoeuvering through the unfamiliar legal reality (Bierbrauer 1994). The values reveal themselves in migrants' dealings with immigration services (Home Office), the Inland Revenue and welfare offices, but also with the labour market, where contemporary economic migrants are most visible (relationship between employers and employees, tax matters, health and safety provisions, etc.). Yet, as with the adaptations of South Asians documented by Ballard (1994), the values are not static and fixed, but dynamic and changing. New ideas emerge from their antecedents; migrants as active agents engage with state legal frameworks which result in the internal dynamics of their values, attitudes to law and patterns of accustomed behaviour.

Therefore, with no strong premises for the adoption of the legal pluralism lens, one could turn to legal consciousness/culture denoting and best capturing the subtleties and nuances of migrants' values, attitudes to law and patterns of behaviour towards the state and the legal institutions. To put it differently, Menski observed that:

> it came as a shock to 'Asians' to discover, in the early 1970s, that their customary marriage rituals did not create legally valid marriages in the UK; the result was a speedy process of 'learning the law', to the extent that all 'Asians' will now register their marriages. (Menski 1988: 219)

An immediate question arises: was this behavioural turn to the law, while initially probably inspired by instrumental considerations, accompanied by any changes in values and attitudes to the state law?

Legal Culture, Legal Consciousness

Legal culture and its aspect, legal consciousness – inspired by the social constructivist vision of law – have been successfully employed in order to understand how people interpret and relate themselves to law.[7]

The foundational studies in the field focused on ordinary people and their attitudes and behaviour towards the law in formal institutional settings. The research examined ordinary people who brought their problems to small claims courts (Merry 1990; Yngvesson 1993) and their interactions with the welfare bureaucracy (Sarat 1990). The early empirical studies looked into people's attitudes to legal institutions (Sarat 1977) when they were filing cases seeking a divorce (Sarat and Felstiner 1995) or when they were the subjects of sex and race discrimination (Bumiller 1988).

In a trendsetting study of the perception of law by lower-class Americans, Sally Engle Merry (1990) framed her observations in terms of legal ideology. *Getting Justice, Getting Even* provides an insight into legal consciousness through a thoughtful and rich ethnographic portrayal of white working-class American individuals (primarily women) who sought redress for personal wrongs within the lower criminal courts, small claims courts, juvenile courts and their associated mediation programmes in the early 1980s. Merry has taken up the question of the legal meanings that people attach to their court experiences: 'the way that people understand and use the law' (Merry 1990: 5). Lay plaintiffs' definitions of the law frequently differ from those of judges and lawyers, and what lay plaintiffs want, neither the court nor mediation can give.

This strand of empirical research concerning legal consciousness/legal culture is helpful in understanding and subsequently researching the similar mechanisms that many international migrants are faced with in the context of their beginnings in the host country. On arrival they have to attend to immigration matters (or not) and register with the police or local authorities. If migrants want to start working, they need to arrange for an appointment to get a National Insurance number (or its equivalent) and attend the interview. They must liaise with the tax offices with respect to tax contributions. They must also contact local authorities or welfare

7 The distinctions between the concepts of legal culture and legal consciousness have been the subject of much debate in socio-legal studies. I understand legal culture as comprising both the behavioural *and* cognitive spheres of people's relationship with the law. It encompasses values and attitudes to law, as well as legal behaviour. Legal consciousness is therefore treated here as an aspect of legal culture – a theoretical concept relating to the cognitive sphere of people's relationship with the law, their values and attitudes to law, but also images, myths and understandings of it. However, this analytical distinction is not reflected by much of the empirical research reviewed here, where on various occasions the terms 'legal culture' and 'legal consciousness' have been used interchangeably. It is beyond the scope of this research to engage in the division between the subjects studied under the legal culture and legal consciousness discourses, respectively, as the overlap of issues is quite extensive and the same – or similar – topics were successfully studied under both approaches.

agencies when applying for benefits. Careful examination of these situations enables us to see the meanings and interpretations that migrants attach to their 'formal' experiences of law in the host country – from immigration offices via courts to welfare bureaux.

A substantial shift in the studies on legal consciousness was initiated by Patricia Ewick and Susan Silbey (1998). *The Common Place of Law* looked at how ordinary people interpret and relate themselves to the law outside of the legal and welfare offices, courtrooms and other formal or laboratory settings, and focused on everyday life in commonplace locations like workplaces, schools and neighbourhoods. Theoretically, Ewick and Silbey's account offered an interesting conceptual fusion between legal consciousness and the understanding of legality. The authors contended that legality, understood as 'the meanings, sources of authority, and cultural practices that are commonly recognized as legal, regardless of who employs them for what ends' (Ewick and Silbey 1998: 22), manifests itself in various forms of legal consciousness.

Ewick and Silbey (1998) show how ordinary people – citizens of New Jersey – sometimes saw themselves as 'before the law', sometimes 'with the law' and sometimes 'against the law' (Ewick and Silbey 1998). For instance, when people described the law as magisterial and remote (before the law), they saw themselves as supplicants. When they described the law as a game (with the law), they perceived themselves as players. And when they described the law as an arbitrary body of rules constructed to assist the powerful (against the law), they cast themselves as resisters. Ewick and Silbey further maintain that these three modes of consciousness are not entirely separate or even opposed, but instead are inter-related in practice. The contradictions and tensions revealed in the presence of various forms of legal consciousness sustain its very power and durability in social life (Ewick and Silbey 1998: 224).

The shift in the studies of legal consciousness has found many followers, including Hull's (2003) research on the cultural enactment of legality in the case of same-sex marriages (Hull 2003), Marshall's (2003) insights into the frames that women use to understand their experiences of sexual harassment (Marshall 2003) and Hoffmann's (2003) examination of how workers perceive the laws and rules that regulate their workplaces (Hoffmann 2003).

The socio-legal perspective of *moving the law into the common place* offers a useful reference point for investigating migrants' understandings, interpretations and invocations of law and legality: their experiences of law at work (registering with employment agencies and businesses, making use of their social security numbers (or not)); using public services (opening bank accounts, sending money home, registering with a GP, looking for a flat with an agency or joining the queue for a council flat); or within their community (relationships with flatmates, neighbours, informal codes of conduct, borrowing money and etiquette).

Researching Migrants' Relationship with Law: Towards an Integrated Approach

The review of the traditional approaches to the incorporation of migrants into the host society brought the study to the concept of integration. Integration, especially when considered within the transnational framework, portrays migrants as agents who are not merely passive recipients of the opportunity structures available to them upon arrival but – analytically and methodologically – possess a certain degree of freedom in choosing how to respond to the new environment of the host country.

The cultural approach to researching migrants in the host societies strongly accentuated the role of symbolic understandings, links and pre-migratory cultural legacies which migrants employed in shaping their responses to the new environment.

In building the premises for this study, this chapter, by focusing on the socio-legal perspective of researching migrants in the host country, has highlighted existing gaps and certain shortcomings in the current knowledge on the various aspects of socio-legal integration.

The legal assimilationist approach to migrants' integration in legal and civic matters tended to overstress the role of nation states and their immigration policies as the main actors in the socio-legal integration process. Therefore, legal integration has so far been researched either from the perspective of the host state's institutions (the role of nation states) or the perspective of the legal status of migrants (the consequences of particular immigration laws already in place). The research focused primarily on the legal opportunity structures produced by the states and available to migrants upon arrival: immigration policies, naturalization laws and legalization programmes (Hofinger 1997; Huddleston 2008).

Suffice to say that this does not hold true, especially in the current world of globalized, polysemic migration flows, with people constantly on the move, crossing various national, state or local borders. Indeed, it has to be stressed that migrants, in fashioning their responses to civic and legal matters, have been largely influenced by the structural factors of the host country's laws and immigration policies, but, at the same time, this did not happen solely with reference to these factors (Coutin 2000; Hagan 1994). Very often, different groups of migrants faced with the same (or very similar) laws in a host country would demonstrate different ways of responding to them, from distinctive relationships with law, with some of the groups following the laws more closely than others, avoiding different laws and, more importantly, presenting a variety of nuanced interpretations and understandings of law and legality.

Therefore, this review points to a conclusion that the different outcomes of socio-legal integration between various groups of migrants cannot be explained solely with regard to the institutional and legal structures available to immigrants in the host country upon arrival. This study argues that the socio-legal integration of migrants is also worth considering from the perspective of migrants' agency in responding to the legal environment of the host country, researching their values, attitudes to law and legal behaviour.

In the literature that looked at migrants' responses to the host country's laws and legal institutions (Abrego 2008; Coutin, 1998; Hagan 1994) migrants might have been perceived as making choices regarding their immigration status, engaging in a battle to win legal permanent residency, and yet the culture as a factor that many migrants drew upon in fashioning their responses to the legal environment was largely neglected. Whenever migrants' culture was mentioned in the literature relating to legal integration, migrants were portrayed as carriers of certain deeply embedded cultural values, traditions and traits. Migrants' culture and their attitudes to law were in turn mainly presented as given, stable and almost resistant to change in the new socio-legal environment and hence as creating a problem, an issue that had to be addressed before or by a judge (Banakar 2008; Hein and Beger 2001a, 2001b; Hamed and Moore 1999; Sellin 1938).

The cultural perspective, if applied without nuances and qualifications, might of course be prone to abuse: it is usually the behaviour of 'they', the others (the immigrants or members of minority groups) which tends to be regarded as culturally conditioned, while the behaviour of the dominant majority is 'just normal' – 'culture' might be envisaged as the antithesis of normality (Ballard 2010). While the accounts of how South Asians re-built their community life 'on their own terms' (Ballard 1994), including the order, legal hierarchies and means of dispute resolution, provide rich insights into the means of legal adaptation, the main focus remains inward-looking on the community itself. The legal pluralist perspective on legal adaptations was usually intermediated via minority communities' distinctive 'rules of the game' and tells us little about their members' values or attitudes to the state law of the host country – how immigrants perceive the host state, its institutions and enforcement agencies, and whether these views, values and attitudes undergo a change. The communities are not homogeneous but are complicated by those characteristics of their members other than 'cultural' ones (class, education levels and socio-economic positions, to name but a few).

Apart from South Asians, which legal pluralists focused on as a distinctive immigrant population, many different immigrant groups are now facing the questions of legal adaptations. Eastern Europeans (e.g. Poles, Ukrainians, Lithuanians and Romanians) or Latin Americans (e.g. Brazilians and Colombians) in the UK, for example, with no traditional or colonial ties to the country have over the last 20 years substantively enriched the British ethnic mosaic. Between 2003 and 2010 the Polish-born population alone increased from 75,000 to 532,000 to become the second largest group of immigrants in the UK, placed between immigrants of Indian (at 684,000 in 2010) and Pakistani origin (419,000 in 2010) (Office for National Statistics 2011).

While the literature on the subject is scarce, the available empirical evidence (Abrego 2008; Coutin 2000; Kubal 2009) suggests that whilst more recent migrants do not rely on systems of personal laws or distinct codes with regard to family formation or dispute resolution, their individual responses to the legal system of the host country, be it in everyday life or when facing public institutions, are very much intermediated by different values and attitudes to law, different understandings of what the law is for and different meanings attached to legality.

This research, engaging critically with the reviewed literature, offers a new approach to studying socio-legal integration, based on the case study of Polish post-2004 EU enlargement migrants in the UK. It proposes a focus on migrants as agents responding to the new socio-legal environment and yet in their choices being influenced not only by the structural factors stemming from the host country's legal environment, but also by their legal culture background – the values, accustomed patterns of legal behaviour and attitudes to law – in the process of shaping (and possibly re-shaping) their relationship to law in the host country.

This study therefore makes the claim for the proper recognition of the cultural background of immigrants, taking into account the cultural patterns of values and attitudes to law stemming from the different legal cultures in which migrants were socialized to prior to their arrival and residence in the host country. The research calls for the re-definition of legal culture from stagnant, homogeneous, deterministic sets of values and attitudes influencing behaviour to more flexible repertoires of habits and toolkits (Swidler 1986), allowing people to exercise their choice and agency while designing their responses toward the legal system of the host country. This research acknowledges legal culture as a more significant factor in empirical research, accounting for nuances and bringing out the subtle differences and therefore revealing the bigger, richer picture of immigrant socio-legal integration, than one solely relying on structural factors and government policies of immigrant incorporation. The approach to culture adopted in this book acknowledges the diversity of sub-cultures and sub-groups within it, at the same time stressing a general, distinguishable and largely shared pattern of accustomed behaviour, thinking and experiences of law.

Chapter 3
Polish Post-2004 EU Enlargement Migrants in the UK: Case Study

Polish migrants' lives in the UK are intertwined with law in a threefold way. Firstly, as 'new' EU citizens, they are subject to European regulations on European citizenship (Article 18 of the EC Treaty) and safeguarding the principle of free movement of persons as laid out in the Treaty of Accession (2003). Secondly, Polish migrants are subject to how these European regulations are depicted in British legislation.[1] Finally, Polish immigrants, whilst living and working in the UK, have to comply with British national legislation in all other areas not specified or covered under the European legislation, particularly employment law, labour law, health and safety provisions, welfare benefits, etc.

The intermediate area, comprising the British national legislation enacted in response to the conditions specified in the Treaty of Accession (2003) and – more generally – in order to interpret and implement the European provisions on the free movement principle, is particularly important as it clearly illustrates how the British legal system impinges on the lives of the Polish migrant population (as well as other A8 nationals). During the transition period, three pieces of legislation – the Accession (Immigration and Worker Registration) Regulations 2004 (SI 2004/121), the Social Security (Habitual Residence) Amendment Regulations 2004 (SI 2004/1232) and the Immigration (European Economic Area) and Accession (Amendment) Regulations 2004 (SI 2004/1236) – regulated and limited the right of residence for workers from Poland (and other A8 countries) and their family members by imposing compulsory employment registration under the Workers Registration Scheme (WRS), and denied the right to reside for work-seekers.

Under European law, the transitory provisions could not be continued beyond the seventh anniversary of the accession to the EU of the countries to which they applied. As a result, the WRS was closed on 30 April 2011. Upon the completion of the transition period and discontinuation of the scheme, Polish migrants' rights to residence and social security and access to the labour market have finally been

1 During the transition period, between 2004 and 2011, by the way of derogation from Article 39 EC (free movement of workers) and Articles 1–6 of Regulation (EEC) No. 1612/68 on the freedom of movement of workers within the Community, in accordance with the Treaty of Accession, national laws (laws of the respective 15 ('old') EU Member States) were put in place to provide for the situation of workers from eight of the ten new Member States (the A8 countries).

brought into line with the rights of 'older' EU citizens (the EU-15) (Residence Directive 2004/38) and British citizens.

One of the aims of this book is to comprehensively evaluate and assess the impacts that the transitory measures had on the lives and work of A8 migrants in the UK between 2004 and 2011. The Accession Regulations 2004, as an inseparable part of the legal environment, should be considered as an important factor that shaped the relationship of migrants with the law. Despite its discontinuation on 1 May 2011, the effects of the WRS are still visible and are also likely to have a lingering effect on the residence conditions of A8 migrants in the future.[2]

The influence of accession regulations during the transition period was of course far greater. It meant that although Polish migrants arriving in the UK experienced no problems clearing immigration at the airports and sea ports, shortly after arrival they were faced with a detailed body of regulations. The laws put in place by the UK for the migrants from the 'new' EU Member States, although fairly liberal in comparison to the immigration policy of other 'old' EU Member States (Germany or Austria, for example), did not make these migrants full recipients of the free movement of persons principle, but stated a set of conditions to aspire to such status. If the migrants wanted to work legally in the UK, they were required to register their employment with the Home Office under the WRS within one month of taking up a job. There was a £90 fee for joining the Scheme.[3] If they did not register, their work became illegal and migrants 'might' need to stop working (UK Border Agency 2004). Migrants should have remained within the Scheme for 12 months, after which they were no longer required to register and gained full rights as British residents, equal to those of other EU nationals coming from the 'old' 15 Member States. In practical terms, this meant that Polish migrants were included within the welfare and benefits system and passed the right to reside and habitual residence test required for many means-tested benefits only when the 12 month transition period under the WRS was completed.

Within these initial 12 months, however, Polish migrants had to re-register each time they changed their employer. If the time period between two jobs (and two registrations) was longer than 30 days, they were required to work towards the 12-month target from the beginning. Upon registering, they gained access to in work benefits (mainly tax credits) and, as long as they remained within the WRS, their work in the UK was legal.

2 Those particularly affected might be the economically inactive A8 nationals who are not able to work due to health reasons and who never completed 12 months' work under the WRS in the past. Those who were economically active but who were not registered under the WRS for the past five years or those who dropped out of the Scheme are unlikely to be recognized as permanent residents for the purposes of welfare legislation. Those with limited proof of residence (i.e. without a registration certificate between 2004 and 2011) are also likely to face problems in this respect.

3 The fee has risen considerably since 2004, when it was originally introduced. In 2004 A8 nationals were required to pay £60 in order to register (UK Border Agency 2004).

Although the history of the enlargement of the EU had transition periods for the accession states – Greece was to be granted full free movement of workers six years after joining the EC in 1981, while Portugal and Spain were to obtain full freedom of movement of worker seven years following their 1986 admission into the EC[4] – the British response to the 2004 EU enlargement transition provisions introduced a certain novelty. The UK 'opened' its labour market to the migrant workers from the 2004 accession states, but at the same time restricted their right to legal residence (and legal residence of their family members) in accordance with the provisions specified in the national legislation (the 2004 Accession Regulations). Equally, it restricted the participation of migrants in the welfare system to ensure that so-called 'welfare tourism' did not occur. As the WRS knitted together the issues of employment, legal residence and access to social benefits (Currie 2008b: 35), the British immigration regulations towards the post-2004 EU enlargement migrant workers therefore resulted in a very specific legal environment – half-open and half-closed.

How did the Polish migrants respond to the new legal environment during the transition period? The official statistical data on Polish migrants from Home Office reports is not specific, only referring to the migrants who successfully registered their employment with the WRS (1.1 million A8 nationals between 2004 and 2011) (Home Office 2011; Office for National Statistics 2011). However, the registration did not exclude earlier work without registration beyond the 30-day time limit.

Table 3.1 Workers Registration Scheme Applicants 2004–2011

Year	Total A8 applicants	Total approved	Polish	Percentage Polish
2004	134,555	125,885	71,025	53%
2005	212,325	204,970	127,325	60%
2006	234,730	227,875	162,495	69%
2007	217,970	210,800	150,255	69%
2008	166,485	158,340	103,015	62%
2009	118,675	108,920	62,095	52%
2010	122,625	116,760	52,325	43%
2011*	29,240	27,944	12,434	43%
2004–2011	1,236,605	1,181,494	740,969	63%

* Data for 2011 until discontinuation of the scheme on 30 April 2011.

Source: UK Border Agency, the Department for Work and Pensions, HM Revenue & Customs and the Department for Communities and Local Government (2009) *Accession Monitoring Report 2004–2009.* London: Department for Work and Pensions, HMRC, Office of the Deputy Prime Minister; Home Office (2011) *Control of Immigration: Quarterly Statistical Summary, January–March 2011*, London: Home Office

4 However, as no significant movement occurred, these transitions came to an end earlier than originally planned after five years.

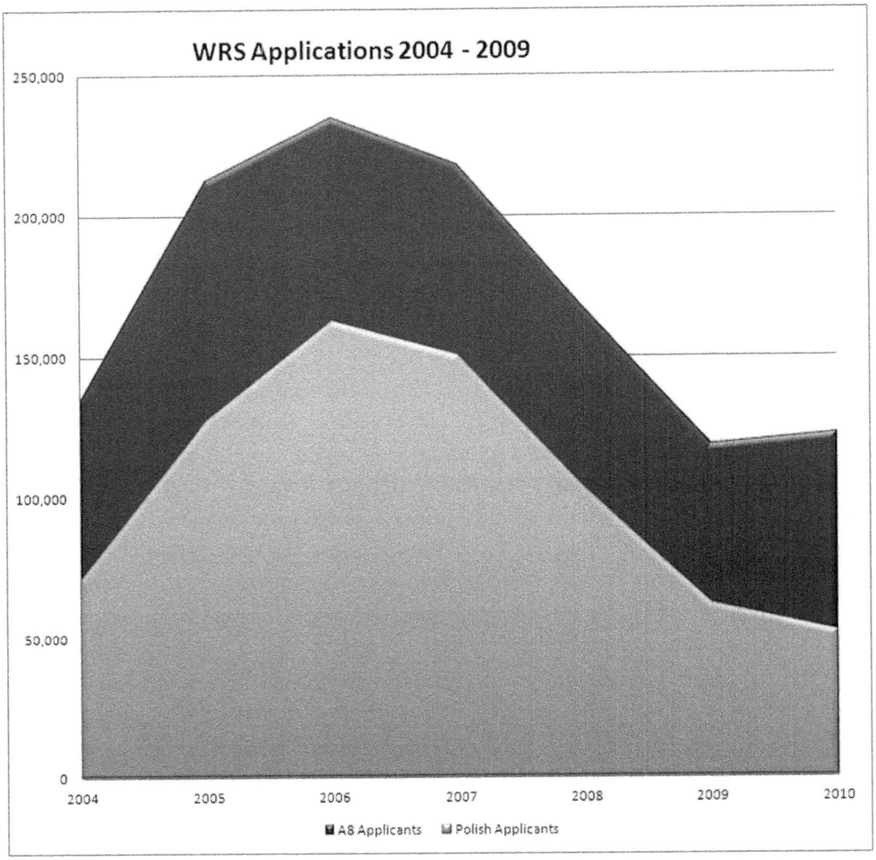

Figure 3.1 WRS Applications 2004–2009

The Home Office therefore did not have information on the numbers of migrants that have actually registered late, have not registered their simultaneously-held jobs or have not re-registered their employment upon terminating a contract (within less than a year) and hence dropped out of the Scheme. As such, the official data does not say much about the real numbers of migrants, apart from giving a very approximate estimate of the scale of migration.

With the circular nature of migration and the numbers of Polish and other A8 migrants leaving the UK since 2007, it is indeed difficult to estimate the numbers. Let us therefore use a snapshot method and focus on a specific period when alternative data to Home Office estimates was published.

The Institute of Public Policy Research (IPPR), combining data stemming from the Labour Force Survey, International Passenger Surveys, Census 2001 and acession monitoring statistics, estimated that between 2004 and 2007 alone, well over one million migrant workers had already come to Britain from the eight Central and Eastern European countries that joined the EU at that time (Pollard et al. 2008). Between 2004/5 and 2006/7, the cumulative total of National Insurance number (NIN) allocations talks 'only' of 711,030 A8 nationals[5] (including 452,630 Poles), whilst cumulative data for the WRS also estimates around 'only' 769,530 registered workers from all the accession countries (A8, including 511,100 Poles).

Table 3.2 National Insurance Number Allocations to Adult Overseas Nationals Entering the UK 2003/2004–2010

Year	Total number of foreign applicants	Polish	% Polish	Total A8 applicants	% Polish	Ranking in relation to other countries (all)
2003/2004	373,500	11,260	3%	28,720	39%	9th
2004/2005	435,350	61,120	14%	116,840	52%	1st
2005/2006	663,060	171,080	26%	276,690	62%	1st
2006/2007	705,840	220,430	31%	317,500	69%	1st
2007/2008	733,090	210,660	29%	332,430	63%	1st
2008/2009	686,110	134,360	20%	257,020	52%	1st
2009/2010	572,740	69,940	12%	182,760	38%	2nd

Source: Department of Work and Pensions 2003/2004–2010

In light of the above statistics, even at a generous estimate, 30–40 per cent of A8 migrants in the UK have not complied – or at some point did not comply – with the British immigration regulations, with Poles constituting the largest group. Other empirical research confirms these estimates (Anderson et al. 2006; Currie 2007b, 2008a).

Therefore, the interesting question to investigate is why did this happen? Why do so many Eastern European migrants decided to remain semi-legal and what were the factors that influenced the choice for semi-legality over legality among Polish post-2004 EU enlargement migrants?

The statistical, quantitative representations signal the problem but do not provide the reader with answers to these questions. As such, this qualitative, 'thick description' study (Geertz 1975) aims to fill in these gaps in our understanding of the socio-legal integration of Polish post-2004 EU enlargement migrants.

5 The number does not disaggregate between employees or those who were self-employed.

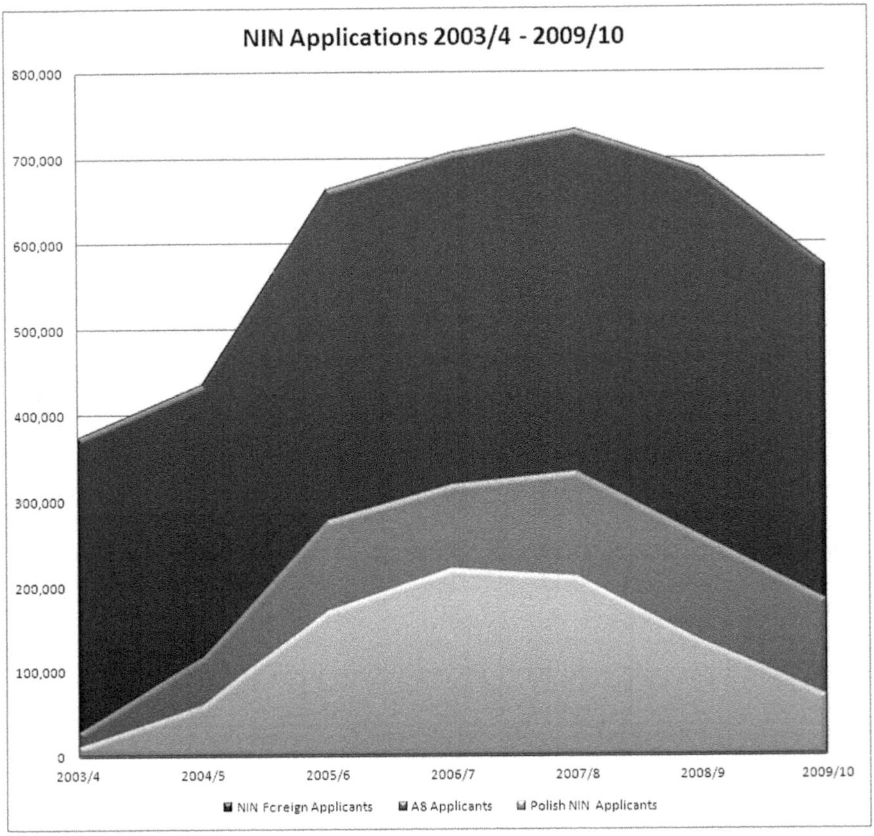

Figure 3.2 National Insurance Number Allocations to Adult Overseas Nationals Entering the UK 2003/2004–2010

Profile of the Group

The 2004 enlargement of the EU resulted in a mass influx of Eastern European migrants into the UK. According to the Home Office figures,[6] a cumulative total of 1,181,494 A8 nationals joined the WRS between May 2004 and March

6 These figures were originally published in quarterly Accession Monitoring Reports prepared by the Home Office, the Department for Work and Pensions, HM Revenue & Customs and the Department for Communities and Local Government between May 2004 and May 2009. They could be accessed from the UK Border Agency's website. Since August 2009 the UK Border Agency no longer publishes separate monitoring reports about A8 worker registrations and associated data. The only summary data for the A8 countries continues to be published in the Home Office's 'Control of Immigration: Quarterly

2011 (Home Office 2011; UK Border Agency et al. 2009). Polish post-2004 EU enlargement migrants constituted the majority of the applicants – 66 per cent of the total (Home Office 2011). Office for National Statistics estimates that between the year ending December 2003 and the year ending December 2010, the Polish-born population of the UK increased from 75,000 to 532,000 (Office for National Statistics 2011). This makes them the most prominent of the already visible group of Eastern European economic migrants in the UK.

The scale of Polish immigration to the UK raises the following question: 'Why did they come?' With no colonial or other historical ties to Britain, people who were not native English speakers might well have been expected to go elsewhere. The main incentive was indeed the opening of the British labour market for the migrant workers from new EU countries marked by the 2004 enlargement. Therefore, the migration reflects the relatively rapid adaptation of Polish citizens to economic transition and the accession to the EU – a willingness to take responsibility for themselves and plan as rational economic actors in an entirely new situation, taking the 'old EU countries' as their framework of choice and calculating the costs and benefits of activities in the informal as well as the formal economies of each country.

Heuristically, one could employ the metaphor of certain discernible 'push and pull factors' stemming from the Polish economy and British labour market respectively that contributed to such a volume of migration. Increased mobility has often coincided with rapid rises in the standard of living in the countries of emigration (Jordan and Duvell 2002: 8) and, indeed, over the last 20 years, the standard of living in Poland has improved; slow but stable economic growth with no major political or economic crises can be seen. Additionally, better transport links, the development of cheap airlines (Ryanair, Wizz Air, EasyJet, etc.)[7] and informational campaigns presented in national mass media and newspapers, e.g. *Praca za Granica* (*Work Abroad*) or *Europa. Praca i Studia* (*Working and Studying in Europe*) by Gazeta Wyborcza, in Poland provided the means that made the idea of economic emigration more attractive, 'within one's reach' and possible.

Among the push factors in Poland, the structural, economic factors also had an impact on the decision to migrate, such as economic restructuring, unemployment (on average around 19 per cent, peaking at 40 per cent in some regions, in 2004, the year of Poland's accession to the EU (United Nations Development Programme 2004)),[8] a weak social security system and wage and currency differentials between

---

Statistical Summary'. The most recent of these summaries, relevant for this publication, is for the first quarter of 2011: January–March (Home Office 2011).

7 In December 2003 some 40,000 passengers flew between three British airports and Warsaw and Krakow in Poland. By December 2007, it was possible to fly from 22 British airports to 10 Polish cities, and passenger numbers between these destinations in that month were almost 385,000 (Pollard et al. 2008).

8 The unemployment was the highest among young people aged between 15 and 24 – 40 per cent in 2004 according to the United Nations Development Programme – *Human*

receiving and sending countries (in 2004 the approximate ratio of sterling to the Polish zloty was 1:7).

Finally, it is important not to neglect the strong culture of working abroad to earn and save, which was sustained by networks of practical assistance and moral support among friends and families. Previous undocumented migratory experiences contributed to the shared knowledge of the British labour market and earning opportunities according to the accounts of skilled workers (building and construction workers, plumbers, etc.) and facilitated the search for jobs after the 2004 enlargement of the EU.

With regard to the pull factors – the way in which receiving countries actually regulate and tolerate (legally, socially and politically) substantial inflows of foreign labour or population – these could be related to the qualitative and quantitative mismatches in the labour market and structural needs for foreign skilled labour, as well as demographic evolution and educational and training output on the British labour market. An important pull factor was the widely announced opening of the British labour market for migrant workers from the new EU Member States on 1 May 2004. Before the enlargement, the UK had been perceived as a country with severe external and internal passport and document controls, complicated and time- and effort-consuming visa and work permit procedures. Since the 2004 enlargement, Polish migrants embarking on a journey across the English Channel experienced no problems entering the UK.

What general, statistical picture of Polish migrants (as well as other A8 nationals) can be gathered from the available official figures? The vast majority of A8 migrants that came to the UK were young (81 per cent of them were aged 18–34, out of which 44 per cent were aged between 18–24 and 38 per cent were between 25 and 34 years old), without dependants and slightly more males than females (the ratio was 56:44). Amongst those who did have dependants (8 per cent), the average number of dependants was 1.5 (UK Border Agency et al 2009: 10–11).

Most of the migrants came to the UK mainly to find work. A great number of them were employed in administration, business and management (41 per cent); however, the majority of workers in this sector work for employment businesses ('employment agencies') and could be employed in a variety of industries. Migrants were also filling in the gaps in the following sectors on the British labour market: hospitality and catering (18 per cent), agriculture (10 per cent), manufacturing (7 per cent) and food, fish and meat processing (5 per cent) (Home Office 2011). What strikes in the above statistics is that the construction sector is placed only at a distant eighth place with 4 per cent of workers employed in it. Whilst the majority of workers in the construction sector might be self-employed and therefore did not need to register with the WRS, it also signals the problem of non-registrations in particular sectors of the labour market.

The biggest group of migrant workers registered with the WRS has been in general occupation, with 28 per cent classified as 'process operatives (other

Development Report 2004, available at http://www.unic.un.org.pl/nhdr/nhdr2004.php

factory worker)' (UK Border Agency et al. 2009: 12–13). This was followed by warehouse operatives (8 per cent) and packers (6 per cent) (UK Border Agency et al. 2009: 12–13).[9]

Polish migrants made up the largest proportion of all Accession States' workers in every sector between May 2004 and March 2011, with 69 per cent of those registering to work in manufacturing, 68 per cent in administration, business and management (including employment agencies) and 64 per cent in hospitality and catering (Home Office 2011; UK Border Agency et al. 2009).

This trend has been constant throughout the post-accession years. The most recent report by the Migration Policy Institute on the changed migration patterns to the UK five years after the enlargement of the EU reveals that Polish migrants work in less skilled occupations than other immigrant groups: in 2008 more than half of migrants with jobs worked in unskilled occupations (Sumption and Somerville 2009: 16). This occurs despite relatively high levels of education. The recent migrants have higher education levels, on average, than those born in the UK: while the median non-immigrant in 2008 finished education at age 16, A8 workers had a median school leaving age of 19 (Sumption and Somerville 2009: 16). Indeed, when controlling for individual characteristics including education, recent A8 immigrants earn the least of any immigrant group (Drinkwater et al. 2007). In other words, many recent immigrants 'downgrade' their occupational status when they come to the UK, working in jobs that do not reflect their level of qualifications (Sumption and Somerville 2009), what has been observed in the literature as de-skilling (Currie 2007b).

The data shows that migrants' main activity in the UK is work, with 86 per cent working more than 35 hours a week in 2009 (UK Border Agency et al. 2009: 16). However, the earnings of the majority of migrants vacillate around the National Minimum Wage: 75 per cent of the workers stated that their hourly rate of earnings was £4.50–5.99 per hour, while 19 per cent stated an hourly rate of £6.00–7.99 (UK Border Agency et al. 2009: 16).[10] The Migration Policy Institute report confirms the lower wages of accession workers in comparison to British workers and other immigrant groups (Sumption and Somerville 2009: 26). A figure of 89 per cent of A8 workers (and A2 workers – Romanian and Bulgarian nationals – following the 2007 enlargement of the EU) earned less than £400 per week in 2007, compared to 57 per cent of UK-born workers (Pollard et al. 2008). While the average non-A8

9 The last Accession Monitoring Report by the UK Border agency et al. (2009) included the most recent socio-economic characteristics of the Polish post-2004 EU enlargement migrants in the UK. When the reports were discontinued and replaced by the general Quarterly Statistical Reports, the available figures talk only about the total numbers of WRS applicants by country of nationality and sector of employment. Unfortunately, they are silent about the broader characteristics of registered migrants. However, the latter are believed to have remained stable.

10 These figures varied between May 2004 and May 2011 following the changes in the National Minimum Wage legislation.

or non-A2 immigrant worker earns more than those born in the UK, Eastern European migrants during the first years following accession earned an average of 12.5 per cent less (Blanchflower and Lawton 2008). Recent A8 migrants have typically earned between 60 and 70 per cent of the median wage of native-born workers in the same year (Sumption and Somerville 2009: 26).

Yet, despite being clustered on the low-skilled, low-paid end of the labour market, the new migrants have been quite successful in accessing employment in general. About 95 per cent of male accession migrants and 80 per cent of female accession migrants found work upon entering the UK (Dustmann et al. 2009).

According to the report by the Migration Policy Institute on the working profile of the post-2004 EU enlargement migrants in the UK, in the 2008–2009 economic crisis, A8 workers' unemployment rates remained low, in contrast to rising unemployment among British-born workers and other immigrant groups. By the third quarter of 2009, the unemployment of British-born workers had risen to 7.8 per cent, while that for A8 workers fluctuated around 5 per cent (Sumption and Somerville 2009: 26). This lower vulnerability to the recession was likely to stem in part from the fact that the flows of migrants to and from Central Europe (particularly Poland) appear to have responded strongly and flexibly to economic circumstances. In general, various migration studies demonstrated that Polish migrants have been widely praised for their superior 'work ethic' and 'flexibility' (Anderson et al. 2006; Spencer et al. 2007; Sumption and Somerville 2009).

'Work' was also stressed as the most popular motivation for coming to the UK, based on the accounts of Polish migrants interviewed for this study. The migrants emphasized earnings and the opportunity to save for the future, due to the fact that work prospects and earning opportunities in their home country, Poland, were limited. Personal growth and development prospects (studying in the UK at a college or university, pursuing a Bachelor's or Master's course, or simply learning English) were emphasized mainly by young migrants (those in their mid-twenties). They hoped that the combination of studies and work experience in the UK would increase their job prospects in Poland upon their return.

The labour market characteristics of migrants, reflected in their motivations and aspirations to move to the UK, are also confirmed by the figures analysing the benefit claims of A8 migrants. According to the Home Office, the numbers of A8 nationals applying for tax-funded income-related benefits and housing support, although increasing, still remain very low in relation to the total number of claimants in the UK. Between May 2004 and March 2009 among A8 migrants, there were 13,989 applications for Income Support, 332 applications for the income-related Employment and Support Allowance, 27,366 applications for the income-based Jobseeker's Allowance and 889 applications for State Pension Credit. A total of 10,760 applications (including 494 allowed on reconsideration or appeal) were allowed to proceed for further consideration of whether the claimants met the other conditions of entitlement (UK Border Agency et al. 2009). According to the most recent statistics – between 2007 and 2010 – on average 29 per cent of applications were allowed and the vast majority (71 per cent) were disallowed on the basis of the right to reside and habitual residence tests (Home Office 2011). The information about the nationality of applicants comes from the Accession Monitoring Reports (the latest was in 2009); however, there are no bases to anticipate changes in the trends: most applicants were Polish (51 per cent), followed by Lithuanian (14 per cent) and Czech (12 per cent) nationals (UK Border Agency et al. 2009: 23).

Polish Migrants in the Migration Research

Polish migrants have been an object of interest to migration researchers for more than a century. There is substantial research on the early assimilationist tradition (Sword et al. 1989; Thomas and Znaniecki 1974) and the transnational approach (Iglicka 2007; Jazwinska et al. 2007; Okolski 2007). The following sections review the contemporary research on Polish migrants and, at the same time, identify the gaps and issues that still need to be addressed.

Research on emigration from Poland dates back to before 1918, i.e. the re-establishment of the Polish sovereign state after 123 years of partitions. 'The Great Emigration' left the country after the November Insurrection (1830–1831), yet consistently influenced the cultural and political aspects of their home country (e.g. through various cultural foundations established in France, Switzerland, the UK or the USA, as well as publishing houses and journals targeting elites in Poland) (Iglicka 2007: 14). The Polish diaspora, called *Polonia*, is believed to embrace account for 15 and 20 million people scattered throughout the world, with the largest centres in Brazil, Germany, the UK and the USA. It was produced by the mass migration of the nineteenth and twentieth centuries, composed of a variety of migration streams and pushed out by multiple reasons (mainly economic but also political, and individual: Kicinger and Weinar 2007).

The Polish Diaspora in Assimilation, Acculturation and Integration Research

The first mass economic migration from the Polish lands at the turn of the twentieth century to Western Europe and the USA was documented and analysed in the famous five volume opus by William I. Thomas and Florian Znaniecki (1974). *The Polish Peasant in Europe and America* figures prominently among the classic approaches of assimilation, acculturation and integration to studying migrants in the host country.

Thomas and Znaniecki focused on the change in American society that took place under the influence of immigration and other factors such as cultural assimilation, the increased rapidity of social evolution, the breakdown and isolation of groups, and the processes of democratization (Blumer 1949: 7). The authors approached the study of social change in the context of Polish migrants' assimilation from the perspectives of values (the objective cultural elements of life) and attitudes (the subjective characteristics) and the relations between them

(Thomas and Znaniecki 1974). Thomas and Znaniecki viewed values and attitudes as categories enabling them to tackle the fundamental problem of the dependence of the individual upon social organization and culture, and the dependence of social organization and culture upon the individual (Blumer 1949: 8). Changes in social life were therefore to be accounted for in terms of the interaction of attitudes and values (Blumer 1949: 9).

This book, reviewing the extensive work of Thomas and Znaniecki, also proposes a combined focus on values and attitudes observed in the wider context of socio-legal integration among the Polish post-2004 EU enlargement migrants in the UK. Where this study diverges from the stance adopted by Thomas and Znaniecki is by narrowing its focus to concentrate on migrants' values and attitudes to law, including images, myths and understandings of law that migrants were socialized to prior to their experience of migration and arrival in the UK. It also goes beyond the focus on the cognitive sphere only (values and attitudes) and proposes the inclusion of the analysis the legal behaviour of migrants, that is, the strategies they devise to deal with the body of law upon their arrival in the UK (i.e. their responses to British immigration regulations, labour laws, workplace regulations, health and safety at work provisions, etc.).

Another important contribution to the study of the Polish diaspora from the assimilation and acculturation perspectives is that of Sword et al. (1989) documenting the arrival and the formation of by far the largest Polish community (in Europe) in the UK between 1939 and 1950.

In the subject literature, this group of post-Second World War Polish migrants to the UK is known as the 'First Wave of Immigration'; the 'Second Wave' comprises political migrants escaping the authoritarian regime in Poland between 1953 and 1989, who, towards the end of the regime and after 1989, became more visible as migrant workers (Okolski 2007). The 'Third Wave' of Polish migration to the UK in the twentieth century – and by far the largest of all – is the post-2004 EU enlargement migration.

Yet, of the many thousands of Poles who found themselves in the UK during and immediately after the Second World War (around 142,000: Sword et al. 1989: 49), very few made the journey directly from Poland. The general pattern of movements of these Polish migrants was compared by Sword to a string of 'star-shell' explosions, each of which dislodged them from their temporary resting places and scattered them again due to successive crises (Sword et al. 1989: 21).

After the Second World War, the Polish community in the UK consisted mainly of former and exiled government officials, military servicemen and political migrants, together with their dependants. It was a complex amalgam of people with varied social, geographical, ethnic and political backgrounds, conditioned by wartime experiences in many different countries, who in the UK faced a fresh set of adaptational challenges (Sword et al. 1989: 82).

The research by Sword et al. (1989) focused on the relationship between the Polish migrants and the local population in the context of the new socio-legal environment, as plans to resettle former Polish combatants into civilian life and civilian jobs experienced early problems not only due to the intransigence of the trade unions or slow administrative procedures and unnecessary bureaucratic inflexibility, but also to the fact that the legal situation of the Polish armed forces after the Yalta Conference was a complicated and confused one (Sword et al. 1989: 295). Government reports mentioned the growing gloom and scepticism of the Polish men and an increasing distrust towards both the British and their own officers. The creation of resettlement corps was an attempt to overcome the ambiguous legal situation and to subject the Polish troops to the King's Regulations. Those Poles who did not want to join were by the power of the Polish Resettlement Bill to be deported to the British zone of Germany and discharged (Sword et al. 1989: 298).

This research demonstrated that, despite some early problems (like the initial recalcitrant issue: Sword et al. 1989: 302), the British resettlement plans were gradually accepted by the Polish population without major disturbances to law and order. Most of the offences for which Poles were appearing in British courts during the period 1946–1948 were of a petty nature and were perhaps to be expected in a settlement community of such numbers (Sword et al. 1989: 302). Cases reaching the courts included domestic troubles, driving offences, failures to register as an alien with the police, the illegal possession of firearms and fighting with the local population (Sword et al. 1989: 302). Yet the authors prompted the reader to remember that the frequently hostile attitudes of the host population towards the Polish migrants in reality meant that the Poles were as often victims of violence as they were perpetrators (Sword et al. 1989: 302).

The new migrants, often anxious to prove themselves in their new surroundings, frequently got involved in the struggle to achieve better standards of living and work productivity with eagerness and determination, often exceeding the customary production norms. The research portrayed in detail the Stakhanovite tactics (named after Alexei Stakhanov, the Russian working-class leader from the 1950s) among the Polish workers, which, sooner or later, raised the hackles of their British fellow workers and often resulted in social ostracism or compulsory dismissals of Poles from their respective workplaces. The newcomers had to be taken aside by more experienced Polish workers in order to be kept out of trouble (Sword et al. 1989: 382).

Despite these early hindrances, the First Wave of Polish migrants to the UK has been documented in the literature as being rather well integrated in terms of civic and legal matters into the community. An interesting illustration of this conclusion was found in the *Dziennik Polski* (*Polish Daily*) in an article 'Do Not Borrow', which contained a cautionary tale of a Polish lodger in the house of a British engineer (Dziennik Polski 1947, quoted in Sword et al. (1989)). The Pole enjoyed a good, friendly relationship with his British hosts until on one occasion, being short of money, he asked his landlord to lend him £1 until the following Monday. The British family expressed incomprehension and then concern, fearing that some catastrophe had befallen him. Consequently, a noticeable cooling of the relationship occurred between the lodger and the hosts. The author of this article concluded that without doubt the Pole was guilty of breaching etiquette. In Britain, he explained, a financial loan was regarded as a formal transaction, accompanied by a signed agreement, a set rate of interest, etc. An 'informal' loan, based on a verbal agreement and which benefited only the borrowing party, must have been seen from the British perspective as something 'abnormal, unhealthy' (Dziennik Polski 1947, quoted in Sword et al. (1989)). Sword added that it probably indicated that the lodger was not capable of keeping his financial affairs in order or was irresponsible due to living above his means.

Parallel to the settlement of the Polish community in the UK, the mass movements in Poland also eased. According to Okolski, they were reduced to virtually exceptional cases – for instance, in 1953 only 2,800 emigrants and 2,000 immigrants were recorded (Okolski 2007: 11). Not only did international migration come to a halt, but any cross-border mobility was effectively stopped. In his fundamental book on the population of Poland, Edward Rosset (1975) justified the absence of the analysis of ongoing migration by quoting from Soviet demographers, who declared that, contrary to capitalist countries, no international migration existed under socialism (Rosset 1975). In real life, however, it was not so much forbidden but rather impossible to conduct research on migration in Poland due not only to the 'official political line' but also simply because no data was collected on international population mobility on Polish territory and particularly through Polish borders (Iglicka 2007: 14).

With time, however, and with the softening of the authoritarian regime, a variety of forms of the out-movement were observed – an alternative to 'regular' emigration. These movements, which were heavily controlled by the authorities, reflected a specific pattern which was concomitant with an internal political cycle. In particular, compared to a 'norm', many more people were allowed to leave Poland at times of political turmoil and a shift in the political leadership (Okolski 2007: 11). Step by step, more and more residents of Poland travelling abroad became the residents of foreign countries – as immigrants or temporary workers, refugees, or irregular 'overstayers' (Okolski 2007: 11). All over non-communist Europe, the USA and elsewhere, old Polish migrant communities were revitalized and new ones established which greatly facilitated further out-movements. Finally, the outflow took on a massive scale in 1980–1989 when more than one million Poles emigrated and several other millions were engaged in 'there and back' circular migration between 'the West' and Poland (Okolski 2007: 12).

Polish European Economic Migration from a Transnational Perspective

In the 1980s and 1990s, while the vast majority of migrants from Poland sought employment in foreign countries – and that was by far the greatest motive for their migration – it was difficult to conduct official research on these migration movements due to their concealed motives and forms (Okolski 2007: 12). However, there is a substantial body of research that used the transnational approach to document Polish migrants' international labour sojourns (circular migration:

Okolski and Jazwinska 2001), whilst being prevented from settling 'in the West' by restrictive immigration laws. The specific shape of the legal environment at that time locked them into an unstable and disadvantageous, if not precarious, situation in terms of the labour market and social life in general. Even after 1989, when the exit from Poland became unlimited and Polish residents could easily enter many countries (France, Germany, Greece, Italy, the UK and the USA), Polish migrants as a rule could legally only be tourists in those countries, which rarely was their actual motive of their journey.

After 1989, two broad research streams on Polish economic migration in the transnational perspective could be distinguished (Jazwinska et al. 2007). The first one, continuing the traditions of research on the Polish diaspora (Babinski and Chalupczak 2006; Dopierala 2003–2005; Kubiak 1975; Kubiak et al. 1988; Nowicka 2000; Pilch 1984; Walaszek 2001), focused on the new emigration to the countries of traditional settlement, especially Australia, Canada and the USA, yet devoted more attention to the very mechanisms of the migration processes, establishing migratory networks and transnational ties (Sakson 2005; Slany 2002; Wlodarczak 2005).

The second stream of research focused on seasonal migrants and 'tourist' migrant workers in European countries, both in the traditional destinations (especially Germany) (Morawska 2001) and relatively new countries on the migration map, such as Greece (Romaniszyn 1996), Belgium (Grzymala-Kazlowska 2001; Kuzma 2004), Italy (Rosinska-Kordasiewicz 2005), Spain (Matejko 2004) and Ireland (Grabowska 2005).

Until the EU enlargement in 2004, migration to the above-mentioned countries was mostly seasonal, with Polish migrants usually placing themselves in the shadow economy without legalizing their status (Jazwinska et al. 2007: 32), falling into a limbo between work (abroad) and life (at home). As a consequence, the starting point of many studies were migration regulations and legalization programmes, migrants' rights, the possibilities of residence and regular employment (Grabowska 2005; Kuzma 2004; Rosinska-Kordasiewicz 2005). These studies stressed the link between the legal status of Polish migrants and their labour market performance, remittances and relationship with Poland within the communities of receiving countries. As a result of their irregular immigration status, Poles located themselves in market niches, creating scarce opportunities for promotion and assistance from social services, but at the same time being afforded the relative safety of functioning without the regularization of employment or residence. Such niches were the construction/decoration sector, agriculture for male migrants and domestic work for female migrants (Jazwinska et al. 2007: 32).

The issues generated by Polish migration were undertaken not only by domestic scholars but also attracted the attention of foreign migration researchers. Anna Triandafyllidou edited an important volume on *Contemporary Polish Migration in Europe: Complex Patterns of Movement and Settlement* (2006). Adopting the technique of a life-story interview (which could be dated as far back as the famous work by Thomas and Znaniecki), she gave Polish immigrants a voice across various countries, where they led their transnational lives: Germany, Greece, Italy and the UK. This book also analytically focused on the gendered nature of East to West migrations, the negotiation of migrant identities, the transnational mobility of *earners* and *learners* in Europe, and the impact of globalization on the immigrant labour force (in the situation of the flexible and deregularized labour market) (Triandafyllidou 2006).

Polish Transnational Experiences of the British Labour Market

In the 1990s and early 2000s Polish nationals in the UK were identified by the Immigration Service Enforcement Directorate for their illegal strategies of joining the labour market almost in equal numbers with those who were documented by the work permit section of the Home Office (Jordan and Duvell 2002). In 1996 Polish nationals came third amongst those being identified as having entered illegally (*Hansard*, 19 December 1996). In 1998 East Europeans accounted for 10 per cent of the cases of the Immigration Service Enforcement Directorate office that Duvell and Jordan were studying (Jordan and Duvell 2002b). However, in general they were perceived as a group that was relatively easy to deal with, a group of migrants identified with irregular work but otherwise regarded as an 'unproblematic nationality' (Jordan and Duvell 2002).

Studying the dilemmas of transnational mobility in the context of migration to the UK, Jordan and Duvell (2002) observed that the Polish irregular migrant population largely consisted of nationals – perhaps legal entrants – who lived without the support of institutions designed to sustain the lives of lawful members of that society, including welfare systems, regulatory bodies and agencies for the protection of people and property (Jordan and Duvell 2002: 8).

As the Polish migrants – despite often having documented entry – remained in the UK in breach of the conditions attached to their immigration status, I would see in them the origins of the behaviour strategies and attitudes to law observed widely (perhaps *learned*) within the semi-legal, semi-compliant Polish post-2004 EU enlargement migrant group which forms the focus of this study.

Jordan and Duvell characterized the group of Polish international yet undocumented sojourners in the UK in a deep and diligent manner. They were interested to learn why the Polish migrants in the 1990s and 2000s (prior to 2004) arrived in the UK, despite clear immigration regulations, how they managed to enter the UK, how they were able to obtain employment and stay in irregular employment in the country, and subsequently how they evaded detection (Jordan and Duvell 2002b). Through their rich empirical study of the undocumented workers themselves and of the reactions of host society organizations, they presented a strong body of evidence of how Polish migrants explained their reasons for coming, interpreted their experiences of irregular employment in the country, and interacted with each other, largely evading detection. The research reveals a close reliance on distinct informal networks – which are rather weak in terms of social capital – taking the shape of small *commercial* systems of partly underground institutions ranging from 'Polish houses' – Polish-owned, run and populated premises – to Polish corner shops as a source of information, Polish sub-contractors as a source of obtaining employment and Polish brokers, who provided migrants with information, NINs or jobs (Jordan and Duvell 2002: 12). The migration dynamics included a constant fear of denunciation as part of a culture of unrestrained competition within the group (Jordan and Duvell 2002: 12). The research also showed the complex links and structures of transnational entrepreneurism, informal economic activity and the shadow labour markets of the host economy, which for many Polish undocumented migrants nevertheless resulted in considerable upward mobility (Jordan and Duvell 2002: 11).

What distinguished Poles from other migrant groups from Central and Eastern Europe was their sheer volume and potential of migration. This Polish 'specificity' has been confirmed since 1 May 2004, when the citizens of eight Central and Eastern European countries could benefit from the freedom of movement within the EU and, especially, from access to the labour market of selected EU countries. The number of Poles was much greater than the numbers of migrant workers from the other accession countries (Okolski 2007: 12).

The specifics of the 'continuity and change' in East to West European mobility after 2004 have been addressed in a volume edited by Kathy Burrell (2009). The quantitative picture of the recent migratory trends and the socio-demographic profile of the *Polish Migration to the UK in the 'New' European Union* set the scene for more indepth, qualitative analysis, with chapters on Polish migrants in a fictional film (Mazierksa 2009), migrants' material worlds (exploring links between Polish food, Polish shops, home and ethnicity: Rabikowska and Burrell 2009), the negotiation of gender and ethnic identity among the Polish migrants in cyberspace (Siara 2009) or the narratives of Polish masculinities among construction workers in London (Datta 2009).

Ryan et al. (2009) provide useful and fresh insights into the experiences of recent Polish migrants in the UK by using the social networks perspective, focusing on how these migrants access, use, form, maintain and expand their networks. The authors also attend to the under-studied – albeit very popular – phenomenon of arriving without networks. This is true with regard to professional mobility, but is also often attributed to the idea that 'the Poles do not help each other' and instead 'may deliberately compete and undermine each other' (Ryan et al. 2009: 161). In this context, the authors seek an explanation for the importance of trust in social relationships, but in my opinion they address the issue only partially. More helpful would be a closer analysis of the functions of bridging and bonding trust and social capital (Putnam 2000). Placing this interpretation into the post-communist socio-political context (with strong family ties but a weak civil society and social vacuum at the intermediate level) might be one of the ways to explain why the levels of bridging trust with the 'generalized other' are indeed so low.

Where my study steps in is to fill the gaps in the most recent scholarship on Polish post-2004 EU enlargement migrants in the UK concerning the socio-legal dimensions of their migratory experiences. The current research on the legal situation of these migrants particularly focused on how the British legal environment impinges on migrants' experiences in the UK, resulting in 'Regular Migrants in the Irregular Workplace' (the top-down approach) (Coyle 2007; Currie 2007b, 2009). Currie (2009) perceived the UK's Immigration Regulations and the restrictions they imposed on free movement of accession state nationals as the sole factors responsible for the de-skilling and devaluing of the performance of migrants on the labour market – locking migrant workers (especially women) in irregular, poorly paid and highly insecure jobs typically associated with 'illegal' workers (such as domestic work in private homes) (Currie 2009: 5).

My research instead inquires into migrants' responses to the new socio-legal environment (the bottom-up approach). It looks at a specific group of migrants – the Polish post-2004 EU enlargement migrants in the UK– in specific migratory conditions, that is, in the new socio-legal environment created by the laws enacted by the UK in the 2004 Accession Regulations. It presents not only an analysis of the ambiguous legal status of Polish migrants in the UK resulting from the provisions included in the Treaty of Accession (2003), but also stresses the agency of migrants towards the legal framework – what do Polish migrants themselves make of it, how do they respond to law when do they follow and when do they avoid and contest the law?

The identification and analysis of a significant group of semi-legal Polish immigrants among all Polish post-2004 EU enlargement migrants in the UK acknowledges that migrants nowadays come as representatives of a far more diverse set of cultures than did earlier generations and they arrive in a society that is itself far more diverse. It also indicates the complexity of the actual responsiveness of migrants to the new social, cultural and legal environments.

A Note on Methods

Analysing the responses of Polish migrants towards the British body of law that governs their work and residence in the UK, I relied on four sources of empirical data. The first comes from the fieldwork conducted among Polish migrants in southern England[11] between 2007 and 2008 in the form of indepth, semi-structured interviews (lasting between 2 and 2.5 hours) and a number of shorter interviews among post-2004 EU enlargement Polish migrant communities in Oxfordshire and Berkshire.

Snow-ball and chain-referral sampling were used to select respondents. The structure of each interview was threefold. It was aimed, firstly, to re-trace the migration experience of the interviewees. These stories reflected and sustained the institutional and cultural arrangements to which migrants were socialized in

11 Following the settlement patterns of Polish migrants: cf. UK Border Agency et al. 2009.

Poland and, at the same time, with which they were bridging the gap between daily social interactions and the large-scale social structures of British law and society.

Secondly, the interviews aimed to disentangle the strategies and tactics employed by migrants in order to follow, avoid or manipulate the law. I employed the narratives of immigration experience as a form of social action. Did they register with the WRS? Did they prefer to work in an unauthorized manner and ignore the registration altogether or work for employers who did not pay much attention to their legal status? When did Polish migrants decide to register? Did they keep to the 30-day limit? What were their priorities in terms of registration and, more generally, in terms of legalizing their stay in the UK? Did they re-register their employment if they changed employers during the initial 12-month period? What about the practices of Polish migrants who were not employees but worked for employment agencies?

The questions about their legal behaviour were, of course, intertwined with questions about their values and attitudes to law – that is, how migrants argued, motivated and made sense of their experiences with the law upon their arrival in the UK. If Polish respondents registered their employment with the WRS, what motivated this? Was it because legal status was important to them or because of instrumental considerations (e.g. they wanted to gain access to benefits)? If they did not register, what was their reasoning for that, as – objectively speaking – registration was actually in their interests. These questions helped to cast some light on migrants' interpretation of the law and focused on the nuances in Polish attitudes to law and legality, as migrants negotiated their new lives in an unfamiliar legal context.

Finally, the interview focused on the consequences of Polish migrants' behavioural and attitudinal responses to law – on the shape of their relationship with the law in the new socio-legal environment. What were the consequences of their preference for certain types of behaviour over others or of certain interpretations of legality over others? Did they result in changes of their behavioural patterns with regard to law? Were these particular behavioural choices and strategies of dealing with the law followed by respective changes in values and attitudes popularly held about the law?

This source of primary data was then supplemented by observations among Polish communities in southern England over a period of 12 months. I underwent legal training with a non-governmental organization (NGO) that helps people to resolve their legal or law-related problems by providing free information and advice. Their areas of expertise include debt, benefits, housing, discrimination, employment, immigration, consumer and other matters. The focal point of the NGO policy was that the advice is impartial, confidential and available to everyone regardless of race, gender, sexuality, age, nationality, disability or religion. During the fieldwork period, I became particularly active on Polish Internet forums and community pages. I was contacted by people who wanted to share their experiences or needed advice.

The third source of empirical, qualitative data used in conjunction with interviews and observations comes from eight focus groups held in Poland with Polish citizens, eight focus groups held in the UK with British citizens and one focus group with Polish migrants in London. The focus groups concentrated on the image of law, values and attitudes towards law among the respondents. The focus groups were conducted in Poland and the UK in January and February 2008 as part of a larger, comparative research project: 'Legal Cultures in Transition. The Impact of European Integration and the War on Terror' funded by the Norwegian Research Council.[12]

The fourth source of empirical data stems from two quantitative surveys conducted in Poland among Polish citizens and in the UK among British citizens in February 2009, which was also part of the 'Legal Cultures in Transition' research project. Each survey consisted of a thousand participants (N=1,000) randomly selected in terms of age, gender, education, financial position and experience with law in order to secure the representativeness of the sample. The results of the survey have been weighted.

The variety of empirical data sources has been used to better serve the main purpose of case study methodology: an indepth investigation demonstrating a multi-perspective analysis. Understanding the various aspects of socio-legal integration, I gave voice to its main actors – Polish post-2004 EU enlargement migrants – in deciding when, why and how to respond to the various rules and regulations in the UK.

As the migrants did not arrive in a vacuum but in a specific socio-legal environment, the following chapter turns to the particular features of the receiving context – European free movement principles – and how they were depicted in British legislation during the transition period of 2004–2011.

12 Each group, in each city, consisted of eight to ten discussants. I am very grateful to the project partners for allowing me to consult the transcripts. For the complete list of locations and timetables for the focus groups, please see the Appendix.

Chapter 4

The British Legal Environment in the Context of the 2004 EU Enlargement Free Movement Regime

The importance of the broader legal environment – the extra-personal factors such as migration laws and the labour market that together shape the opportunity structures for migrants – is well known (Menjivar 2000; Portes and Rumbaut 1990; Portes and Zhou 1993). The immigration laws determine who stands inside or outside of the law (or in-between) and also dictate whether migrants have access (or partial access) to resources, to what kind and for how long. The legal, political and economic contexts into which migrants arrive result in either a favourable or an adverse reception.

As the origins of the legal environment for Polish post-2004 EU enlargement migrants in the UK lie in the European legislation on free movement, this chapter substantively analyses European primary and secondary legislation in this field.

With regard to the primary European legislation, it examines:

1. the Treaty on the Functioning of the European Union (formerly the Treaty establishing the European Community);
2. the Treaty of Accession 2003, specifying the transition provisions regarding the free movement of persons between the 'old' and 'new' EU Member States.

In the area of secondary European legislation, the chapter draws on the following documents, establishing provisions necessary for the implementation of the principles of the above treaties:

1. Regulation 1612/68/EC, which is concerned with the entry conditions of access to the labour market for workers, their eligibility for employment, residence, equality of treatment within employment and right to remain with their families.
2. Directive 2004/38/EC, which stipulates the right of citizens of the EU and their family members to move and reside freely within the territory of EU Member States.

The chapter then moves to the level of national immigration legislation of the UK in order to investigate the British 'response' to the transitory provisions contained in the 2003 Treaty of Accession. It investigates the 2004 Accession Regulations which comprise the first set of legal requirements that migrants had to face and respond to upon their arrival in the UK. As the Polish migrants mainly arrived in the UK as workers, the workplace regulations therefore present another area of requirement requiring immediate response and have an effect on migrants' experiences of the law and their relationship with it in the UK.

The introduction of the above legislation brings the discussion to the concept of law. The interpretation of law for this purpose is as the Polish migrants (interviewees and focus group participants) understood it: the law as legislation, the state, state officials, governors, public administration and bureaucracy; the law as law enforcement; the law as workplace regulations and employment arrangements. Taking a step further and looking at law analytically, there are two contexts in which migrants' experiences of the law are particularly informative for this socio-legal Integration study: (1) immigration; and (2) workplace regulations. These two contexts embrace both the legal architecture – rules – and how the rules are enforced in the UK. Together they form the unique *legal environment*, which is the subject of this chapter.

Free Movement of People in the EU Primary Legislation

The provisions on the free movement of people in the EU primary legislation can be found in the Treaty on the Functioning of the European Union (TFEU). This treaty was formerly known as the Treaty establishing the European Community (TEC). It was amended by the Treaty of Lisbon, which entered into force in December 2009. In the amended Treaty one can broadly distinguish three articles setting the principles for the free movement of persons: Article 20 (formerly Article 17 TEC) establishing European citizenship; Article 21(1, 2) (formerly Article 18(1, 2) TEC) giving citizens the right to move and reside freely within the EU; and Article 45 (formerly Article 39 TEC) securing the freedom of movement for workers within the EU.

Citizenship of the Union

Article 20 of the Treaty on the Functioning of the European Union (formerly Article 17 TEC) introduces European citizenship and confers this status onto: 'Every person holding the nationality of a Member State [who] shall be a citizen of the Union. Citizenship of the Union shall be additional to and not replace national citizenship.'

The status of the European citizen is important as it precludes that every citizen of the EU shall have the right to move and reside freely within the territory of the Member States, subject to the limitations and conditions laid down by the Treaties and by the measures adopted to give them effect (Article 21(2) (formerly Article 18(2) TEC)).

From the structure of the new treaty, one can see that the articles relating to the citizenship of the EU and, subsequently, the right to reside within the territory of Member States take precedence over Article 26(2) (formerly Article 14(2) TEC), which established the internal market, indicating that it 'shall comprise an area without internal frontiers in which the free movement of goods, persons, services and capital is ensured in accordance with the provisions of the Treaties'. This was used to set out the context for reading and interpreting the articles relating to citizenship and free movement.

The former structure of the treaty, which was nonetheless still in place at the time of the 2004 EU enlargement and Poland's accession, led many to observe that the development of citizenship has essentially taken place alongside the development of the Common Market-driven mobility rights: 'In the absence of mobility, citizenship of the Union contributes little to the social status and day-to-day experience of Community nationals' (Ackers and Dwyer 2002: 16–18).

It may seem that the new structure of the Treaty and the symbolic precedence given to citizenship rights over the 'market' could be interpreted as the EU's response to the criticism brought about by the limitation of free movement and residence provisions to the economically active citizens of the EU. Citizenship of the EU was labelled an 'unfinished business' due to its clearly visible benefits which were however attainable only by those citizens of the EU who were and remain economically active (workers, service providers, etc.: Guild and Carrera 2005; Spaventa 2007). Therefore, the reading and interpretation of EU citizenship in the context of the internal market was actually considered by some to be a barrier to full European integration, not adding anything significant to the situation of individuals who were not pursuing economic activity, students, employed or self-employed individuals who had ceased to work, or individuals of independent means.

Free Movement

Aside from the citizenship articles, the other legal provisions governing the free movement in the primary legislation are contained in Article 45 of the Treaty on the Functioning of the European Union (formerly Article 39 TEC). This treaty has not brought about any changes in the qualification and precedence of that article, again confirming the close link between the mobility rights and the evolution of the common market. In brief, Article 45 stipulates as follows:

1. the right of economically active EU citizens to freedom of movement to another EU Member State to take up employment and to reside in the host country with family members;[1]

1 Family members are defined as the spouse, the partner in a registered partnership (if recognized in the host Member State), children under 21 or dependant children (of the spouse, registered partner or worker); dependant relatives in the ascending line of the worker, spouse or registered partner. Cf. further Article 23 of Directive 2004/38/EC.

2. EU Member States are precluded from discriminating, whether directly or indirectly, against migrant workers and their families on the basis of nationality;
3. EU migrant workers and their families are entitled to equal treatment in matters relating to employment, remuneration, social and tax advantages, and other conditions of work and employment;
4. the right is subject to limitations justified (if invoked by particular EU Member States) on the grounds of public policy, public security or public health.

Subsequently, Article 45 gives workers the following rights:

1. to accept offers of employment actually made;
2. to move freely within the territories of Member States for this purpose;
3. to stay in a Member State for the purpose of employment in accordance with the provisions governing the employment of nationals of that state as laid down by laws, regulations or administrative action;
4. to remain in the territory of a Member State after having been employed in that state, subject to conditions which shall be embodied in implementing regulations to be laid down by the Commission.

The provisions on non-discrimination mean that individuals seeking work have similar rights to individuals taking up an offer of a job in another Member State. They enjoy the right of entry into, and the right to move freely within, Member States for the purpose of seeking employment. In addition, they are permitted to reside in a relevant Member State for a reasonable period of time whilst they are actively seeking work and have a genuine chance of being employed (Weiss and Wooldridge 2002: 49).

Yet, although all EU nationals have been afforded the right to move freely to other Member States and reside there for the purpose of seeking employment, the legal status and the right to residence of 'work-seekers' are considerably less secure when compared to the rights of 'workers'. Member States might deport an EU national if he or she had not found employment within six months, unless he or she has provided evidence that he or she was continuing in the search for employment and had a genuine chance of engagement (Weiss and Wooldridge 2002: 50). The European Court of Justice held in *Dimitrios Tsiotras v. Landeshauptstadt Stuttgart*[2] that a Greek national who had been unemployed at the time of Greek's accession to the EU and had remained unemployed since that time had no right to reside in Germany. The limitations of free movement with respect to economically inactive individuals who are citizens of the EU became particularly visible in the context of recent Roma deportations from France in 2010.

2 Case C-171/91, (1993) ECR I-2975.

Free Movement of People in the EU Secondary Legislation

Regulation 1612/68/EC

Regulation 1612/68/EC completes and implements the free movement rights already provided for in the Treaty with respect to access to the labour market and eligibility for employment (Articles 1–6), as well as the non-discrimination principle and equal treatment (Articles 7–9).

Reiterating the labour market access rights, Article 1 stipulates that:

> Any national of a Member State shall, irrespective of his place of residence, have the right to take up an activity as an employed person, and to pursue such activity, within the territory of another Member State, in accordance with the provisions laid down by law, regulation or administrative action governing the employment of nationals of that State.

The regulation then reasserts that access to the labour market itself shall take place in accordance with the non-discrimination provision: 'the right to take up available employment in the territory of another Member State [should take place] with the same priority as nationals of that State' (Article 2), as:

> provisions laid down by law, regulation or administrative action of the Member States which restrict by number or percentage the employment of foreign nationals in any undertaking, branch of activity or region, or at a national level, *shall not apply* to nationals of the other Member States. (Article 4) (emphasis added)

Therefore, upon having obtained access to the labour market, workers benefit from the following non-discrimination provisions (Article 7, Regulation 1612/68/EC):

1. They may not, in the territory of another Member State, be treated differently from national workers by reason of nationality in respect of any conditions of employment and work, in particular as regards remuneration, dismissal and, should they become unemployed, reinstatement or re-employment.
2. They shall enjoy the same social and tax advantages as national workers.
3. They shall also, by virtue of the same right and under the same conditions as national workers, have access to training in vocational schools and re-training centres.
4. Any clause of a collective or individual agreement or of any other collective regulation concerning eligibility for employment, remuneration and other conditions of work or dismissal shall be null and void insofar as it lays down or authorizes discriminatory conditions in respect of workers who are nationals of other Member States.

The Regulation asserts workers' equal entitlement to trade union membership (Article 8) as well as to social housing (Article 9) and to family reunion (Title III). With regard to the provisions on family unification, however, Regulation 1612/68/EC has been amended and supplemented by Directive 2004/38/EC.

Apart from implementing existing treaty rights, the importance of this Regulation is that it also defines their scope and conditions. Non-discrimination, as outlined in Article 5, obliges Member States to provide the same quality of assistance to work-seekers coming from a Member State and seeking employment in another Member State:

> A national of a Member State who seeks employment in the territory of another Member State shall receive the same assistance there as that afforded by the employment offices in that State to their own nationals seeking employment.

In other words, Polish nationals seeking work in the UK are entitled to the same priority as British nationals with regard to access to available employment and to the same *assistance* as that afforded by the UK's employment offices to their own nationals seeking employment. Recruitment may not be dependent on criteria (medical, occupational or other) which discriminate on the grounds of nationality.

Therefore, this article was largely opposed by the 'old' EU Member States during the accession negotiations prior to the 2004 enlargement of the EU. Member States were clearly concerned about the possibility of the mass movement of work-seekers looking for unemployment benefits ('welfare tourism') and sought to exclude from the right to reside those who would be unable to support themselves and their families upon arrival.

Residence Directive 2004/38/EC

Directive 2004/38/EC on the right of citizens of the EU and their family members to move and reside freely within the territory of the EU was adopted by the European Parliament and the Council on 29 April 2004. It brought together the complex body of legislation that existed in this area. The basic premise of the Directive reinforced and implemented the right of European Economic Area (EEA) citizens to free movement and residence across the EEA.

The Directive reiterates the residence rights as provided for in the European citizenship legislation. Reading the Treaty itself (Article 45), it becomes clear that Member States are required to grant the right of residence in their territory to EU citizens (and their families) who entered as economically active persons. The importance of the Directive for the free movement legislation is that it also supplements the not so explicit residence provisions with regard to economically inactive persons: however, their right of residence is only valid *as long as they do not become an unreasonable burden* on the social assistance system of the host Member State during the initial period of residence (Article 7(1) of Directive 2004/38/EC).

Therefore, for stays of less than three months, while the only requirement on EU citizens is that they possess a valid identity document or passport,[3] the right of residence for more than six months remains subject to economic activity (and therefore supports the interpretation of residence and free movement rights as being the function of the common market).

The Directive therefore reasserted that EU citizens wanting to reside in the territory of another Member State for more than six months must:

1. be engaged in economic activity (on an employed or self-employed basis);
2. or have sufficient resources and sickness insurance to ensure that they do not become a burden on the social services of the host Member State during their stay. The Member States may not specify a minimum amount which they deem sufficient, but must take account of personal circumstances;
3. or be following vocational training as a student and have sufficient resources and sickness insurance to ensure that they do not become a burden on the social services of the host Member State during their stay;
4. or be a family member of an EU citizen who falls into one of the above categories (Article 7 of Directive 2004/38/EC).

Only upon fulfilling the above conditions are those persons to be granted the right of residence in the territory of a different Member State. A member of the family who is not a national of a Member State is to be issued with a residence document having the same validity as that issued to the worker on whom he or she is dependent (Article 11 of Directive 2004/38/EC). Completion of the formalities for obtaining a residence permit must not impede the immediate implementation of contracts of employment.

The main conclusion that could be drawn from the Directive is that the Community law status of 'worker' precludes extensive citizenship rights in the form of secure residence in the host society and, furthermore, contingent social rights such as family and welfare entitlement. The extensive nature of migrant workers' citizenship (somehow in opposition to a citizenship of economically inactive persons) is illustrated further by the ability of the status to have continuing effects after the employment relationship has come to an end.[4]

---

3 The host Member State may require the persons concerned to register their presence in the country within a reasonable and non-discriminatory period of time (Article 6(1) of Directive 2004/38/EC).

4 The Directive therefore re-asserts the interpretation of the treaty right (Article 45) discussed earlier, stipulating that a valid residence permit may not be withdrawn solely on the grounds that the worker is no longer in employment – either because he or she is temporarily incapable of work (sickness or an accident) (Article 7(3) of Directive 2004/38/EC) or because he or she is involuntarily unemployed (Articles 7(3)(b), (c) of Directive 2004/38/EC) or because he or she embarks on vocational training. Unless he or she is

The Directive also spells out the provisions relating to the expulsion of EU citizens from the territory of another Member State. As long as the beneficiaries of the right of residence do not become an unreasonable burden on the social assistance system of the host Member State, they should not be expelled (Article 14(1) of Directive 2004/38/EC). Therefore, an expulsion measure should not be the automatic consequence of recourse to the social assistance system (Article 14(3) of Directive 2004/38/EC). The host Member State should examine whether it is a case of temporary difficulties and take into account the duration of residence, the personal circumstances and the amount of aid granted in order to consider whether the beneficiary has become an unreasonable burden on its social assistance system and to proceed with his or her expulsion. In no case should an expulsion measure be adopted against workers, self-employed persons or job-seekers as defined by the European Court of Justice, save on grounds of public policy, public security or public health.

The Treaty of Accession 2003: Transition Provisions

The reason behind presenting in detail the provisions and principles relating to the free movement of persons contained in the European primary and secondary legislation is that the legal situation of workers and work-seekers as economic free-movers as set out above became particularly contentious during the Treaty of Accession negotiations preceding the 2004 enlargement of the EU to the east.

The 15 Member States of the 'old' EU (the EU-15) expressed their concern over the possibility of a mass influx of workers (and work-seekers) crossing their borders from the eight Central and Eastern European accession countries. In response to these fears, the fundamental rights of freedom of movement discussed above were questioned and the final Treaty of Accession included certain pre-determined transitional arrangements, which allowed for derogations from the *acquis communitaire* applicable to the EU-15 ('Fifteen') and the new Member States (Inglis 2004).

According to the Treaty of Accession (the relevant provision is found in Part 4 – Temporary Provisions, Title 1 – Transitional Measures, Article 24 of the Act of Accession 2003) the EU-15 were entitled to derogations from Article 45 of the Treaty on the Functioning of the European Union (formerly Article 39 TEC) on the 'Free movement of workers' and the first paragraph of Article 56 (formerly Article 49 TEC) on the 'Freedom in the provision of services within EU'.

By the terms of the Annexes to the Treaty of Accession, the EU-15 were also allowed to derogate from Articles 1–6 of Regulation 1612/68/EC on the freedom of movement for workers within the EU, which specified the conditions of access to the labour market that could be limited in the transition period, and certain

involuntarily unemployed, the retention of the 'worker' status shall require the training to be related to the previous employment.

provisions of Residence Directive 2004/38/EC with regard to legal residence rights.

In summary, what the transitory provisions meant was that:

1. the restrictions to freedom of movement were applicable only to migrant workers (and not to other EU citizens, e.g. the self-employed, persons of independent means, students, etc.);
2. the restrictions (with implicit discrimination on nationality grounds) only applied to obtaining access to the labour market;
3. once access had been obtained by the migrant worker in an EU Member State, there could be no discrimination on nationality grounds, and such a worker was entitled to equal treatment in respect of wages, employment rights and social and tax advantages.

The limitations resulting from the transition provisions can be broadly divided into two categories: (1) limitations in *access to the labour market*; and (2) limitations in *access to legal residence* (which has consequences for equal access to welfare) for migrant workers from the A8 countries in an EU Member State applying the transitory provisions.

Limitations in Access to the Labour Market

The derogations can be summarized as follows. Through the suspension of Article 45 (formerly Article 39 TEC), Articles 1–6 of Regulation 1612/68/EC and the corresponding provisions of Directive 2004/38/EC, there was a basic five-year period after accession during which each existing Member State could continue to apply its own *national rules* on access to the labour market (i.e. until 2009).[5]

These national rules (or bilateral agreements) could have meant anything between no and full rights to free movement and residence for accession state nationals for the purposes of taking up employment within any given Member State. In other words, the transitional arrangements envisaged that Member States were allowed to impose restrictions on immigration for employment purposes and to discriminate on grounds of nationality with regard to access to their domestic labour markets.

However, accession state nationals, once admitted to the labour market of an existing Member State for an uninterrupted period of at least 12 months (whether at the time of accession or during the transitional regime), would have secured the right of access to the labour market of that Member State, although not a right to free movement as a worker across the rest of the EU (Dougan 2004: 123).

After the basic five-year period had elapsed (after 2009), full free movement of workers would extend to relations between all Member States subject to two

5 Subject to the review for each accession state before the end of its second year (2006) by the Council on the basis of a report by the Commission.

provisions. Firstly, where there were serious disturbances on the domestic labour market (or the threat thereof), those existing Member States which were still applying their own immigration rules could continue to do so for a further period of two years (i.e. until 2011), having again notified the Commission.

Secondly, any existing Member State applying the Community *acquis* on the free movement of workers (whether having decided to shorten or terminate the transitional regime following a Commission review or upon the natural expiry of the basic five-year period) could still invoke a safeguard clause until the end of the seventh year following accession (i.e. 2011) to cope with exceptional situations (Dougan 2004: 124). As a result of the transitional measures, the fundamental principle of the freedom of movement of workers could have been deferred for a period up to a maximum of seven years.

Limitations in Access to Residence

In the light of the current legislation, only EU citizens who *lawfully reside* in another Member State are entitled to equal treatment in respect of all benefits falling within the scope of EU law.[6]

However, in the light of the transition arrangements in the 2003 Treaty of Accession, the *lawful residence* of accession state citizens exercising the right to free movement in another Member State was not derived from the more liberal *European citizenship* legislation[7] but was governed by the rather restrictive *national residence rules and regulations*.

The limitations in the access to legal residence had important consequences for the equal access to social security provisions. From among the three 'old' Member States (Ireland, Sweden and the UK) that provided migrant workers from the accession states with access to their labour market in 2004, only Sweden duly applied the European law resulting in equal access to welfare for migrant workers. Ireland and the UK imposed restrictions regarding legal residence, which resulted in limited access to social security benefits. Therefore, in the opinion of some researchers, the 2004 enlargement of the EU brought to the surface not so much the recognition of the right of Member State nationals to move of other Member States, but the extent to which these other nationals might become active claimants of social welfare provisions (Currie 2007a, 2008b; Spaventa 2007).

The 2003 Treaty of Accession conferred EU citizenship onto nationals of the accession states and made no transitory provisions in this respect. However, as the implementation of citizenship rights (*lawful residence*) was kept as a prerogative

6 This made Dougan and Spaventa conclude that the 'equal treatment not only flows from lawful residence; it also makes the latter status more meaningful in practice' (Dougan and Spaventa 2003: 708).

7 Liberal, as observed in the ECJ case law jurisprudence in *Grzelczyk*: Case C-184/99, *Grzelczyk* [2001] ECR I-6193; *Sala*: Case C-85/96, *Martinez Sala* [1998] ECR I-2691; and *Bidar*: Case C-209/03, *Bidar* [2005] ECR I-2119.

of national governments of particular Member States, the citizenship status of 'new' EU members between 2004 and 2011 was downgraded, as they occupied a lower citizenship status than their EU-15 counterparts (Currie 2007a: 13). Currie's analysis of the role of EU citizenship in the context of EU enlargement points to the conclusion that the new EU members were 'denied full membership and participation in the community that they have, formally, joined and are, accordingly, not fully incorporated into the EU "society" while restrictions are in place' (Currie 2007a: 13).

In this context, Maas makes a strong point about the changing nature of EU citizenship as triggered by the enlargement:

> Usually, the concept of citizenship is seen as a status that is unitary; either one is a citizen or one is not. That is not the way to think of citizenship in this case; the current enlargement will feature a gradual process of extending rights to individuals. (Maas 2005: 9)

The entrenchment of differentiated citizenship rights for all EU citizens under EU law led Currie to observe that:

> citizenship of the Union, in the sense of the formal provisions, was introduced to increase the EU's legitimacy and bring Europe 'closer to its citizens' but the very existence of transitional arrangements on free movement suggests that Europe does not desire to be close to all of its citizens or at least not as close to some as it is to others. After all, it is predominantly through exercising rights of mobility that Member State nationals experience meaningful citizenship. As a consequence of this selective intimacy, the legitimacy of the EU may be damaged irrevocably as a result of transitional mobility restrictions. (Currie 2007a: 41)

British Response to the Transition Provisions: The 2004 Immigration Regulations

To reiterate, after the 2004 enlargement, most of the EU-15 relied on the derogations provided by the Treaty of Accession with regard to free movement: their labour markets remained closed until 1 May 2011, so the right to residence remained conditional upon obtaining a work permit.

In the UK on 1 May 2004, in compliance with the derogations stipulated in the Treaty of Accession 2003, free movement rights were generally extended to the nationals of the 10 new Member States and their family members; however, this was done *under the conditions specified in British legislation.*[8]

---

8 The laws provided for the situation for citizens – workers, work-seekers and their family members – from eight out of the ten newly joined Member States (A8: the Czech

A significant introduction to the UK's 2004 immigration regulations has already been given earlier in the book. This section expands on the particularities of the legislation without which it would be difficult to fully comprehend the British legal environment towards the migrant workers from A8 states during the transition period 2003–2011.

The three pieces of legislation which the British government introduced were:

1. the Accession (Immigration and Worker Registration) Regulations 2004 (SI 2004/1219);
2. the Social Security (Habitual Residence) Amendment Regulations 2004 (SI 2004/1232); and
3. the Immigration (European Economic Area) and Accession (Amendment) Regulations 2004 (SI 2004/1236).

These regulations, known as the Accession Regulations 2004, amended the 2000 EEA Regulations to include within their scope the 10 new Member States from 1 May 2004. In a nutshell, they limited the right of free movement for workers, work-seekers and their family members from the A8 countries in the UK in the following ways:

1. A8 workers were lawfully resident in the UK during their first year of employment only if they had registered their employment with the WRS and were working for authorized employers.
2. A8 workers who ceased to work during their first year of employment were only lawfully resident for the remainder of the month in which they ceased working.
3. Work-seekers from the A8 countries were not 'entitled to reside in the UK'.
4. Family members of A8 workers during the first year of employment were not granted residence permits (Rogers and Scannell 2005: 404).

The Accession Regulations, by binding together access to employment, legal residence and access to the welfare system (Currie 2007a: 5), limited free movement in a threefold way. Firstly, migrant workers upon finding employment were *required to register* under the WRS within a 30-day grace period. The registration was designed by the Home Office for the purpose of monitoring the numbers of migrants and not to limit their access to the labour market; however, if a migrant failed to register within the 30-day period, their work became illegal and the migrant 'might need to stop working' (the Accession (Immigration and Worker Registration) Regulations 2004).

Secondly, the Accession Regulations limited *the right to residence* of the workers admitted to the labour market and their families. As discussed above,

---

Republic, Estonia, Hungary, Latvia, Lithuania, Poland, Slovakia and Slovenia – excluding Malta and Cyprus, which were granted full access immediately from 2004).

the right to residence was thus not derived from the European legislation but was made conditional on complying with national legislation. Non-compliance with the Accession Regulations brought the consequence of *unlawful residence* and – at least in principle – exposed migrant workers to the risk of deportation (Currie 2008b).

Thirdly, the Accession Regulations limited A8 nationals' *participation in welfare* by making access to many benefits dependent upon compliance with 12 months' continuous employment and registration under the WRS. Work-seekers and workers without WRS registration were indefinitely excluded from access to welfare support and benefits.

Therefore, the UK seemed to go part of the way with regard to free movement, as it opened its labour market to workers from the new EU Member States in 2004, but at the same time limited their rights to residence and equal access to welfare on the basis of national legislation until 2011.[9] As Rogers and Scannell observed:

> It might be suggested that Member States that do open up their labour markets are acting generously and ought not to have the detail of the regime put in place analysed too critically. However lest any regime be exploitative such Member State cannot provide less protection or afford less social rights to A8 nationals than would be afforded to any other EU national. Non-discrimination is a fundamental principle of Community law and … if Member States wish to enjoy the benefits of labour migration, Community law would expect them to take on the attendant social responsibilities involved. (Rogers and Scannell 2005: 404)

The WRS

The Accession (Immigration and Worker Registration) Regulations 2004 created a legal requirement for A8 nationals to register their employment with the Home Office and join the WRS within 30 days of starting work. Failure to register resulted in the person working in breach of immigration laws and an offence being committed by the employer (s. 9 of the EEA Regulations). There was a £90 fee for joining the Worker Registration Scheme.

---

9 What remains questionable, however, is whether the UK legislation was compliant with the European principles of equal treatment and non-discrimination on the grounds of nationality (Article 18 Treaty on the Functioning of the European Union, formerly Article 12, TEC). The provisions of the Treaty of Accession 2003 do not permit derogations from Articles 7–12 of Regulation 1612/68 on equal treatment. For example, A8 nationals who obtain employment in the UK should be entitled to the same treatment as British nationals and other EU nationals with respect to terms and conditions of employment (Article 7(1) of Regulation 1612/68), access to housing (Article 9 of Regulation 1612/68) and, importantly, the same social and tax advantages (Article 7(2) of Regulation 1612/68).

Between 1 May 2004 and 1 May 2011, the scheme applied to workers from A8 countries who:

1. started a new job on or after 1 May 2004;
2. have been working in the UK before 1 May without authorization;
3. were working on a short-term or temporary basis;
4. were students and also working (European Commission 2009).

There were some categories of A8 workers who were exempt from registration (like the self-employed, those working legally in the UK for 12 months or more in their current job on 1 May 2004 and those who were given leave to enter the UK as a participant on the Seasonal Agricultural Workers Scheme (SAWS) before 1 May 2004). The differentiation between A8 workers required to register and those not required to register has therefore brought about some confusion regarding the application of the scheme.

With regard to the general requirements, registered workers were required to remain within the Scheme during the first 12 months of employment in the UK. If they held two or more concurrent jobs, all their jobs had to be registered under the Scheme. Each time they changed their employer during these initial 12 months, they had to re-register their employment. If the period of employment was interrupted (e.g. they lost their job within the initial 12 months), workers were obliged to start a new job within 30 days and re-register for it to be treated as continuous employment, otherwise they 'lost' the months accumulated when working under the Scheme and (with the new employer) they would be compelled to start the registration anew.

Only A8 nationals who duly registered their employment were lawfully resident, as were their spouse and other relatives (as defined in the national legislation).[10] A8 nationals who have worked in the UK but who lost their jobs or ceased to work, perhaps through no fault of their own, during the first year of residence in the UK became unlawfully resident if they had not obtained alternative employment within one month. As discussed earlier in this chapter, EU law requires that Member States grant work-seekers at least six months to find work (Weiss and Wooldridge 2002: 50). Therefore, provisions requiring that alternative employment is found within a month appear to fly in the face of EU law (Rogers and Scannell 2005: 406).

Only after the first 12 months of registered work could A8 nationals apply for an EEA residence permit in accordance with the EEA Regulations 2000,

10 The introduction of the WRS as a condition of lawful residence during the first 12 months of residence in the UK purported to deprive work-seekers from the A8 countries of any right of residence in the UK unless they were self-sufficient and could meet the conditions laid down in Directive 90/364/EEC.

confirming their right to live and work in the UK. Their spouse or other relatives were also able to obtain residence permits at this point.[11]

Social Security Limitations

The Social Security (Habitual Residence) Amendment Regulations 2004 dealt with entitlement to means-tested benefits. These Regulations transformed the social security eligibility criteria to the effect that persons needed to satisfy a 'right to reside' test in addition to the standard habitual residence test (Currie 2007a: 9).

A8 workers who came to the UK to work after 1 May 2004 could only have a right to reside if they were working and registered under the WRS or they have completed the initial 12-month period as a registered worker in continuous employment (European Commission 2009). EU-15 nationals in the UK were considered to be 'legally resident' both as work-seekers and former workers who became unemployed (the Immigration (European Economic Area) Regulations 2000 and 2006). As a result of this test, A8 migrants were automatically excluded from consideration, while UK nationals and EU-15 migrants in a comparable situation were not (Currie 2007b).

The Social Security (Habitual Residence) Amendment Regulations, when read together with the Accession Regulations, made clear the intention that certain categories of A8 nationals (job-seekers, workers and their family members during the first year of employment) were not eligible for means-tested benefits such as income support, income-based Jobseeker's Allowance, housing benefit, council tax benefit and pension credit, which were dependent on the satisfaction of the right to reside test. In addition, exclusion from homelessness assistance was stated in the Allocation of Housing and Homelessness (Amendment) Regulations 2004. Moreover, reg. 5 of the Accession (Immigration and Worker Registration) Regulations sought to make unlawful the residence of an A8 national if he or she ceased to work during the first year of employment, thus depriving him or her of access to social security benefits (or any other social and tax advantages that he or she might otherwise have obtained as a worker) (Rogers and Scannell 2005: 408). This provision directly discriminated against A8 nationals (Currie 2008a) and exceeded the derogations expressly provided for in the treaty (Article 39 TEC).

When comparing UK transitory provisions with the EU legislation on the access to welfare, one clearly observes that in the EU law any limitations mainly concern economically inactive persons. Workers and economically active persons fully benefit from access to the welfare system of a particular Member State on an equal footing with its nationals. With the transition provisions in the UK, the restrictions were directed towards the migrant workers themselves (the *spiritus*

11 Accession state nationals could apply for indefinite leave to remain under para. 255B of the Immigration Rules (HC 395), provided they lawfully resided in the UK for the necessary period of four years prior to applying for indefinite leave to remain (Rogers and Scannel 2005: 407).

movens of the EU principle of free movement) and therefore exceeding the principles set up in the EU law.[12]

It can therefore be concluded that the post-2004 EU enlargement regime imposed by the UK (and Ireland) – opening the labour market yet limiting the workers' access to social welfare – lay beyond the scope of the derogations permitted by the 2003 Treaty of Accession.[13] As Spaventa observes, on the one hand, the Member State had a legitimate interest in protecting its limited welfare resources from undeserving claims, but on the other hand, EU citizens might well have had reasonable expectations to enjoy *some* benefits in the host welfare society by the virtue of their employment and contribution to the national economy (Spaventa 2007: 115).

NGOs dealing with the rights of migrant workers (AIRE Centre and Migrants' Rights Network) have long been sceptical about the compatibility of the restrictions on A8 nationals' access to benefits with EU law. The courts and tribunals in the UK have upheld these restrictions. However, the European Commission, which is responsible for overseeing the implementation of EU law, deemed that at least some aspects of the restrictions on A8 nationals were unlawful. The Commission in 2010 sent the UK government a 'reasoned opinion' and, whilst its content remained confidential, it appears that the Commission was challenging the fact that A8 workers who had not yet completed 12 months of registered employment were excluded from out-of-work benefits if they became temporarily unable to work due to illness or accident, were made involuntarily unemployed or began vocational training (Migrants' Rights Network 2011).

Accession Regulations as a Compromise of Interests

The analysis of the Accession Regulations revealed that UK's 'opening' of its labour market to workers from the 'new' EU Member States was not a straightforward process. It was accompanied by initiatives to impose restrictions on the social

---

12 According to the 2003 Treaty of Accession, transitional derogations were permitted only from Articles 1–6 of Regulation 1612/68 (in the area of access to the labour market) and *not* with regard to the equal treatment provisions relating to social security: Article 7(2) of Regulation 1612/68 – *the same social and tax advantages*. Therefore, economically active citizens from the 'new' EU Member States, upon being admitted to the labour market on the basis of national laws, should enjoy equal treatment in relation to access to contributory and non-contributory benefits on an equal footing with UK nationals.

13 During the initial 12-month period, an A8 worker was only entitled to child benefit and in-work benefits such as tax credits (e.g. working tax credit or child tax credit). A8 nationals could qualify for non-means tested and contributory benefits (e.g. statutory sick pay, maternity pay, maternity allowance and disability living allowance or attendance allowance) in the same way as UK and other EU nationals, that is, provided that enough UK National Insurance contributions had been paid in the relevant period (contributions paid in another Member State could be taken into account under EC Regulation 1408/71) (European Commission 2009).

welfare entitlement of A8 workers, the main objective being to prevent 'welfare tourism'. Although the common perception was that the UK's open labour market access was tantamount to a liberal or even generous policy, Currie, in her analysis of post-accession migrant workers in the UK, challenged this view and deemed this regime to be the 'one of the more exploitative post-accession free movement regimes to have emerged' (Currie 2008b: 23).

In the academic discourse on the British immigration rules, two interpretations seem to be dominant. EU optimists say that in the Accession Regulations the UK has sought a way to reconcile the potentially conflicting interests of acting in line with the EU principle of freedom of movement and preserving the public benefit system (Kubal 2009). EU pessimists see this legislation as being dictated solely by the national interest, aiming at receiving the benefits from labour migration without acquiring the social responsibility for migrant workers.

The Accession Regulations were put in place as a compromise – to monitor the scale of migration and to limit access to the welfare system for A8 workers, but not to reduce the number of migrants. The final shape of the Regulations was dictated by various – often conflicting – interests that had to be considered.

On the one hand, there was a need in the UK for foreign labour. David Blunkett, Secretary of State for the Home Department, announced publicly on 23 February 2004 that:

> We currently have more than 500 000 vacancies and will benefit from the skills, flexibility and willingness to work of those new migrant workers, (David Blunkett, quoted in Currie 2008b: 34)

Indeed, the Accession Monitoring Reports prepared quarterly by the UK Border Agency, the Department for Work and Pensions, HM Revenue & Customs and the Department for Communities and Local Government suggested that A8 workers help to fill the gaps in the labour market, particularly in administration, business and management, hospitality and catering, agriculture, manufacturing and food, fish and meat processing (UK Border Agency et al. 2009: 1). In many cases A8 nationals are supporting the provision of public services in communities across the UK.[14]

Concurrent with the government's declarations of vacancies, in the run-up to the enlargement of the EU, a negative perception of potential migrants from the new accession countries was portrayed in sections of the British media, where much emphasis was placed on the 'threat' posed to the benefits system by migrants (Smith 2004). *The Sun* 'warned the UK against the 1.5 million Slovakian Gypsies'

14 According to the most recent Accession Monitoring Report, in the 12 months prior to March 2009, 815 A8 nationals have registered as bus, lorry and coach drivers, 2,660 as care workers, 790 as teachers, researchers and classroom assistants, 55 as dental practitioners (including hygienists and dental nurses) and 720 as GPs, hospital doctors, nurses and medical specialists (UK Border Agency 2009 et al.: 1).

who would exercise their right to use 'scarce and British' health, education and welfare resources, while other tabloids presented equally alarming scenarios of the UK being flooded by welfare seekers from the poorer accession state countries:

> The Daily Mail upped the numbers coming to Britain from tens of thousands to 100,000 and derided the government's plan to fatuously propose an advertising campaign telling would-be migrants not to come to Britain ... The Daily Express believed there were 1.6 million Gypsies 'ready to flood in' and said they were already counting the benefits they would be paid. (Smith 2004)

The scale of the collective paranoia portrayed in the British tabloid press put pressure on the UK government to impose restrictive measures. The influences exerted internally were additionally heightened by the fact that the majority of the Member States announced transitional restrictions. As a result of the above pressures (stemming from the labour market as well as echoing the tabloid threats), the British government had to design a scheme that would accommodate the need to fill labour shortages but at the same time respond to the concerns connected to the benefit system.

Equally, the UK government had to consider the sets of pressures stemming from the European Commission on the final application on EU law on free movement in the UK (Rogers and Scannell 2005). Romano Prodi, the President of the European Commission (1999–2004), told 'old' EU Member States who decided to open their labour markets for migrant workers from the accession states that they 'must set aside their national interest and abide by policies decided by majority voting in future' (Horsley 2004). He referred to equality of treatment and non-discrimination as the fundamental principles of EU law. It was extremely unlikely that the EU would turn its back on decades of progress and permit Member States to benefit from labour migration without acquiring at least some social responsibilities for migrants: 'Member State[s] cannot provide less protection or afford less social rights to accession state nationals than would be afforded to any other EU national' (Rogers and Scannell 2005: 404).

The overall character of the British legislation in the transition period 2004–2011 therefore resulted from the struggle to compromise between the national interest and the EU principle of free movement. The political and economic consensus of the Home Office involved, on the one hand, fulfilling the need for temporary migrant workers to ensure competitiveness, increase labour market flexibility, control inflation and underpin economic growth. This set of interests re-legitimized low-status labour migration into the UK. These economic interests, on the other hand, were confronted with the fear of 'benefit tourism' skilfully amplified by tabloid propaganda, and the pressures from the European Commission on the equal treatment of workers exercising their free movement treaty rights. The Accession Regulations were therefore created as a political balancing act. The normative internal contradiction of law resulting from its aim to accommodate various, conflicting interests has weakened its meaning.

Enforcement of the Accession Regulations

The burden of enforcement of the Accession Regulations (particularly the WRS) was passed to the employer. The employer was obliged by the UK Border Agency to keep a copy of the worker's completed application form to prove they had applied for registration within one month of starting work and to keep a copy of the valid registration certificate once it had been issued by the Home Office.

On 1 May 2004, the British government introduced measures to strengthen the enforcement of s. 8 of the Asylum and Immigration Act 1996 (as amended by s. 147 of the Nationality, Immigration and Asylum Act 2002), which made employers in general responsible under the regulations for ensuring that they were authorized to employ a worker from one of the A8 states affected by the WRS. Section 8 made it a criminal offence to employ an individual over the age of 16 who did not have the entitlement to be in the UK or whose status precluded them from undertaking the employment in question (Ruhs 2006). The employer was also committing a criminal offence and faced legal sanctions of a fine of up to £5,000 (UK Border Agency 2010).

In 2006 the newly introduced Immigration, Asylum and Nationality Act 2006 (ss. 15–25) changed the legal qualification of employing illegal workers from a criminal to a civil offence (it came into force on 28 February 2008). As a result, the UK Border Agency can issue 'on the spot' fines to employers if the latter are found to employ an illegal worker and has not copied and kept the right identity and work permit documents. If a UK employer is found to be employing illegal workers, he or she is issued with a notice of potential liability by UK Border Agency officers. The civil penalties compliance team will then consider the evidence and decide whether to issue the employer with a notice of liability and a civil penalty of up to £10,000 per illegal worker.[15] The criminal charges still hold for those employers who knowingly employ illegal workers. These carry a maximum custodial sentence of two years and/or an unlimited fine.

Between 1998 and 2005, 17 employers (including eight employers in 2004) were successfully prosecuted for illegally employing migrants under s. 8 of the Asylum and Immigration Act 1996. More than half of s. 8 convictions in 2004–2005 resulted in fines of less than £700, with four employers fined the maximum of £5,000 (Home Office 2005).

With the introduction of the civil penalty scheme, the prosecution rate of illegal workers under the Immigration, Asylum and Nationality Act 2006 significantly increased. In the whole of the UK, 660 employers received a notice of liability and civil penalties for the use of illegal migrant labour in the last quarter of 2009 only, with 29 businesses being fined £20,000, one £40,000 and three £50,000.[16]

15 The maximum charge for employing an illegal A8 worker was set at £5,000 (UK Border Agency 2010).

16 The lists of fined employers were published on the UK Border Agency's website and were made available for the public to view until the change of government in May 2010;

However, the numbers do not disaggregate between EU (A8 and A2) and non-EU illegally employed migrant workers. Therefore, it is impossible to work out the actual number of employers prosecuted for employing unregistered A8 migrant workers. Nevertheless, the qualitative evidence has it that the prosecution rate against employers employing A8 nationals without proper registration remained low. The vast majority of the penalties were issued to employers illegally employing migrant workers from outside the EU (UK Border Agency 2010).

Anderson and Ruhs argue that this is because in practice the enforcement of immigration laws remains influenced by its perceived economic costs and benefits (Anderson and Ruhs 2010: 207). Lack of WRS registration in the light of not-so-clear executive rules (in terms of who is required to register and who is not) presented itself as arguably less harmful to public order than working without a valid work permit, for example. The low prosecution rates against unregistered A8 workers could also be explained by the fact that the employers had a defence if they could demonstrate that during the first month of employment, they were shown a document which 'appeared … to establish either that the A8 national was not required to register, or that they had applied to register [Regulation 9(2)a]' (Ryan 2008: 86).

According to the Home Office 2006 report on employers' use of migrant labour, employers expressed no knowledge of illegal working, whereas actually some of them were (or had been) recruiting illegally. This was reportedly owing to their ignorance of registration procedures and their responsibilities as employers. Some employers admitted the procedures were too time-consuming to deal with and sometimes 'turned a blind eye' to workers of unknown legality (Dench et al. 2006). On the other hand, many employers who recruited through recruitment agencies assumed that the agencies had undertaken the appropriate checks on the WRS registration of their clients (Dench et al. 2006).

At the same time, when the employers actually attempted to take steps to enforce the registration of their workers, they were faced with a bureaucratic and informational maze that they had to navigate. The details of the registration system were complex and information regarding the WRS was not readily accessible. The rather 'last minute' nature of the UK's response to the enlargement of the EU – the

currently, the website has been archived. The most recent data is available for the last quarter of 2009, with the website last being updated on 4 February 2010. The data reveals that the prosecution rates grew steadily after the introduction of the civil penalty scheme. In the first year of its operation (between February 2008 and January 2009), 236 employers were fined for employing illegal workers; between January and June 2009, 1,166 employers were fined; and between June and September 2009, 670 employers were fined. The lists include details of employers from whom no appeal or objection was received within the stipulated 35 days after the serving of the notice of liability (NOL) and no extension request was received or granted, and the appeal process against the service of the NOL was fully exhausted. Cf: http://webarchive.nationalarchives.gov.uk/20091212072532/http://www.ukba.homeoffice.gov.uk/sitecontent/documents/employersandsponsors/listemployerspenalties/

government passed the law in February 2004, three months before the impending accession – meant there was very little time for any widespread publicizing of the scheme (Currie 2007a: 6).

This resulted in uncertainty among migrant workers and UK employers alike; the latter in particular were unaware of the specific details of the WRS. Currie, looking at the situation of the new European 'free-movers' in the post-accession regime in the UK, reported that the Home Office indeed seemed to have experienced some 'teething problems', particularly in the initial stages of the operation of the WRS (Currie 2006). Drawing from her extensive fieldwork, she provided multiple examples of employers who were aware of the need to find out about the status of A8 nationals working for them after 1 May 2004, but where the Home Office was 'not yet sure how to answer their questions':

> My employer chose me for the position before 1st May and he did absolutely everything to find out. He phoned the Home Office every day and they kept saying 'We do not know yet, you have to be patient'. But it was a week until 1st May and they still said they did not know. (Currie 2008b: 46)

The lack of information with regard to the registration rules for migrants from new EU Member States at the grassroots level resulted in inconsistent law enforcement. This suggests that the British state itself adopted a 'soft' approach towards enforcing this legislation. The WRS was put in place to monitor the scale of migration and not to limit the number of migrants. Paradoxically, recent reports show that it even failed to deliver accurate figures and artificially reduced the actual numbers of Eastern European migrants by not taking into account those working and living in the UK who dropped out of the Scheme before the completion of 12 consecutive months of employment. These inconsistencies made the Scheme less relevant and less important from the perspective of the British authorities. Additionally, enforcing these rules could prove to be a very time-consuming and costly project, and as such not very beneficial to the state.[17]

The lack of clear executive clauses in the Accession Regulations – 'the unregistered worker *might* have to stop working' (UK Border Agency 2004, emphasis added) – point to a conclusion that it was a 'soft' law, a law which lost

17 Despite the low prosecution rates and the 'soft approach' to the enforcement of the WRS, it was however possible to observe the 'tightening' of the immigration discourse by the British authorities. When the British government in April 2009 decided to keep the WRS in place for the next two years, the UK Border Agency announced that 'strict working restrictions for Eastern Europeans will not be scrapped' (UK Border Agency 2010). At the same time, Phil Woolas, the Minister of State for Borders and Immigration, for the first time in this context gave evidence of deportation cases of European nationals: 'We are determined to remove people that harm our communities – wherever they are from. That is why we are making it easier to kick out European criminals and stop them from returning. In 2007 we removed over 500 European nationals' (UK Border Agency 2010).

its coercive power and was implemented by negotiation and reasoning, rather than using the prospect and fear of punishment. If a migrant worker from the accession state did not apply to join the WRS, the employment should have become illegal within a month. There was, however, no mention of any legal consequences for the worker of failing to register, apart from the practical issue that all the time that a worker spent working outside the WRS would not count towards the 12-month qualifying period to become exempt from registration. As the law did not have the quality of prohibition, non-compliance did not feel as if one was actually breaking the law.

With no real coercive power and no power of punishment, all the law was left with was its power of exclusion. The exclusionary character of the law was particularly visible in the part of the Accession Regulations directly concerned with social security. When migrants from the new EU Member States failed to register their employment, they would become indefinitely excluded from full participation in the welfare system. In this way, the law acted as a barrier to benefits and social support. As such, it was there rather to exclude those who did not comply with it than to impose rules in general.

The recent case law – the House of Lords' decision in *Zalewska v. Department for Social Development* [2008] UKHL 67 – confirmed the thesis of the inconsistent nature of law enforcement and the exclusionary character of the Accession Regulations 2004.

Case Law Evidence: Zalewska v. Department for Social Development

Ms Zalewska is a Polish national who arrived in Northern Ireland on 1 July 2004. On 9 July 2004 she began working as a mushroom picker and, as this job was registered with the WRS, at this point she was both lawfully employed and lawfully resident in the UK.

On 7 January 2005 Ms Zalewska ceased her original, registered employment and, via a recruitment agency, started a different job the following day. She remained in work until 10 July 2005. What is important here is the fact that the work carried out since January had not been registered with the WRS. Therefore, according to the Accession Regulations, she was neither lawfully employed nor resident from February 2005 when the 30-day grace period provided by the law to re-register one's new employment with the Home Office expired (reg. 2(4) of the Accession (Immigration and Worker Registration) Regulations 2004).

Between January and April 2005, Ms Zalewska was joined in Northern Ireland by her daughter and partner (the child's father). However, in June 2005 she left her partner after experiencing domestic violence and moved to a Women's Aid hostel. It was around this time that she also stopped working and ultimately, on 22 July 2005, applied for income support for herself and her daughter. Her income support application was refused on the basis that she did not have the right to reside in the UK – she had accumulated only six months of registered employment.

Ms Zalewska appealed against this decision and her appeal with the Social Security Appeal Tribunal was successful on the grounds that she was entitled to rely on Article 7(2) of Regulation 1612/68/EC in order to access social advantages. This decision was overturned in August 2006 by the Social Security Commissioner and, in May 2007, the Northern Ireland Court of Appeal affirmed the Commissioner's decision ([2007] NICA 17). Finally, Ms Zalewska submitted her appeal to the House of Lords on two grounds:

1. that her entitlement to claim access to income support was derived directly from Article 7(2) of Regulation 1612/68/EC, on which migrant workers have the right to access the same social advantages as British nationals;
2. that the Workers Registration Scheme rules (especially the provisions regarding the re-registration of employment) were incompatible with EU law, in particular because they did not satisfy the proportionality principle.

The House of Lords, by a majority of 3:2, upheld the decision of the Court of Appeal in Northern Ireland. Ms Zalewska's first ground for appeal – non-discrimination on the grounds of nationality with regard to social advantages – was overruled by the argument that this was contingent on the worker complying with the national measures put in place by the Member State in the first place. As Ms Zalewska had not satisfied the conditions of the WRS which the UK had put in place as part of its entitlement to derogate from Articles 1–6 of Regulation 1612/68/EC, she had not been 'admitted to the labour market' under the terms of the Treaty of Accession and therefore could not rely directly on Article 7(2) of that Regulation either (House of Lords 2008: paras 25–8).

With regard to the proportionality principle, the court acknowledged the relevance of this principle, but at the same time argued that the actual requirement to register with the WRS was not disproportionate in itself (para. 36). The court justified the WRS in the light of the potential 'influx' of migrants and the possibility of disruption to the UK's social security system, which thus also justified the re-registration when changing employment, as satisfying the proportionality principle (House of Lords 2008: para. 44).

The court also made a strong reference with regard to the enforcement of the re-registration provisions, which are valuable from the perspective of the argument presented in this chapter. Lord Hope recognized that the enforcement of the rules would 'come with a cost, depending on the circumstances' (House of Lords 2008: para. 44). By this, he directly pointed to the fact that the rules might well not be imposed in general, but would rather exclude those who did not comply with them. Ms Zalewska's exclusion from 'lawful residence' and hence her disqualification from an award of income support, despite having worked for over a year in the UK, was presumably conceived by Lord Hope as a necessary price to pay to ensure the protection of the social security system.

Baroness Hale (who together with Lord Neuberger dissented from the verdict of the court) had no difficulty pointing to the paradox of Ms Zalewska's case relating to inconsistent law enforcement. Ms Zalewska's new employer, for whom she started working in January 2005, had committed a criminal offence by recruiting a worker without ensuring that she had re-registered (reg. 9 of the Accession (Immigration and Worker Registration) Regulations 2004) and yet it was Ms Zalewska who bore the full and serious consequences of the application of the law (House of Lords 2008: para. 51). Baroness Hale's justification supports an argument made earlier in this chapter that very few checks were conducted on employers and employment agencies with respect to their own obligations and enforcement of the WRS. Generally, the levels of prosecution against employers for violations of immigration law are low, and this also prevailed after the introduction of the WRS (Anderson et al. 2006).

The commentary to the judgment that 'employers and agencies were likely to be in a better position to be aware of their duties than the workers themselves, and therefore it would make more sense to *impose* the (re)-registration obligation on them' (Currie 2008a: 56, emphasis added) also confirms the argument about inconsistent law enforcement. This points to a conclusion about the selective imposition of law ('depending on the circumstances': House of Lords 2008: para. 44) and its exclusionary character.

Workplace Regulations in the UK

As most of the A8 nationals came to the UK to work (or to find work), workplace pegulations constitute part of the British legal environment even beyond the post-2004 EU enlargement transition period (2004–2011). Employment law, labour regulations – concerning contracts, National Insurance contributions and tax regulations – and health and safety provisions are the first ones migrant workers had to respond to upon their arrival in the UK.

Employment Contracts and Employment Status

Employment law in the UK stipulates that all employees have an employment contract with their employer, although the contract regulations are quite flexible – the contract may not be in writing. Lack of a written employment contract does not exclude an existing employment relationship, which would have automatically been created when one starts working for a particular employer.

The bottom line is a specific understanding of 'a contract' in the British legal tradition; a contract is not a document that has to 'be signed' upon commencing employment but an agreement that 'is made' as soon as the acceptance of the job offer is undertaken (HM Government 2009b).

In reality, however, the lack of written employment contracts complicates the execution of employment rights and responsibilities, especially in the event of a dispute. There is therefore a widely popular practice (and understanding) of contracts as being mostly in writing. In addition, the employer is obliged to deliver to new employees – within two months of commencement of the employment – a written statement of employment particulars. The written statement sets out some of the main rights and duties relating to the employment.

The flexible nature of the British labour law also differentiates between contracts *of employment* and contracts *to provide services*. The latter are particularly popular among temporary agency workers (and self-employed persons). A contract to provide services is usually an agreement between the worker and an agency (or another person) to undertake some work, but not on a permanent basis and with restricted rights.

For any person working in the UK, it is therefore important not only to have a contract or written employment particulars but also to be aware of the type of contract. This is the case because the type of contract holds particular significance for the person's employment status.

Labour law in the UK differentiates between 'an employee' and 'a worker'. However, it is often difficult to clearly state whether one is an employee or (only) a worker. If the written agreement includes the phrase 'contract of employment', it is probable that it has been established between an employer and an employee (ANIMATE et al. 2008). However, how does one determine one's status if there is no written agreement between the parties?

This general confusion led to the development of different tests to clarify one's employment status. If there is no written contract, one may still be an employee if it is the employer who controls the overall work and specifies how it should be carried out, who supplies the equipment and tools required for the job, requires the employee to work regular hours and pays tax and National Insurance on behalf of the employee (ANIMATE et al. 2008: 27–8).

At the same time, agency workers also have tax and National Insurance paid on their behalf by the agency, their work is controlled and specified by the agency's client, and it is the client who delivers the tools required for the job and requires them to work regular hours. And yet, as a general rule, agency workers are not considered agency employees (or employees of the agency's client). There is a grey area between being an employee or a worker beyond the scope of contract wording, the supply of tools and freedom of work.

The definitional qualifications have a bearing for the analysis of the British legal environment for Polish migrant workers in the workplace, as the scope of rights and duties at work depends on a person's employment status and differs distinctively between employees and workers (including agency workers). As a general rule, employees enjoy more rights and a more secure position than workers.

Consequences of Employment Status for Rights at Work

Both categories – workers and employees – are guaranteed the following rights: they have to be paid the National Minimum Wage (the National Minimum Wage Act 1998), they have the right to not have unlawful deductions made from their pay, they have to receive itemized payslips showing earnings and deductions such as tax, they have the right not to work more than 48 hours a week (the maximum working week) and to four weeks' holiday a year (the Working Time Regulations

1998), they have the right not to be discriminated against,[18] they have the right to join a trade union and they have the right to health and safety protection, protection relating to pregnancy and Statutory Sick Pay (ANIMATE et al. 2008: 28).

Employees also enjoy some additional rights, such as the right to maternity leave and the right to return to work at the end of the leave period, the right to protection from dismissal as a result of pregnancy or because of trade union activity, the right to equal pay and the right to paid or unpaid time off work in certain situations (ANIMATE et al. 2008: 31–2). Employees are also guaranteed certain rights depending on the length of employment with a given employer.[19]

Although there is no separate definition of 'agency worker' (in addition to the distinction between employees and workers) in British law, the law grants special rights to agency workers (workers for employment businesses). These include the right not to be charged fees by the employment agency merely for finding work or putting the agency worker on their books (Carby-Hall 2007: 112) and certain rights relating to wages (the employment agency has no right by law to withhold the agency worker's wages because the hiring company has not paid the agency). Furthermore, agency workers also have a right to receive from the employment agency a written statement of terms and conditions of employment before they start work. This applies whether the agency is attempting to find permanent or temporary work for the worker (Carby-Hall 2007: 112). Special rights and duties also exist in the health and safety areas.[20]

However, despite the existence of the above laws regulating the situation of agency workers, their rights and duties at the workplace are still considered a 'grey area'. The legal framework for agency workers does not cover the use of agency work (e.g. length of assignment, sectoral bans, permitted reasons of

---

18 This protection was afforded by the Sex Discrimination Act 1975; the Race Relations Act 1976; the Disability Discrimination Act 1995; the Part-time Workers (Prevention of Less Favourable Treatment) Regulations 2000; the Employment Equality (Religion or Belief) Regulations 2003; the Employment Equality (Sexual Orientation) Regulations 2003; and the Employment Equality (Age) Regulations 2003.

19 These are: after one month, the right to one week's paid notice of dismissal and pay in cases of suspension on medical grounds; after two months, the entitlement to a written statement of terms and conditions of employment, including hours, pay and holiday entitlement; after six months, the right to maternity pay (providing that an employee has worked a certain number of weeks before the maternity leave); after one year, the right to protection from unfair dismissal (in cases where the employment was terminated without good reason or dismissal took place without proper procedures being followed); and after two years, the right to claim redundancy pay if the person's position is no longer needed and no one else has been employed to do the same job (ANIMATE et al. 2008: 32).

20 The employment agency is obliged to find out from the hiring company what known risks exist and the steps which have been taken to avoid or control them. It also has a duty to check that the hiring company has carried out a complete health and safety risk assessment and that agency workers are made aware of the risks before they are placed with the hiring company (Carby-Hall 2007: 113).

use and number of agency workers per company), the form of the contract (e.g. project, fixed-term, special contract, open ended, etc.) or social security benefits (Arrowsmith 2008). No licence is required (since 1995) to open an employment agency.[21]

As a result, agency workers prove to be the most vulnerable to the precarious employment and work conditions in the era of labour market de-regulation. Legal practitioners – legal advisers, Citizens Advice Bureau consultants and Trades Union Congress (TUC) representatives – working with agency workers (many of whom are migrant workers) have raised these points on numerous occasions, attributing the grey legislation area to the fact that agency workers are considered to be the main feature of the flexible British labour market (TUC Commission on Vulnerable Employment 2008). In response to the frequent abuse of their rights and discrimination, as highlighted in the reports by the above-mentioned agencies (TUC Commission on Vulnerable Employment 2008), the UK government attempted to clarify the situation of agency workers in law in the Temporary and Agency Workers (Equal Treatment) Bill. This 2007–2008 proposal was replaced by the EU Agency Workers Directive (Directive 2008/104/EC on temporary agency work), the purpose of which was to ensure that the principle of equal treatment is applied to temporary agency workers. The Directive entered into force on 1 October 2011 and introduced equal treatment rights for agency workers with permanent workers in the agency's client enterprise concerning employment and working conditions. After 12 weeks in the same role with the same employer, agency workers will be entitled to the same payment, overtime, shift allowances, holiday pay and bonuses attributable to individual performance, as well as maternity rights. However, the Directive does not protect workers from unfair dismissal. How the rights introduced by the Directive will be enforced remains to be seen.[22]

National Insurance and Tax Regulations

Aside from the employment contracts and different rights linked to one's employment status, workplace regulations also cover deduction of tax and National Insurance contributions. For the purposes of administration relating to tax and National Insurance, a special number is required – the National Insurance number (NIN). The NIN is a personal number used to record a person's National Insurance (NI) contributions and credited contributions, and it is needed when applying for social security benefits and tax credits. A NIN is specific to one person and must only be used by that person.

21 However, the Employment Agency Standards Inspectorate (EAS) has the power to investigate complaints and to undertake random checks on temporary employment agencies (Arrowsmith 2008).

22 There have been fears that some agency workers will simply be laid off after 11 weeks so that they do not benefit from the increased rights.

In order to receive a NIN, it is necessary to attend an interview with officers of the Job Centre. This is part of the procedure to establish the identity of the applicant and, in an employment-related application, to prove that they have the right to work in the UK. If the application is successful, a NIN is allocated to an applicant shortly after the interview, along with a special card with the NI number embossed on it. The NIN registration date is sometimes thought of as a proxy for when migrants become active in the labour market. However, migrants can legitimately seek and take up employment before being allocated a NIN; however, once employed, it is the duty of the individual employee to apply for a NIN at the earliest opportunity. Employers are required to ensure that they only employ those with a legal right to work in the UK

Flexibility and Deregulation of the British Labour Market

From the various reports and academic research (Arrowsmith 2008; Carby-Hall 2007; Currie 2007b; Jayaweera and Anderson 2008; Lane and Bachmann 1996) into the nature of the British workplace and employment regulations, two of its features appear to be most dominant.

Firstly, the contemporary British labour market is a 'flexible' one, as are the employer–employee–worker relations and the rules regulating them. Consequently, the British labour law encourages flexibility through light regulation – short-term and temporary contracts, a lack of employer commitment to job security, low levels of training – rather than the stability of employment relations.

As Michie and Sheehan observe, at the employer level, there are different means of securing flexibility. Numerical flexibility delineates the ability of firms to change the number of people they employ by making use of part-time, temporary and seasonal employees, and short fixed-term contracts, freelance work and homework or outwork (Michie and Sheehan 2003: 126). Numerical flexibility is not conducive to the safety and stability of employment but results in the greater popularity of temporary work. These practices are particularly visible among migrant workers, which led Neil to the conclusion that the use of 'flexible' work forms came as a dramatic challenge to the traditional labour law regulation and the ability to ensure fundamental social rights in the workplace (Neil 2003: 24).[23]

The flexibility of the labour market is intertwined with its de-regulation – 'low road' practices: the use of short-term and temporary contracts, a lack of employer commitment to job security and low levels of available training (Michie and Sheenan 2003: 138). In Britain, historically grown political structures and institutions have created arm's length relations between the state and industry and have fostered flexibility in state–industry and inter-firm relations (Lane and

23 The third form of flexibility used by employers – wage or reward flexibility – is the ability of payment systems to respond to labour market conditions and to reward and encourage improved performance (e.g. performance-related pay) (Michie and Sheenan 2003: 126).

Bachman 1996: 374). This has manifested itself in comparatively low levels of regulation, both of a legal and non-statutory kind.

As British labour and employment laws form part of the common law heritage and thus, by definition, are not highly codified (Lane and Bachman 1996: 376), the state law is therefore more absentionist, stepping in as a last resort and leaving the regulation of business relations to private initiatives. Voluntarism still rules supreme (Lane and Bachman 1996: 376) and the low level of regulation has resulted in a high degree of diversity in the forms of business relationships and the paucity of universal norms and standards governing inter-form relations. This makes for less consistency and, hence, predictability of legal business practices, and might be seen to provide a less stable context for business relations (Lane and Bachman 1996: 376).

Low state intervention has particularly affected large and medium-sized enterprises, which often enter into relations with migrant workers, as they sub-contract their services to employment/recruitment agencies. A lack of risk sharing by the state has negatively affected medium-sized firms' access to capital, skilled labour and R&D (Research and Development), inhibiting investment and innovation; therefore, many of them rely heavily on supplies of unskilled or semi-skilled migrant labour provided by the agencies. In their study on the relationships between the labour market de-regulation (de-regulatory techniques of human resource management) and the innovative activities of companies in the UK, Michie and Sheenan (2003) observed that practices encouraged by labour market de-regulation were negatively correlated with innovation. The workplace and employee relations surveyors revealed negative associations between the use of 'flexible', 'non-standard' workers – and the use of temporary agency workers in particular – and the proportion of employees who were trained to be functionally flexible (prepared to move from one task to another). While labour market de-regulation might have 'restored management's right to manage', the ease of use of the 'flexible' labour market through part-time and temporary contracts and the like 'proved to be less innovative than to those firms who have declined to take such a route' (Michie and Sheenan 2003: 136).

Enforcement of Workplace Regulations

When analysing the workplace regulations as an inseparable part of the British legal environment, it is important to see how these laws and regulations are actually enforced with regard to migrant workers. The next chapter provides empirical accounts of the enforcement of workplace regulations based on the experiences of Polish post-2004 EU enlargement migrants in the UK who were interviewed for this study. The following section therefore mainly focuses on introducing and developing the argument that the enforcement of the host country's workplace regulations (as part of the larger legal environment) should be considered as a factor in the socio-legal integration of migrants. It also reviews the existing empirical research on the enforcement of workplace regulations towards migrant workers in the context of a flexible and de-regulated labour market.

The statutory rights of both employees and workers in the UK are enforced through the Employment Tribunals (Carby-Hall 2007:117). They appeal on questions of law to the Employment Appeal Tribunals, the Court of Appeal and the House of Lords. Employment Tribunals have wide jurisdiction in employment law matters. Although they were originally designed to have a more informal procedure than a court of law, solicitors or barristers tend to represent employers in particularly complicated matters (Carby-Hall 2007: 118). In less complex cases the employee may be represented by a trade union official, a friend, an advice agency or may present his or her own case.

However, my research suggests that many migrant workers have limited access to Employment Tribunals (cf. Anderson et al. 2006; Carby-Hall 2007), which contributes to the inconsistent enforcement of their rights and the uneven execution of workplace regulations. The main way for migrants to access an Employment Tribunal is to seek legal help from the Citizens Advice Bureau. The 'grassroots level' evidence demonstrates that many migrants do this when it is already too late. A three-month limitation period (from the date that the event happened) exists for most complaints. Employment Tribunals are very strict in observing this limitation period and the outcomes of many cases have been affected by a failure to file the case within the three-month period.[24]

With regard to agency work, there are two UK regulators: the Gangmasters Licensing Authority (GLA) and the Employment Agency Standards Inspectorate (EASI). The former gained full legal powers in late 2006 and governs a limited number of industries (agricultural, horticultural, food packing/processing and shellfish gathering/processing industries). The latter, by contrast, has a much longer history and is charged with regulating agencies across the whole UK economy.

However, according to Arrowsmith's report on 'Temporary Agency Work', rights to representation for agency workers (as well as information and consultation) are very limited in most recruitment agencies or their user companies (Arrowsmith 2008). This is because representation rights are largely associated with the recognition of trade unions and are additionally hindered by the absence of collective agreements for agency workers and the typically short duration of assignments with user enterprises (Arrowsmith 2008).

As a result, flexibility and de-regulation, as inseparable features of the contemporary British labour market, do not seem conducive to the consistent enforcement and application of the law, particularly in the low-skilled, low-wage sectors. These echelons of the labour market – 'regular by name but not by nature' (Currie 2009) – are characterized by informality, precarious working conditions and therefore semi-legality, even with regard to migrants with regularized immigration status.

24 In the case of redundancy claims, a six-month limitation period exists (s. 111(2) of the Employment Rights Act 1996).

There is ample research evidence suggesting that many migrant workers can, upon arrival in the UK, become trapped in lower paid jobs with poor working conditions – the so-called '3D jobs' (dirty, dangerous and demanding) (Anderson et al. 2006; Clarke and Drinkwater 2008; Currie 2009; Markova and Black 2007; Spencer et al. 2007). There is a high demand for workers in jobs designated as 'low skill' and these sectors have long relied on the labour of contingent workers, mostly migrants. In these sectors, however, workers' wages remain low (with a significant group being paid wages that appear even to be below the National Minimum Wage, and migrant workers especially are often found to work longer, unpredictable or anti-social hours on average: Anderson et al. 2006). Drinkwater et al.(2007) even went on to suggest that the majority of post-enlargement migrants from accession countries have found employment in low-paid jobs, despite some (especially Poles) having relatively high levels of education (Drinkwater et al. 2007: 1).

The low-wage, low-skills sectors, where majority of accession state migrant workers found employment in are well documented for low legal awareness and law enforcement (Dench et al. 2006). The research by Anderson and Rogaly demonstrated that 'migrants were often engaged through a bewildering array of subcontracting chains and agents, all of which could make it difficult to claim and safeguard their basic human and labour rights' (Anderson and Rogaly 2005: 6). With regard to post-2004 EU enlargement migrant workers, the authors pointed out that some employers had even refused to register A8 workers with the WRS as they preferred to keep their workers away from the 'legitimacy' associated with registration, making it easier to impose poor work and pay conditions (Anderson and Rogaly 2005).

Inconsistent law enforcement has also been acknowledged to be an ever-present feature of the construction industry (Spencer et al. 2007: 11), where work is often carried out on a flexible, project-by-project basis. Contractors bring together teams of workers to work together on a project and then they disperse. The project timeframe and long time spells between periods of employment do not allow many A8 workers to complete 12 months of continuous employment under the WRS. Many construction workers (if they are registered at all under the WRS) are therefore more likely to drop out of the Scheme or not bother with subsequent re-registrations. As a result, many of the migrant workers who work in the construction industry share a precarious working status.

A wide variety of grey area practices were exemplified in the *Report on the Treatment of Polish and other A8 economic migrants in the European Union member states* by Jo Carby-Hall (2007) prepared for the Commissioner for Civil Rights Protection of the Republic of Poland and included, *inter alia*, health and safety irregularities, long working hours, no rest periods, unlawful deductions from wages, excessive rents for accommodation, inflated transport costs, removal of documents, denial of holidays, unfair and unjustified dismissals, discrimination of various kinds, unlawful and inflated fees being demanded by employment agencies, dishonest financial practices, unpaid overtime, work involving unsocial hours, dangerous work, unsavoury work, intimidation and violence (Carby-Hall 2007: 222).

A report by the Trades Union Congress (2007) focusing on migrant agency workers in the UK found that migrant workers were more likely to be working in sectors or occupations where there are health and safety concerns and that their status as new workers may place them at additional risk. It found that few checks were made on migrant workers' skills and qualifications for undertaking the work they were doing (Trades Union Congress 2007: 3). Even in cases where workers were performing skilled and potentially dangerous work like scaffolding, work was being offered to those who had no previous experience in the task.

The authors of the report found out that in food production and catering, most workers were not tested on their knowledge of food hygiene and only a minority of them was offered training (Trades Union Congress 2007). Those working with chemicals generally had little knowledge of what they were composed of and formal training was not always sufficient, especially where technical language was used to explain the nature of the risk (Trades Union Congress 2007: 3). Of the 200 migrants interviewed for the Trades Union Congress' Health and Safety Executive study, a relatively high proportion (one in four) had either experienced an accident at work themselves or had witnessed accidents involving migrant co-workers (Trades Union Congress 2007: 3).

The above research points to the conclusion that regular immigration status does not necessarily shield A8 migrant workers from precarious labour market patterns and conditions associated with informality. The research evidence presented seems to support the observation that quite often it is the inconsistent law enforcement of workplace regulations in the low-wage, low-skilled sector of the labour market which is more likely to lock migrant workers in low-status, informal and irregular work than their undocumented immigration status (cf. Ruhs 2008).

Beyond the Legal Environment

The analysis of the British legal environment, resulting from the transitory provisions of the 2003 Treaty of Accession, points to the conclusion that the British 'opening of its labour market' to nationals from post-2004 EU enlargement Member States was neither complete nor straightforward.

The Accession Regulations adopted by the British government placed a number of requirements on migrant workers from the EU accession states, primarily by conditioning their right to legal residence with registration of employment and limiting their access to social security and welfare by a compulsory and documented minimum 12-month contribution period. A lack of registration made their employment and residence in the UK illegal. As a result, even upon completing 12 months of continuous work (with the payment of taxes and national insurance contributions) they could not claim the right to reside in the UK, were excluded from participation in welfare and had to work towards exemption from the scheme anew.

Insights into the immigration regulations demonstrate that they were introduced as a compromise between the EU principle of free movement – which corresponded to the nation-state economic interest of filling numerous job vacancies – and the need to control the access to welfare, intensified by tabloid-driven paranoia over 'benefit tourism'. As a result of this compromise, during the transition period (2004–2011), Polish migrant workers (as well as other A8 migrants) were not completely free in their 'free movement' within the UK, as, arguably, they were not completely EU citizens (in the context of equal access to welfare).

Furthermore, the enforcement of the Accession Regulations was complicated due to confusion over who was required to register and who was not, the level of bureaucracy involved and the inconsistent system of checks and balances on employers, who often 'turned a blind eye' to workers of unknown legality.

The workplace regulations resulting from the recent changes towards increased flexibility of the British labour market have made many workers, including migrant workers, uncertain of their employment status. This has implications for their entitlement to rights and safety of employment. Although labour laws do not formally require a written contract for the employment relationship to be recognized, in practice a lack of written agreements between the parties often results in poor and inconsistent enforcement of rights at work (especially in the event of a dispute). The de-regulation of the labour market and 'low-road' practices contribute to the fact that great numbers of migrant workers in low-skilled, low-paid sectors actually find themselves working on a temporary basis in 'flexible' and often semi-regular employment via employment agencies. The inconsistent enforcement of the workplace regulations, especially in the 3D niche of the labour market, does not inspire much confidence in the law and leaves many with the feeling that this sector is perhaps 'regular by name, but not by nature' (Currie 2009).

This points to the conclusion that the post-2004 EU enlargement British legal environment – comprising immigration and workplace regulations and their enforcement – is a precarious one. The legal environment produced uncertainties about legal interpretations and did not afford protection or security of residence and employment to many migrants who arrived in the UK between 2004 and 2011. Compliance with immigration regulations did not shield migrant workers from the irregularities and exploitative practices associated particularly with the lower echelons of the flexible and de-regulated labour market. In light of the above analysis, it is therefore justifiiable to say that the legal environment itself encourages – or at least does not effectively discourage – non-compliance with the law.

However, what were the actual responses of Polish post-2004 EU enlargement migrants towards the immigration and workplace regulations? The next chapter turns to migrants themselves and their initial *responses* towards the British legal environment. It investigates how the Polish migrants followed, avoided or contested the immigration and workplace regulations while negotiating their relationship with the new socio-legal environment.

Chapter 5
Polish Migrants in the British Legal Environment: The Question of Semi-Legality

Upon their arrival in the UK, the first priority for many Polish post-2004 migrants, as expressed in my interviews with them, was to find a job. Only a few of the interviewees had a job pre-arranged for them or arrived having received a strong job offer – most of them came to the UK as work-seekers.

Only some of the Polish migrants had the financial means to support themselves for a longer period of time; for the vast majority, the reality was to find a job and register with the WRS within 30 days of commencing employment, otherwise their residence would become illegal (according to the Accession Regulations 2004).

The Polish migrants I interviewed either had accommodation arranged for them or were coming to stay with their friends during the initial period. Some of them at first relied on a network of friends or relatives; others came individually, making the British labour market a framework of their choice:

> England and me, it was like a blind date. One thing I had was a room, a place to stay, which I arranged through a letting agency back in Poland. It was a room in London. I did not speak English, I had few pounds in my pocket. There was one thing I knew though – if you wanted to work in the UK, you would find work there. It was common sense, since the labour market was opened to Poles after 2004, there must have been lot of vacancies there. (Interview No. 11)

Finding a job, however, very often proved to be more difficult than initially anticipated:

> I came after I graduated from university, I spoke English quite well, but could not find a job for over a month. (Interview No. 15)

The most popular strategies of looking for work among the newly arrived migrants were to contact potential employers directly in response to job adverts placed in shop windows in cafes, bars and restaurants or looking for job offers through friends or via local newspapers:

> First thing I did upon arrival in London was thinking how to find a job without knowing the language. I walked across the whole of London and was looking for adverts in Polish on shop windows. After two weeks I found a job advert in Polish

> on a Pakistani shop it said: 'I can help to arrange a job and accommodation.' I said why not? (Interview No. 11)

> I was looking for job adverts on shop windows and cafes, going in, leaving my CV, trying to speak to the manager. (Interview No. 9)

The success of strategies, especially at the initial stage of work-seeking, very much depended on the people who migrants themselves knew, whether they had contacts, knew other people and their access to the migrant networks:

> People were saying 'go there', 'don't go there', and 'avoid this guy, as he is lazy, go talk to her instead, as she might help you'. People have all that information. And they pass it around. It's a mouth to mouth exchange. And that's how it's working. (Interview No. 30)

Some of the migrants were looking for job offers in local Job Centres; however, for many of them, due to their low levels of English and unfamiliarity with the system of Job Centres, the experience was rather daunting and not particularly successful:

> I did not look for jobs via [the] Job Centre directly from the beginning, due to the language barrier. It's a pity, as they have many interesting job offers. Now, when there are more Polish consultants employed there, it's easier, but at the beginning when I did not speak English at all, there was no one who could help me, hence I did not use it. (Interview No. 3)

Another popular strategy (usually employed in parallel) was registering with an employment agency or employment business. With no extended networks of family or relatives and no business contacts, many Polish migrant workers turned to the most vulnerable and flexible labour market practices performed by many employment agencies in order to find any kind of employment. Most of my interviewees (excluding those who were coming to the UK to start a previously arranged job) directed their first efforts at employment agencies. They knew about them from friends, colleagues and other migrants who had previously settled in the UK:

> First thing I did was to register with an agency. (Interview No. 8)

> I arrived in the UK on Wednesday, Friday I registered with the agency. (Interview No. 16)

The British agency sector (also known as the employment sector) is the largest agency sector in Europe (Arrowsmith 2006: 6), which has increased fourfold in size since 1994 and is worth an estimated £25 billion (Demos 2007: 26–7)

–£ 29.3 billion (EMAR 2008: 2) (prior to the recession). The sector involves at least 16,000 companies and between 200,000 and 225,000 individuals employed as recruitment personnel (EMAR 2008: 2). The best estimates for the number of workers come from the Recruitment and Employment Confederation (REC) 'census', the Survey of Employment Agencies conducted by Department for Business, Enterprise and Regulatory Reform (BERR) and the Labour Force Survey (LFS); the number of workers varies between 1.1 million and 1.5 million with the mid-point being 1.3 million (EMAR 2008:1). At the same time, it is one of the most fragmented temporary agency sectors in the EU, with a significant proportion of small, local operators forming the bottom-end of a two-tier sector (Coe et al. 2007).

The agency sector in the UK is increasingly migrant-dominated: in the food industry, for example, one is now 'more likely to encounter an agency in the UK employing temporary Eastern and Central European workers than an agency employing indigenous workers' (Geddes et al. 2007: 90). Also data from Labour Force Survey (for 2007) demonstrate that agency workers are more likely to be younger, from an ethnic minority group but with broadly similar qualifications compared with all employees (EMAR 2008: 1). Home Office data reveals that a large number of A8 migrant workers have found employment either via employment agencies or have worked for employment businesses: approximately 40 per cent of all the workers that registered with the WRS between May 2004 and March 2011.[1]

Polish workers (alongside Portuguese and Lithuanian workers) dominate the UK agency industry (Scott 2009: 2). Whilst Polish workers – according to the Home Office data – made up the largest proportion in every sector between May 2004 and April 2011, their presence in administration, business and management – in other words, the employment sector – was particularly prominent at 67 per cent (UK Border Agency 2009: 21).

My interviewees largely fit this quantitative evidence. Most of my Polish respondents either were, or at some point had been, working for an agency or recruitment business. From the respondents I gathered that most of the agencies offered work placements (assignments) for skilled, semi-skilled and low-skilled workers – warehouse staff, machine operatives, assemblers, forklift drivers for the main UK supermarkets (Tesco, Sainsbury's, Waitrose, etc.), packers, rubbish pickers, factory workers, kitchen staff, porters, bar and restaurant staff or cleaners. The job opportunities suitable for women, however, were comparatively limited.

---

1 In a 2008 poll of Polish workers in rural areas, for example, the most commonly reported reason for living in a rural area was recruitment by an employment agency (Chappell et al. 2009). The difference between the employment agency and employment business arrangements is explained in British law: a business that arranges temporary work with a 'hiring company' is legally known as an 'employment business', while an 'employment agency' is a business that introduces job-seekers to employers (e.g. a recruitment consultant) (HM Government 2009a).

They were also mainly recruited as warehouse staff, factory workers or for waitressing.

Agency work was associated with particular types of jobs with a view that certain jobs (and low-paid jobs in particular) were 'for agency work'. For some large food-processing employers, agencies were reported to be the only route into employment (Fitzgerald 2007).

For the interviewed Polish agency workers, registration with an agency took from a couple of days to a couple of weeks. A work-seeker was required to fill in an application form, including supplying the agency with references. The references were usually very difficult to obtain, especially for workers who had previously not been working in the UK. In Poland, for example, there was not much of a 'reference' culture in the recruitment process:

> Many people think: 'OK, I will put anything', but no, it should be five years of documented work, we check the references, I make calls to Poland, Africa, Australia, everywhere. It's not like you could put a name of anybody. For instance Poles at the beginning, before they realized that I am really checking, all that they were putting were non-existent phone numbers, made up dates, made up names and surnames, made up companies, all different things. (Interview No. 24 with agency personnel)

When the references had been checked, the prospective workers were sometimes required to undergo an interview, the main purpose of which was to assess their level of English. Some agencies also offered jobs where a communicative level of English was not required, but over time, fewer such jobs were available.

The time between submitting the job application form and the first job or job assignment (in the case of agency workers) was considered very important and was recalled by many of the interviewees. It was like a transition, being suspended 'in-between' before the actual initiation to work was completed:

> I was visiting the agency [a] couple of times per week. It was very frustrating, it was as if I was begging for a job. Each time I went, all the people there were polite, were smiling, and waving to me assuring me that the job would be available soon. But nothing was coming. And they never stopped waving in this friendly English way. It was so frustrating. If I knew at least that they were looking for it. I was reminding them about me. The gentleman there was smiling to me all the time, saying that he was looking for [a] job. (Interview No. 18)

> Before I was sent to any job I would come to the agency [a] couple of times a week asking for it. There would always be one person who would smile, take a note, and say that they are looking for [a] job for me. After three weeks this was driving me mad! (Interview No. 36)

The feelings of uncertainty when dealing with the agency sector (on the part of my interviewees) could have been amplified by the fact that the British agency sector has historically been subject to light-touch regulation compared to the situation in other EU Member States (Arrowsmith 2006: 22) and sits within one of Europe's freest labour markets (Demos 2007: 10).[2]

This allows different groups subject to regulation to operate according to their own 'rules of the game', even though such interactions might not be compliant with the legal system. Usually, no documents, apart from a passport, were required in order to register with an agency. Although the application form had a field for the NIN, whether the field was left blank or was filled in by the applicant did not have much effect. Recently, more and more agencies have insisted on applicants having a bank account opened in the UK prior to their registration. Very few agencies, upon registration, supplied the applicants with booklets on the general rules and regulations relating to working for the agency.

Some interviewees therefore invoked the informal 'code of conduct' of an agency worker that usually preceded an offer of employment:

> In the agency there were two people directly responsible for the recruitment: two guys. And you have to bribe them to get any kind of job. I am not sure how it looks now, but when I came three years ago, you had to have something with you if you wanted a job, some alcohol or Polish sausages ... without the gifts it was very difficult to get a job. (Interview No. 3)

The informal codes of conduct, gifts and favours underlined the imbalance of power between the migrants and the agency personnel, which, in this particular context, was calculated to induce the allocation of scarce resources – with work constituting the main item. The flow of attention and favours in the direction of individuals who had it in their power to allocate labour was often considered as the price of allocation. Despite the official possibility and choice to de-register with a particular agency, there were strong pressures to comply with this system of exchange, which were additionally supported by a lack of other resources, both material assets and human capacities, which could be used by migrants to enhance their bargaining power (such as language, human capital, skills, support networks and legal knowledge). Migrants' lack of awareness about their rights and confusion about their status (worker vs. employee) were combined with the vulnerability accorded due to a more 'patron–client' relationship rather than a work relationship:

2 The general character of employment businesses in the UK does not give rise to an employment relationship in law between the employment business and a worker or work-seeker, which makes work security regulations very difficult to enforce and makes it easy for the agencies to drift into the grey area of employment legislation that is subject to abuse of rules and power (cf. Chapter 4).

> Dave was calling me to come and work at the flower job more often than he did with other workers. I always wanted to be in his good books, hence I would bring him some sweets or traditional Polish stuff from my holiday at home. (Interview No. 4)

> We do not give jobs to everyone who we have put on our books. We need to see that they care. Therefore first we would send to work people that come to the agency frequently and 'remind us' of their desire to work. (Interview No. 24 with agency personnel)

The grey area qualifications of the many practices performed by the agencies specializing in temporary employment could be mentioned among the important factors in increasing the risks and fierce competition that migrants faced in the sector:

> Even when I was not called to wok, I would go early in the morning and queue at the bus stop in front of the minibus that was taking us to work. There were many of us there, but I would make sure that I got in. As long as I got into the minibus, I was safe to work. At the factory they did not care who came to work, but whether the numbers were OK. (Interview No. 3)

The first type of employment for many of the interviewees was hardly ever a long-term one; the first jobs or work assignments provided by the agency were usually on a short-term, temporary basis: one or two times a week, a week in a month. By and large, the agency sector equals temporary employment – in the 12 months to March 2009, WRS applicants who indicated temporary work represented 78 per cent of the registered workers who applied to work in administration, business and management (UK Border Agency et al 2009: 16).[3] The interviewees generally admitted:

> The Agency started sending me for different works. First I worked for H. I was checking the quality of screws. I worked there [for a] couple of days. Then [a] couple of days I worked for someone else, I was packing cosmetics, two days maybe. It was to test me, whether I was a reliable and good worker. (Interview No. 29)

The reasons for increasing reliance on agency labour as provided by employers could largely be grouped around two basic concepts: (1) in response to skill/labour shortages or to deal with peaks in production (functional flexibility); and (2) to make hiring and firing less problematic (numerical flexibility) (McKay 2009: 37).

3 Among the workers who registered under the WRS between May 2004 and April 2011, 51 per cent were in temporary employment and 46 per cent were in permanent employment (Home Office 2011).

From the perspective of the employers interviewed by McKay (2009), employment relationships at a distance – i.e. though agencies – were seen as offering specific advantages: the employer had no involvement in the setting of workers' terms and conditions; there was a minimal obligation to control workers, thus reducing the involvement of human resources (HR); and also the agency workers were hired on different, and inferior, terms (McKay 2009: 37).

In contrast to the employer perspective, the research on temporary workers in the EU indicates that a high percentage of them (48 per cent) were in temporary work because they could not find permanent work (Leighton 2009). This data suggests that for the majority in temporary employment, the intrinsic insecurity, associated financial and other problems, and sometimes poor working conditions made it largely unattractive (Leighton 2009: 135). Anderson et al. (2006) reported that agency work was viewed less positively than being directly and permanently employed by a business: 'insecurity of employment was consistently referred to, not being guaranteed a job and, when there was work, not knowing how long it would last or how many hours it would be for' (Anderson et al. 2006: 52). This was largely confirmed by my interviewees:

> They were calling me on weekly or daily basis and saying whether I have [a] job or I have a day off. (Interview No. 19)

> It is difficult to earn money that way, not to mention plan for [the] future. They call you in the morning, or evening the previous day to say whether you go to work or stay at home. (Interview No. 39)

At the same time, most of the agencies did not provide means for workers to transfer from agency to direct employment, with only a very small number having a transparent system in place or encouraging the movement of agency staff into direct employment (McKay and Markova 2008: 43). The desire for permanent, long-term employment was reflected by many of my interviews:

> Everybody was waiting for a permanent contract like for some sort of a revelation. (Interview No. 18)

> Finally I was bought by the employer … Yes, bought – the employer paid a fee to the agency and from then I could work for him only. The uncertainty of temporary job was over! (Interview No. 17)

The temporary employment had become a stepping stone on a job mobility ladder toward the more preferred permanent employment however not for all interviewed migrants. Many were locked in the agency assignments for a much longer period of time.

Responses to the Immigration Regulations

The nature and character of initial employment – either found via various advertisements or arranged through an agency – brought about the first questions about migrants' responses to the immigration regulations, especially the requirement to register with the WRS. What were the migrants' experiences with the WRS? What did they think of it and what were the motivations behind applying for a registration certificate (or not)? From the interviews with Polish migrants in the UK, the following attitudes to the WRS seemed to prevail.

For some of the interviewees, registration was smooth, as it was performed on their behalf by the employer who collected the documents from the applicant and offered help with filling in the application form. Subsequently, the employer took the responsibility of posting the registration and collecting the certificate:

> There was no problem at all. All that registration was done on our behalf by the administration team. We just supplied them with our data, passport and when the documents arrived we were handed it along with the payslip. I even did not need to pay for the registration. There was an agreement between me and the Care Home that if I resign from work before a one year time [period], then they could deduct it from my salary, but they did not have to. It sort of depended on their good or bad will to a certain extent. (Interview No. 14)

Some migrants performed the registration themselves, as they were aware of the requirement to register their employment with the Home Office. The fact that the registration certificate made their work in the UK legal was sufficient justification:

> I knew I should register; I had money prepared to pay for my registration before I had left Poland. Generally I am a very organized person, and I don't like surprises. I registered, as I try to live according to the law. (Interview No. 21)

However, more than half of my respondents questioned the purpose of the registration process altogether. These migrants' responses towards the WRS varied from non-registration to late registration (i.e. beyond the 30-day grace period) to incomplete registration (some migrants did not renew their registration when they changed employment within the first year or did not register simultaneously held jobs).

Some interviewees justified their non-registration with the lack of immediate consequences attached to the WRS:

> I realized very well that there are no consequences … There is no formal punishment for not registering; they can remind you of registering but they cannot force you to register by, for example, making you to pay a fine. (Interview No. 34)

There were indeed no legal consequences for failing to register within one month, apart from the practical issue that any time that an A8 migrant worker spent working in the UK outside the WRS would not count towards the 12-month qualifying period to become exempt from registration and gain equal access to full social security provisions. The close interconnection between the WRS registration and social security benefits paradoxically became another justification for non-registration. Living and working in the UK without registering was considered legitimate as long as the person did not plan to apply for benefits:

> Generally, you have the right to live in the UK and to work. I did not feel pressured to register, or anything. The registration comes in handy only when you want to claim any benefits. (Interview No. 6)

From the migrants' point of view, the nature of the WRS registration – especially the lack of practical, legal consequences for the worker who failed to register, as well as the initial cost of registration (between £50 and £90) – acted, to a certain extent, as a deterrent to complying with this regulation. As a result, many of the migrants, due to financial constraints and scarce resources, especially upon their arrival in the UK, preferred to postpone registration until later, when it became more feasible, after the initial priorities and instrumental needs were taken care of (e.g. steady income, bank account and accommodation):

> I was working for an agency, it's a temporary job, one day I have the job, the other day I have off. It was really difficult to find £90 to pay for the registration. This is the only thing that was left, I have the insurance number, I pay the taxes. I only need to register. I will do it, when I'll get round to applying for benefits for my son. (Interview No. 25)

Others resented the form of registration, the amount of the paperwork involved and the fact that registration under the WRS meant that they had to part with their passport or identity card for a usually unspecified period of time:

> One has to find time to find and fill in the application form … Above all they want your passport! Explain to me, how can the Home Office imagine that I will send them my passport? What if they lose it? How will I find it? (Interview No. 4)

These responses brought with them a hint of deeply embedded animosity and distrust towards the state institutions, often combined with previous experience of their ineffectiveness:

> [The] Home Office is an institution, you know what a mess there is in Poland when you try to talk to institutions, when you go to ZUS [National Insurance

> Office] or the Tax Office. Perhaps English institutions work differently, but why would I like to take this risk? (Interview No. 8)

The uncertain migratory plans – especially at the beginning of Polish migrants' experience in the UK in terms of staying in the UK, going back to Poland or moving elsewhere – also played a part in Polish respondents explaining why they had postponed their WRS registration until later (or indefinitely):

> Why should I register, since I did not even know whether I would stay in England or go back? (Interview No. 11)

Many of those Polish migrants who registered late developed their own sense of what the WRS was for and justified it through the prism of practical gains – access to benefits. The question whether to register or not was no longer a legal issue for many of the migrants; it became a practical issue:

> A friend who did not register at the beginning, after a year of continuous employment was trying to claim a housing benefit and only then she applied for the registration. In the letter of support from the employer – we were working for the same company – they've stated that she's been employed with them for over a year. So upon the registration, she immediately gained the rights to benefits. (Interview No. 21)

Another group of migrants confused the WRS with the registration required for the NIN:

> I started needing the registration … I registered later only, it was later. It was a tax issue, I could get a smaller tax if I had registered or wait, maybe it was not about the Home Office it was about some number – National Insurance Number. (Interview No. 36)

Confusing the WRS registration with other immigration or work-related requirements imposed on Polish (as well as other) migrant workers in the UK was quite a popular response. Whilst the late introduction of the registration requirement (February 2004, only three months before the pending enlargement of the EU on 1 May) and therefore lack of a sufficient timeframe for the successful dissemination of the new immigration requirements might explain why some migrants who arrived immediately in the aftermath of the enlargement did not register their employment, its explanatory capacity diminishes with time. One needs to look deeper to understand why Polish migrants who arrived in 2006 or 2007 – two years after accession, when information about registration became widely available – did not comply with the regulation.

One possible explanation was that the new immigration rules became an informational maze not only to the migrants themselves but also to British employers. As a result, some of the employers did not know about the requirement of having their A8 migrant workers registered with the WRS. This in turn might have influenced migrants' peculiar interpretation of the immigration rules – many of them did not consider it important or even necessary to register (as registration as such was neither enforced by the British authorities nor required by the employers themselves):

> After the first year I had been working for the cafe, they wanted me to register with [the] WRS. So after the year they were sending me strong signals to do it, to register. So I finally did it. But later on they employed another person, who did not have WRS, who did not have [a] NIN and it was OK. (Interview No. 12)

> I started the new job and I had to re-register with the WRS. I received the documents from the lady in our office, but I was not in a hurry to fill them in and to post them. Then the office lady had left, and the new one was not particularly interested in my case, so I also gave up. (Interview No. 23)

Partially, therefore, it was the inconsistent enforcement and popular practices among the employers of 'turning a blind eye' to migrants of unknown legality which did not inspire migrants' confidence in the WRS.

However, many other migrants admitted that they postponed registration until later as a matter of choice. To young Poles who arrived in the UK without dependants and with no interest in benefits, the registration requirement was perceived as *pro forma* – as an unnecessary burden and trouble.[4] They did not feel pressured to register. They could not see registering as being in their own interests, either due to practical difficulties with the registration process or due to their unspecified plans for the future. To them, working without registration was acceptable as long as their employer did not request proof of registration or until registration became justifiable to them (by their intention to apply for benefits).

Responses to the Workplace Regulations

Migrants' attitudes towards the immigration regulations show only one aspect of their initial responses towards the British legal environment. Apart from the WRS introduced especially for A8 nationals working in the UK, there were other general laws like workplace regulations which all workers in the UK (including Polish migrant workers) fell within the scope of and should comply with.

---

4 Only one of the interviewees was threatened by the employer for registering late with the WRS, and the issue of late registration was raised mainly due to the specific circumstances of this particular case: the employee started a formal grievance procedure against the company for unauthorized deductions from wages while being employed and working without the WRS.

Experiences of National Insurance and Tax Regulations

With regard to migrants' experiences of National Insurance contributions and tax regulations, most of them were initially working in the UK without a NIN or on the temporary insurance number supplied by their employers:

> When I was employed by the agency, I was receiving the weekly wages in cash. There was a tax on the payslip, only the national insurance number was theirs [this refers to a temporary NIN]. (Interview No. 12)

> They employed me without [a] National Insurance Number. And I was working in C for about a year, before I applied for my permanent National Insurance Number. They were not even pressuring me to do so. (Interview No. 36)

When applying for a NIN, one has to undergo an interview at a Job Centre. There are certain documents which applicants were required to bring for the interview in order to establish their identity and right to work in the UK. These fell into two categories: general documents (passport, identity card, etc.) and employment documents (payslips, Home Office documents, the WRS certificate, letter from the employer, contracts of employment, etc.). Therefore, obtaining a WRS certificate was considered to be a pre-condition for applying for the NIN, as it acted as proof of the right to work in the UK for A8 nationals.[5] Some of the migrants indeed followed the procedure and applied first for WRS registration with the Home Office and subsequently for the NIN:

> I followed such order: first the Home Office and WRS, then the Insurance Number as they would ask for my registration during the interview. (Interview No. 2)

However, almost half of the respondents decided to bypass the WRS registration for (among others) the reasons outlined in the above section and applied only for the NIN. Having a NIN results in a practical gain – a reduction in the tax rate. Workers without a NIN are very often required to pay the basic rate of income tax, which is also called emergency tax (at a rate of 22 per cent). Upon obtaining their personal NIN, workers are assigned a personal tax code at a lower rate which depends on their earnings and reflects the annual tax allowances. Therefore, applying for a NIN was considered a priority among the migrants and as much more important than the WRS:

> During the interview for [the] NIN I had a story prepared that I sent the documents for [the] WRS, and I hoped they would believe me. I did not go

---

5 Self-employed persons applying for a NIN were additionally required to bring with them examples of invoices, letters from accountants or letters from clients.

> round to registering, as I work not on [a] regular basis, cash is short, I really don't have time to think of it now. (Interview No. 25)

> People care more about having the national insurance, about paying lower taxes than about getting the work certificate from [the] Home Office, and registering there. Especially when the work and money is not on regular basis. (Interview No. 31)

Experiences of Contracts of Employment

It was usually in the context of the beginnings – of looking for and finding a job – where the initial responses to the workplace regulations were most observable. From the start, the bargaining power of migrants was much lower in comparison to British employers, employment agencies or employment businesses. The majority of them were therefore willing to accept any conditions specified (or not specified) upon being offered a job.

This unequal situation between migrants and their employers left many Polish migrant workers with only one practical strategy to follow: 'take the risk, wait and see what happens next' (Interview No. 4). Not surprisingly, the law was moved further down the scale of importance:

> To be honest, I really needed a job. I was desperate. I found my first stable job only after three months from arrival. It was via an agency. By this time, my only goal was to have this job, have the money coming in. But to be honest I was lucky, even without the papers, I wasn't cheated or anything like that. (Interview No. 18)

The terms and conditions of the job are usually specified in the contract of employment. However, upon arrival in the UK, many of the Polish migrants undertook an offer of employment based on terms and conditions agreed between the parties orally, without a written statement:

> When I found this job, I could make my peace with the fact that the manager in the cafe did not offer me a written contract. (Interview No. 21)

When asked why they worked without a contract of employment, interviewees pointed to the fact that they 'did not feel like they really needed one':

> I knew that the job was legal, I was paying taxes and everything, but I simply did not have a written contract. (Interview No. 33)

Migrants attributed low importance to a written contract. This attitude was often met by the customary practice of working without a written contract in the area of the labour market in which they found their employment:

> In this cafe only the manager had a written contract, even the Polish chef, whom the whole cafe relied on, even he did not have a contract. (Interview No. 21)

Very often, however, the conditions of employment were not even discussed between the parties. The Polish interviewees often expressed that they would 'ask for a job, and if there was any, [they] would have taken it'. Some discussion would usually involve negotiations over the payment, but apart from this, understanding the 'legal side' of the employment was limited; some migrants confessed that it was not particularly important for them, others preferred to rely on their 'legal intuition':

> When you start working in a cafe, you sort of know what they might want from you, don't you? (Interview No. 33)

Generally, many migrants admitted in the interviews that initially they were willing to accept any terms and conditions of the jobs they were offered, including work being paid 'cash in hand' with no weekly payslips, no taxes deducted and no contracts:

> To be honest, I worked there rather illegally. In this job I got paid in cash, at the end of every working week. I realized it only after some time, though. But one had to do something to have money. I also wasn't asked by anybody about the insurance number or Home Office registration. I started thinking about it myself, later on. (Interview No. 22)

This attitude of not paying much attention to the terms and conditions before accepting the job – particularly in the low-wage, low-skilled area of the labour market – proved quite disadvantageous, especially in the event of a dispute. Although in British labour law the lack of a written employment contract is not necessary for the employment relationship to be recognized as existing by law, the lack of any written agreement between the parties made it even more difficult to enforce migrant workers' rights.

Among the native workers in the UK, there is a general expectation of receiving, if not a contract, at least a written statement of job particulars. This stems from the fact that although there is no written contract, there is a set of regulations, usually derived from the statutory provisions, which are not optional for the employer to follow. Polish migrants often do not secure their position by ensuring that both parties agree and understand the job particulars. This makes it easy for employers to ignore the rights of workers and rely on various 'low-road' practices not only with regard to Polish migrant workers, but towards all migrants with restricted employment rights in the UK:

> At some stage I realized that there will be no contract. He [the employer] promised to arrange all the documents within two weeks, when I asked him

> about it after the two weeks, he said he did not do it. So I decided to wait till the end of the month and see whether I was to receive the payment. If the payment was not to be there, then it did not make sense to dwell in this job any longer. (Interview No. 26)

Other migrants, although having received a written contract of employment, recalled an experience of it containing only a set of very basic terms and conditions:

> The contract was saying about only general things, it said I must not join any trade union, I must not take up another job, it regulated the length of my holiday and my hours at work, the load of work, that's all. (Interview No. 14)

The situation of basic and very short contracts of employment in the UK is not unusual, but is in fact quite popular across all the sectors where migrants found employment – hospitality, catering, agriculture, construction, care work, etc. It could be attributed to the fact that, aside from the contractual rights and obligations of workers and employers, both parties are also required to comply with the statutory terms of employment designated by the statutory instruments: acts and statutes of the UK legislature. They, in turn, are not included in the contractual agreements, but are considered the 'minimum' and taken for granted. The statutory rights cover the National Minimum Wage and working time regulations, as well as the non-discrimination provisions, sick pay and maternity rights. The contractual terms are to be built upon them and cannot contravene any of the terms specified in the statutory provisions. However, the de-regulatory practices in the low-skilled, low-wage area of the labour market make it customary to specify particulars of employment almost solely with reference to the basic statutory provisions. The statutory provisions, although considered as the minimum by the legislators, therefore become the 'ongoing' or prevailing terms and conditions in the sectors where most migrant workers find employment.

Migrant workers who were agency workers did not have an employment contract with the agency, as working for an agency did not give rise to an employment relationship in British labour law. However, the agencies were obliged to supply their workers with job particulars (explaining their rights, duties and health and safety provisions), which were usually included in a unified booklet. Nevertheless, not many migrants had access to these booklets, while others were not particularly concerned with them. As a result, many of them did not have any proof of their working relationship with the agency:

> I did not have any papers for my employment with the recruitment agency, apart from the payslips, of course. (Interview No. 19)

Enforcement of Work Contracts

In analysing the relationship between Polish migrant workers and the workplace regulations, the migrants' experiences and attitudes towards the enforcement of their contracts – following, avoiding or bypassing the state regulations – should also be taken into account.

There was a group among the interviewed migrants who, perhaps due to their low level of English, even if presented with a written contract of employment were not in a position to utilize it in order to enforce their rights at work:

> For instance I had a person coming in, saying: 'I heard that I should have 10 days off for holiday'. This is how it usually works. People receive the information from other people, more experienced workers and so on. Mouth to mouth. (Interview No. 24 with agency personnel)

Many migrants admitted in the interviews that as long as their employer was paying their wages, they 'could make their peace with working without a contract'. They did not necessarily see a written contract as a guarantee that their rights would be enforced or that they simply 'would not be cheated'. They did not attach much significance to the contract as:

> It was only a sheet of paper. I knew that if I was getting payslips I had chances of enforcing my rights and I did not need a written contract for that. (Interview No. 21)

Others, by contrast, felt trapped by the official form of a written contract they received whilst at work. Many doubted whether the terms and conditions they were presented with were fair as they did not feel that the contract actually protected their rights (like A, who, by the terms of her contract, was denied the right to join a union (Interview No. 14)). However, due to the fact that such terms were contained in 'a written contract', they felt that they did not have many chances of challenging it without running the risk of losing their job:

> I was wondering how it was possible that the contract did not allow me to join the trade unions. And it had something about how the employer would 'look' at legal group action … it was simply to scare us off. I took my contract and went to the Citizens Advice Bureau, as I wanted to do something about it. The adviser I met was very clear – she said that if I were to join the Union and they find out about it I would be fired. (Interview No. 14)

There was also a distinguishable group of migrants who did not attach much validity to their contracts of employment, as their day-to-day working conditions did not reflect the terms actually contained in their contracts (even the most formal-looking). The interviewed migrants did not therefore consider their contracts as particularly useful tools in protecting them from being exploited by their employers. Within this group, many of the migrants experienced instances of forced labour, poor working conditions contravening the health and safety regulations or working hours regulations, and pay levels below the National Minimum Wage:

> My first work was through a friend, in a Kebab restaurant in K. It was full time, but it was illegal. I was not registered; they also put in my contract, that I was working four days per week, while I was actually working full time. I was working six hours per day, ten hours per day, eight hours. You could not do much in a place like that. You can either accept the conditions or change the job. It was my first job, I did not have much choice. It was bringing money at least. I was paid for eight hours per day, but I had to report to work half an hour before my shift started, then I had to stay at the end of the working day to clean the place. They did not pay more for Sundays or something, it was all one rate. (Interview No. 17)

> I felt cheated. When I started my work in the care home, during the induction week they told us that our work would mean only taking an elderly lady for a walk, or read[ing] her a book. And that there were specially trained carers to look after elderly people. It turned out, however, that people who come here to work as care assistants, like myself, are to wash the elderly people, feed them, change their nappies ... it is not that you have time to read a newspaper to that elderly person. They did not tell me about the MRSA bug, which is a big problem here. You have to put one person on the toilet, change a nappy of another person, someone else wants to go to the toilet, one person is waiting to be changed, and someone else is asking for food. Usually there are not enough assistants, and you have to hurry doing your work. You need to be very careful not to catch the bug yourself or to give it to others. Imagine, you have a couple of people in your ward, who have the bug. And there is only one pair of gloves left. And you have to change all of them. And there is the question – either your health, or theirs. (Interview No. 14)

There is much research evidence relating to migrant workers' exploitation in the UK. As Craig et al. (2007) in the report for the Joseph Rowntree Foundation on modern forms of slavery in the UK suggest, many migrant workers – including Polish post-2004 EU enlargement workers – shared the experiences of exploitative relationships with their employers, as they became subject to forced labour through a mix of enforced debt, intimidation, the removal of documents or an inadequate understanding of their rights. At the same time, the report reveals that some UK-based companies, either knowingly or not, rely on people working in conditions resembling modern slavery to produce goods which they sell – complex sub-contracting and supply chains, managed by agents elsewhere, often obscure this involvement (Craig et al. 2007).

The report by Craig et al. (2007) included a case study of a group of Polish migrant workers who came to work in the UK for a factory that packed chickens for a major UK supermarket (Craig et al. 2007). They were not employed directly by the factory supplying the supermarket but were sub-contracted in a complex supply chain through labour agencies. The report noted a number of formal irregularities relating to general labour regulations: the contracts the Polish workers signed were made without translation. Several workers were given the same NIN. They had tax deducted at a high emergency rate, yet the Tax Office confirmed to the researchers that it had not yet received the corresponding payments (Craig et al. 2007). After deductions, the Polish migrant workers were getting paid £115 a week for 40 hours (£2.88 per hour). On top of accommodation (at £40 per week), an additional £15 was deducted from their payslips without explanation. Most of the Polish workers had not registered with the Home Office because they could not afford the £50 required. This in turn made them vulnerable to deportation. The workers finally managed to escape after a local trade union became aware of their plight (Craig et al. 2007).

Following the same line of argument, recent research by Babiuch-Luxmoore (2008) for the Citizens Advice Bureau conducted in the surroundings of Oxfordshire revealed practices tantamount to bonded labour, by which incoming East European migrant workers were forced to pay deposits which they forfeited if they quit their jobs and assigned accommodation. Dates and times of their work were left uncertain and unpredictable, and regulated rights and benefits were largely ignored (Babiuch-Luxmoore 2008).[6]

The most difficult situation in terms of the exploitation of workers was experienced by agency workers. Most East European workers were signed on to work when needed and were simply dismissed and re-hired after a certain time. My interviews with Polish migrant workers largely confirmed this:

> The agency would send me to one job for three months, and then when the client had problems, or the production stopped, I would be released. Sometimes I had to wait weeks before I was sent to another assignment. (Interview No. 29)

In this manner, the agency workers had no opportunities to accumulate time that would give them more employment rights (12 consecutive months). As temporary staff only, they were required to work long hours, but there was no overtime, night or weekend rates, and no sickness, holiday or pension entitlements (Babiuch-Luxmoore 2008).

Among the interviewed migrants, nearly half did not rely on their employment contracts; however, this was not because of the irregularities on the part of employers or employment agencies (as in the above instances of exploitation). To

6 Under pressure from local government officials, the Citizens Advice Bureau report has been withdrawn from publication. Access to the report and consent for reference was obtained from its author, Jolanta Babiuch-Luxmoore.

this group of migrants, contracts of employment were of no validity as a matter of choice.

They agreed with their employers to terms and conditions that were and were not to be contained in the contracts to ensure that they themselves benefited more from this relationship. These practices between the employers and workers very often challenged the well-established notion in migration literature that illegality is 'produced' by the state, and revealed when and how illegality may become a strategic choice for some migrants and their employers (Anderson and Ruhs 2010: 1).

The most popular practices were to sign contracts which did not reflect real working conditions – e.g. hours of work – but rather were beneficial both to the employees and the employers, and, for example, disguised full-time employment as part-time, whilst the remainder of the conditions (and salary) was agreed between the parties orally:

> I had a contract of employment in my first job, in the pub. I have read the contract and I knew the terms and conditions. I also had an unwritten agreement with my boss, that on the contract it was stated that I was working for 20 hours per week, and I was paying taxes for 20 hours per week. Generally, when you work part-time you pay less tax. So I was paying 4 pounds a week of tax and 4 pounds a week for NI, and the rest of my wages I received cash in hand, as I was working full time. This deal paid off to my employer and it was better for me all in all. (Interview No. 21)

Another strategy that was popular among the migrants who came to the UK with the sole aim to earn money (target earners) was to hold a couple of jobs simultaneously. This in practice meant that, by law, they were required to pay the basic rate tax (the so-called high rate of emergency tax) on all their wages.[7]

A popular way around this was to arrange with at least one of their employers for informal terms of employment in order to maximize their profits and minimize losses from tax and National Insurance contributions. This very often included orally agreed terms of engagement, without any written statement:

> Apart from my day job, once a week I was working in a pub. I did not have [a] contract, I was paid cash in hand. I asked the landlady there how she was going about it, as – as far as I knew – she herself was an accountant. And she told me that she put me in her books as a casual worker. And if I was working as a causal worker, she did not have to pay the tax for me, and I did not need to pay the tax either. If I was to pay emergency tax there, I would have not accepted that job. (Interview No. 15)

---

7 The amount of tax was to be adjusted annually by the HMRC based on the respective P60 forms from all the simultaneously held jobs.

When migrants chose not to (fully) comply with the law or work in conditions contravening the labour or employment law in the UK, they are not necessarily bad-natured.

The strategies of initially avoiding the law due to its problems, complications and ambiguities ('law is a messy reality' (Interview No. 38)) were summarized by one of the interviewees:

> From my experience, the law becomes important for the Poles in the UK when we actually get into some sort of trouble and need help, need legal advice ... we start making a fuss when something is taken away from us, or when someone does not want to give us something, we believe that should be ours. Then we say: 'oh law is this and that, law is unfair'. But to comply with it like that, to think of law on everyday basis, I am not sure whether it works like that. (Interview No. 27)

To clarify and summarize, the interviewed Polish migrants' experiences of workplace regulations could generally be divided into two groups: those who attached some importance to them (and largely worked in accordance with the conditions specified in the labour regulations) and those who expressed indifference towards the workplace rules, as they worked – or at some point had worked – contravening these conditions.

Within the latter group, one could distinguish between migrants who were forced to work on contracts outside the scope of legal regulations due to the exploitative nature of their employers and those who perhaps did not know that they were breaking or not fully complying with the law. Finally, there was a group of migrants who – for all sorts of reasons – had chosen to work in the UK contravening the labour regulations or work on contracts which did not reflect their real employment conditions.

However, this general typology is not a definite or exclusive one: there were migrants who worked without formal contracts, yet they very much would have wanted to regularize their employment and work under a contract (as in the case of many agency workers). There were migrants who expressed no knowledge of the regulations and although one could say that they were not in a position to choose otherwise, they might actually have been unlikely to choose legality in any case (due to various other sets of circumstances – personal interest, uncertainty of stay, etc.). Yet, there were also migrants who were not offered work contracts by their employers and actually considered this to be in their own interests.

Many of my interviewees realized the irregular character of their initial or subsequent jobs. At the same time, they were ready to accept it. The situation was, however, an ambivalent one and on the whole had more to it than being merely a matter of survival. The Polish interviewees felt that they were allowed in the UK as they had no problems clearing immigration upon arrival. There were also no restrictions in place for them to take up a legal job, as they did not require visas or work permits.

How this group of Polish migrants decided to deal with the law in the UK was determined less by their immigration status than as a matter of choice or, more precisely, not making the choice to legalize their stay, of remaining indifferent towards law. Their choices, when combined with instrumental considerations, added weight to their decisions on whether or not to comply with the law or to comply but partially and strategically engage with the state's legal migration and employment frameworks. Their experiences very much challenge the contemporary discourse of an 'illegal' worker as either a *victim* or a *villain* (Anderson 2008) and suggest that the border between the two can be fluid as migrants negotiate their lives in an unfamiliar legal context.

From the review of the initial responses of the Polish post-2004 EU enlargement migrants towards the immigration and workplace regulations, it is possible to distinguish a rather significant, albeit quite diverse, group of migrants who could either:

1. work in the UK fulfilling the general UK workplace regulations (personal NIN, payment of taxes) but violate immigration regulations (the WRS) attached to their status as A8 nationals; or
2. reside in the UK fulfilling the immigration conditions (the WRS) but work in breach of the general UK workplace regulations.

The research reveals that initial responses to law of a substantive group of Polish migrants could be analysed under the framework of 'semi-legality', 'semi-compliance' (Anderson and Ruhs 2010), 'liminal legality' (Menjivar 2006) or 'twilight legality' (Coyle 2007), as, upon arrival in the UK, many Polish migrants did not (entirely) comply with the requirements for legal employment and residence in the UK. Although they had no problems clearing immigration at airports and ports, many Polish migrants found themselves in the grey sphere between the legal categories of documented and undocumented migrants, in the sphere of liminal legality (Menjivar 2006: 1000).

Semi-Legality

The concept of semi-legality is not new. In the common-sense usage of the term semi-legality has often been simply a shorthand for 'not exactly legal.' The perceived irrelevance of the term to describe one's immigration status, because of its vernacular origin and fragmented conceptualizations has bred ignorance among researchers which arises not from the strangeness of the object of investigation, but from its very transparency. Living with the concept, so thoroughly suffused with its assumptions (that it is even hard to recall when we adopted it), one tends to lose the critical perspective which makes the investigation of migrants' relationship with law more than simply a recital of what everyone already knows. The common sense of things, the knowledge everyone is sure to have, is precisely the starting point for the investigations of such order of things.

The academic literature throws at us many such legally ambiguous categories: in-betweens (Schuck 1998), mixed status households (Chaves 1998, Ngai 2004), liminal migrants (Mejnivar 2006), learning to be illegal (Gonzales 2011), semi-compliant (Anderson and Ruhs 2010), legally illegal (Rigo 2011), quasi-legal (Duvell 2008) or semi-legal (He 2005, Kubal 2009, Rytter 2011). These concepts have been used to critically account for and explain the specific, empirically observed case studies – Salvadorans in Temporary Protected Status in the US (Mejnivar 2006), undocumented Mexican parents living with their US born children (Chaves 1998), 1.5 generation of Latinos who discover their irregular status once they leave full-time education in the US (Gonzales 2011), Eastern European migrants working in partial breach of their visa conditions in the UK (Anderson and Ruhs 2010), Polish EU citizens working in the UK without Workers Registration Scheme authorisation (Kubal 2009), or Pakistani families commuting between legal residence in Sweden and their family life in Denmark (Rytter 2011)

The analytical usefulness of semi-legality stems from the fact that it successfully challenges the black and white, binary divisions within the migration and law debate, between legality and illegality (cf. Menjivar 2006). Semi-legality denotes a range of migrants' legal statuses, demonstrating that the divide between legal and 'illegal' is not a strict dichotomy but rather a tiered and multifaceted relationship. The term therefore captures the various shades of uncertainty that leave migrants in different types of legal ambiguity. As analytical construct semi-legality is fuzzy at the edges – so are the borders between legality and illegality. Paraphrasing Benton (1994) setting boundaries between formal and informal law, borders between legality and illegality are: 'difficult, if not impossible to locate' and it is clear that citizens or migrants without much difference operate at times 'as if the boundaries did not exist' (Benton 1994: 229). Semi-legality therefore comes useful as a heuristic device to differentiate between the various forms of statuses on the continuum between legal-illegal.

Under the notion of semi-compliance, it has so far been used by Bridget Anderson and Martin Ruhs (2010), who examined the situation of East European economic migrants in the UK before the 2004 enlargement of the EU. In their research, they investigated the employment experiences of many East European migrants (including Polish migrants) who functioned on the British market especially in the low wage, low-skilled sector (agriculture, construction and hospitality) and the au-pair sector (Anderson et al. 2006).

Their research captured the ambiguous legal situation of migrants who worked and resided in the UK on conditions not covered by their immigration status. They had either been admitted to the UK on student visas or worked more than the visa conditions allowed them to or, having been admitted to the UK on the basis of joining a particular scheme (e.g. the SAWS), found themselves working in a different industry. To fully account for the migrants' legal status – common for many Eastern European migrants in the UK before the EU enlargement of 2004

–Anderson and Ruhs introduced the concept of semi-compliance. They saw semi-compliance as a result and self-reinforcing determinant of both employer demand and the conditions of migrants' employment (Anderson et al. 2006).

'With the 1st of May 2004, the majority of the previously semi-compliant, Eastern European migrants became EU citizens and were allowed to enter the UK and join the British labour market' – in this context, Ruhs talks about an amnesty for the Polish visa over-stayers and semi-compliant immigrants in the UK (Ruhs 2006). However, the change in the migrants' legal status, due to the British legislation put in place by way of derogation from certain provisions of EU law placed in the Treaty of Accession, might have been more ambiguous and less 'overnight' than initially anticipated. In my research on Polish post-2004 EU enlargement migrants, I discovered that semi-legal status was still a widespread phenomenon (Kubal 2009).

More recently, Anderson and Ruhs (2010) looked at semi-compliance and its actors in the UK: the role of migrant workers, employers and the state in constituting the spaces of (il)legality. They observed that although analysis of the state with its laws and policies still remains a key issue, 'a comprehensive conceptual approach to the study of illegality in the migrant labour market needs to acknowledge and theorise the degrees, motivations and processes *of migrants' and employers' engagement* with the state's laws and policies on the employment of migrant workers' (Anderson and Ruhs 2010: 3, emphasis added). The authors therefore included in their analysis the decisions and choices that migrants and employers make when confronted with the legal migration frameworks created by the state.

Therefore, from an analytical point of view, semi-legality, as a framework, recognizes a higher degree of migrants' and employers' agency vis-à-vis immigration laws, while the discourse on 'illegality' in the employment of migrants has tended to be framed in terms of the opportunity structures or constraints on the actions of individuals. In this sense, the change in legal status might also derogate more broadly the decision-making process of migrants (as in this specific case of Polish, post-2004 EU enlargement migrant workers), who are capable of changing their status and whose change of status largely corresponds to the character of their responses and engagement with the state regulatory frameworks. Semi-compliance varies between individuals and depends not only on the character of immigration laws but also on, for example, individuals' characteristics, various personal and impersonal circumstances, as well as on place and time (Anderson and Ruhs 2010: 3).

Semi-legality can also be found in the works of Cecilia Menjivar (2006), who used the concept of liminal legality, originating in Victor Turner's works on liminality.[8] The liminal state is characterized by ambiguity, openness and indeterminacy (Menjivar 2006: 6). Menjivar's interpretation equipped liminality

8 In 'Liminality and Communitas', Turner used the concept of liminality to illustrate the conscious state of being on the 'threshold' of or between two different existential

with a new legal dimension. Liminal legality designates the grey area between the legal categories of legal or undocumented migrants to describe the status of Salvadoran and Guatemalan immigrants in the USA. Menjivar (2006) using the term of liminal legality identified the multiplicity of 'in-between', semi-legal forms that fall between full lawfulness and legal exclusion (at the opposite ends of the spectrum). She recognized such realities as 'the grey area between these legal categories', characterized by ambiguity as 'it is neither an undocumented status nor a documented one, but may have the characteristics of both' (Menjivar 2006: 1008). This study draws from Menjivar's theoretical contribution, which questions black-and-white conceptualizations of documented and undocumented immigration by exposing the borderline area of 'liminal legality'.

Many Polish post-2004 EU enlargement migrants share the experience of legal liminality, especially in the context of their 'beginnings' in the UK. They might comply with workplace regulations but not comply with immigration regulations:

> They have national insurance. But the WRS registration fee – it's a lot for someone who does not work regularly for an agency. They have part of what it takes to be legal here. (Interview No. 24 with agency personnel)

Alternatively, they might register with the WRS but work contravening the general workplace regulations in the UK:

> I did not pay taxes, but it wasn't only me. All the people working there did not pay taxes. (Interview No. 4)

> I was working for 48 hours per week, but I was paying taxes for 20 hours per week. The remainder of my wages I received in cash. (Interview No. 20)

The experience of 'liminal legality' in turn affected how migrants lived their lives outside the workplace, especially with the experience of precariousness accompanying their choices of everyday life:

> I found a job advert in Polish on a Pakistani shop, it said: 'I can help to arrange a job and accommodation.' I said why not. I was lucky I wasn't cheated or anything. (Interview No. 11)

On the other hand, it reflected the precautions one needed to take in order establish networks and circle of people 'to hang out with':

> We prefer to live with Poles, after we had checked them out of course. (Interview No. 27)

---

planes in the anthropological theories of ritual. This 'no man's land' represents the limbo associated with liminality (Turner 1969).

The question of semi-legality – semi-formality – has also been undertaken by Carrie Cobb (2005) in her research on the informal labour market experiences of immigrant workers in Portland, Oregon in the USA. In contrast to Anderson and Ruhs, who addressed the situation of migrants working in violation of the restrictions attached to their immigration status, Cobb used semi-formality to account for the status of Mexican migrants in steady employment with taxes deducted, engaged at workplaces that respect most labour laws, but who possessed false documentation. 'Not Quite Formal' talks about migrant workers, whose labour is registered and therefore to some extent is regulated by the state. However, the very act of working by these undocumented immigrants was a violation of immigration laws and as such was very distinct from formal employment (Cobb 2005).

What are the features and characteristics of semi-legality that emerge from the literature and are supported by the fieldwork? The literature suggests that semi-legality might be placed as a stage within the spectrum of illegality (Cobb 2005: 5), when the latter is interpreted as a continuum of experiences ranging from the most informal types of labour to work better characterized as semi-formal (Cobb 2005: 4). However, this book argues (in agreement with Anderson and Ruhs) that semi-legality itself could be perceived as a spectrum of experiences from steady employment to precarious employment; from taxes deducted to some or no taxes deducted; from engagement at the workplace that respects labour laws to the abuse of basic labour laws such as compensation and payment; from working with false identity documents to working with genuine identity documents but in violation of conditions attached to one's immigration status. Equally, the violation of conditions attached to one's immigration status can vary in degree and severity, e.g. working more than 20 hours per week while being admitted to the UK on a student visa or – in the case of Polish post-2004 EU enlargement migrants – working without WRS registration.

Semi-legality is also characterized by uncodified (not based on a set of laws), yet often mutually beneficial employer–employee relations (Cobb 2005: 4), revealing the degree of agency that both semi-legal migrants and their employers have vis-à-vis legal frameworks of the state. This mutually beneficial relationship between workers and employers was also reflected in many of the interviews with semi-legal Polish post-2004 EU enlargement migrants in the UK:

> I could make my peace with the fact that the manager in the cafe did not offer me a written contract. Ultimately, he was breaking the law only a little bit. (Interview No. 21)

The relationship between workers and employers beyond the scope of state law could be attributed to the fact that migrants, as temporary workers, displayed a target earning strategy and distinctly different objectives from other workers (Cobb 2005: 9), but met the expectations of employers in relation to maximizing their profits. Similarly, many of the Polish post-2004 EU enlargement migrants in the UK often wanted to maximize the hours they worked (including long working hours, exceeding the limits prescribed by labour laws), which allowed them to earn as much money as possible in a short a period of time:

> I worked on a production line together with the Strongman. We nicknamed him Strongman or Stakhanov, as he was working really hard, moving 5 kg boxes with fruits and vegetables as if they were Lego blocks. During breaks he would talk to the supervisor to increase the speed of the production line, so he could pride himself doing more than 100 per cent of the norm. He would also take overtime, and work during the weekends. (Interview No. 1)

In addition, many new migrants did not have the same lifestyles as more established workers; they did not have family with them or obligations in the UK beyond work:

> The three guys, they came here just to earn money, they all work for X now [an automotive company], via an agency of course. Initially they were paid at £8 per hour. Then after getting into X, they managed to register themselves with another employment agency, internal to the X plant. There they are paid at £12–13. But they don't have a life beyond work, it's really hard work. (Interview No. 13)

As a result, many statutory laws, such as those regulating working time and overtime payments, were of no use to those migrant workers displaying target-earning strategies. Even though overtime pay is mandatory when an employee works more than 40 hours a week, the experience of Polish post-2004 EU enlargement migrant workers in the UK was that the employers would rather limit the business week to the prescribed working hour week than give in to requests for overtime work. As a result, most of my interviewees still worked more than 40 hours, but with hours spread over two jobs, having to juggle between different shifts and work schedules:

> There were periods when I was working 60 hours per week. Aside from normal hours, I was working two 11 hour shifts per week, from 8 am to 7 pm, as it was always very busy there. And I also had another job then, I was working in a pub once a week. So after the cafe closed, I would run to the toilet, change there, and catch a bus to my evening job. (Interview No. 27)

The fieldwork revealed yet another mutually beneficial, albeit not codified, arrangement between the semi-legal migrant workers and their employers: non-payment of the National Minimum Wage. Some Polish migrants reported initially receiving less than the National Minimum Wage when they began their first job in the UK. However, since they were paid 'cash in hand' during that period, they managed to take home higher pay than they would have received if taxes had been deducted from the National Minimum Wage (cf. Interview No. 19). Although the payment in cash eroded their legal protection, what the workers valued more was higher pay that they could take home in that scenario.

My analysis demonstrates that semi-legality, as an analytical concept, challenges the stereotypical image of the victimized, undocumented immigrant facing the abusive employer. It reveals that the interactions between migrant workers and employers that arise from these diverse employment strategies are far more complex. Migrants engage in a significant trade-off when they enter into semi-formal relationships that undermine the protection they have been given by labour laws and yet perceive this trade-off as empowering – in their own interests and to their benefit. By this, they challenge the institutional role of the state in enacting laws imposing restrictions on immigrants and they undermine the strong power of the state and its sole capacity to deprive migrants of their rights (Yamamoto 2007: 95).

Cobb's invocations of semi-formality with reference to Mexican migrant workers in Oregon, when compared with and Anderson and Ruhs' insights into the semi-compliance of migrant workers in the UK and conclusions from the study of Polish post-2004 EU enlargement migrants in gainful employment in the UK, demonstrate that semi-legality is a theoretically rich concept with multiple applications in various different legal and migration-related contexts.

Explaining Semi-Legality

This chapter analysed the responses of Polish post-2004 EU enlargement migrants towards the British Accession Regulations and general workplace regulations. The ethnographic inquiry into migrants' experiences, behaviour and attitudes towards the British legal environment revealed that there was a substantial number of Polish post-2004 EU enlargement migrants who did not fully or entirely comply with its requirements. By not making the choice to legalize their stay, they remained indifferent towards the law.

This chapter therefore introduced the concept of semi-legality as theoretically advancing the discussion on the character of Polish post-2004 EU enlargement migrants and migrant workers' relationship with the law in the UK and their experiences of the British socio-legal environment.

Therefore, the legitimate and interesting question to ask is: why did it happen? Why did migrants themselves choose to retain semi-legal status, arguably against their own interests? The lack of WRS registration delayed the process of inclusion into the welfare system and benefit support indefinitely, while working in breach of the employment regulations undermined the protection they were given by labour laws – protection from harassment and discrimination.

The analysis of the British legal environment – in Chapter 4 – demonstrated that the law and its enforcement might very well contribute to solving this puzzle. The legal environment does, of course, matter, yet migrants are not only passive recipients of the opportunity structures provided by the state. Migrants' exploitation by unfair employers or their opportunism cannot solely account for their particular set of responses towards the British legal environment. The situation is much more nuanced than the well-established dichotomy of irregular migrant workers either as victims or villains (Anderson 2008), due to a variety of factors.

This chapter brought to the forefront migrants' agency vis-à-vis the immigration regulations and workplace frameworks. The fieldwork revealed that migrants possess a certain degree of choice – whether to comply with the law, not comply or comply selectively. As EU citizens, they did not face problems entering the country – no work permits and no work visas were required for them to commence employment. These migrants experienced no risk of deportation, therefore they engaged strategically with the legal frameworks and the legal environment according to their priorities and their particular context.

As a result, many of the Polish migrants prioritized compliance with certain rules which benefited them directly (e.g. National Insurance regulations) over compliance with those whose potential benefits could not be seen directly and could be dealt with at a later point in time (e.g. the WRS). The needs of migrant workers – maximization of income and low taxes – met the requirements of many employers, particularly in the low-wage and low skilled sectors. As a result, the negotiations of employment conditions did not take place with reference to the National Minimum Wage or working time regulations, as these seemed redundant from the position of migrants displaying a target-earning strategy.

Polish migrants also developed their own understanding and interpretations of the legal requirements. The law was not considered as a protection, but rather as an unfamiliar reality presenting more of a constraint to a preferred action. Many Polish migrants bypassing the workplace regulations did not necessary mean to break them, but to keep clear of the law or to maintain a low profile. The position of migrants towards the WRS largely delineated their attitude to welfare: the majority of young and single Polish workers who did not consider this a priority ignored the registration altogether.

However, Polish post-2004 EU enlargement migrants, in exercising their agency vis-à-vis British rules and regulations, do not operate in a vacuum (or are influenced solely by the shape and character of the British legal environment). Something else must also be at work. Migrants arrive in the UK with certain values and attitudes to law, understandings of how the law operates and how it is enforced. These experiences are not uniform but constitute a 'luggage', a set of behaviours and toolkits that migrants may draw upon.

The following chapters therefore turn to these 'soft', cultural factors influencing Polish migrants' relationship with the law in the UK. They look into Polish migrants' legal tradition – the historically preserved image of law in society and the role of law as a reference point in shaping the group's identity. The chapters also investigate the current social expectations towards the law, its enforcement and Polish migrants' daily experiences of law prior to their arrival in the UK. Legal culture therefore plays its own role in addressing the issue of the form and quality of Polish post-2004 EU enlargement migrants' socio-legal integration in the UK.

Chapter 6
The Polish Socio-Legal Tradition

While the previous chapters examined the character of Polish post-2004 EU enlargement migrants' socio-legal integration in the UK by looking into the conditions produced by the British legal environment (Chapter 4) interacting and impinging on people's choices of whether to follow, avoid or contest the law (Chapter 5), this chapter turns to another aspect of the complex interplay. It investigates the interpretations, experiences, values, attitudes and the image of law that the migrants brought with them from Poland – their legal culture.

This analysis of the role of legal culture begins with the historical account of Polish socio-legal tradition, as the past very often contributes to understanding the present. Collective past experiences have their impact on individual beliefs, popular myths, group identity and memory as well as, to a certain extent, 'pre-programmed' contemporary individual and collective behaviour. This pre-programming affects the formation of mindsets, cognitive frameworks and emotional dispositions (Kochanowicz 2004: 72). It takes place through socialization within such institutions as the family, the educational system, the state, legal order, etc. Much of this experience is passed on in an informal way, through observing and repeating certain modes of behaviour. As Starr and Collier argue in the introduction to their edited volume, law and legal forms (and thereby also legal cultures) should be seen 'as arising from particular historical negotiations between and among groups, as resulting from particular systems of hierarchy and domination' (Starr and Collier 1989: 24).

There is no doubt that the past also matters in the Polish case. Distinctive social attitudes, dispositions and prescribed patterns of behaviour accepted in the given community and stored in society as a whole have developed in response to certain distinctive and enduring features of the Polish predicament (Podgórecki 1994: 157). They have become sedimentary over generations. Tradition has become the source of identity, as people shape the self-image of the group and their mindsets with reference to representations and interpretations of the past as conveyed in the mainstream version of Polish history. Central among these, and pervasive in their consequences, are characteristic underlying views of norms, the society, the state, law and its institutions.

However, the past's contribution to the understanding of the present should not be confused with the simple and naïve arguments put forward in historical determinism. Therefore, this chapter on socio-legal tradition does not claim to give accounts of contemporary legal culture, but rather to provide the context of its development. It helps to explain the current shape of Polish legal culture not driven by the deterministic forces of the past, but rather tracing back, in the socio-legal history of Poland, the origins and the shape of different relationships with the state law, an understanding of how it operates and how it is enforced. This reveals itself in the historical configuration of political and legal institutions, as well as in the character of human actions. The chapter looks at the socio-legal tradition of the Polish people and their state law, their relationship with state officials and governors and ordinary people's experiences of law enforcement.

Common Sources of Western and Polish Law

Legal tradition in Poland, as in every other society, begins deep in pre-Christian times with the rules of the blood feud upon which a particular form of socio-political organization – which Bardach referred to as military democracy – was based (Bardach et al. 2000: 20). The dynamics of public order were determined by federations and alliances between families within certain clans and often took the form of bloody wars aimed at the subjugation of weaker neighbours. At best it was organized by inter-family customary law and was determined by the rules within a clan. The clan leader was surrounded by a group of warriors and the elders of his clan, which constituted the advisory body – *wiec*.

The politics of conquering new territories transformed the role of the *wiec*. Over time, it expanded to include officials and local noblemen, who advised the ruler on preparing and passing new rules over his lands. Many historians trace the origins of the general conventions – *conventiones generales* – of the nobility to the institution of the *wiec*, which formed the basis of the Polish parliamentary system. The *wiec* also played a jurisdictional role: the prince, who presided over the *wiec*, judged criminal and civil cases. This practice laid the foundations for the later establishment of the Diet Court, the court of highest instance of appeal for the nobility (Grodziski 2004: 138).

Into this social and legal order came Western Christianity. Poland, through Christianization, became an heir to the Roman law of the Holy Empire and the Canon law of the Church. It was under the influence of the Church that the tribal customs were re-stated and reformed. Poland joined the tradition of Western law through the German Holy Roman Empire.[1] The reception of Western models of ruling by the Piast dynasty had a significant influence on the ideology of royal power in Poland, as well as the popularity of Canon law vocabulary in civil and criminal jurisprudence (Chłopocka 1967).

The Piasts regarded themselves as followers of the tradition of the Holy Roman Empire (Michalowski 2005: 40). The early Polish rulers followed in the footsteps of Western Christian kings who used secular legislation in order to induce their

1 During his visit to Gniezno in 1000, the German Emperor Otto III made the Polish prince Bolesław the Brave (reigned 992–1025) his brother and cooperator in the Empire (*frater et cooperator imperii*) (Jasinski 2001) and symbolically crowned him the King of Poland.

subjects to observe the Ten Commandments. This reflected the general trend in Continental Europe at the beginning of the eleventh century of enforcing the norms of Canon law using state power (Michalowski 2005: 34).[2]

The eleventh century in Poland saw the manoeuvres of the powerful nobility against the monarch's power, which coincided with a popular revolt against the landowners and a pagan reaction against Christianity. Stability was restored by the heir to the Polish throne, Casimir (reigned 1040–1058). Thanks to the support he gave the Pope in the investiture conflict with the Emperor (the Papal Revolution of 1075), he managed to regain power. Casimir's success established the channel for the diffusion of Canon law and the importance of the Church in Polish jurisprudence. Known later as 'the Restorer', he eventually succeeded in bringing under his sway most of the Polish lands, reviving the ecclesiastical organization of the Roman Catholic Church and suppressed the pagan tribes that had helped to depose him (Encyclopaedia Britannica 2007).

The Ambivalent Reception of Roman Law

It was the Holy Roman Empire which gave Poland the notion that a state might be organized by law. The state was obliged to give expression to its policy and its administration in public law institutions, embracing governmental institutions, military recruitment, taxation, duties and privileges of various classes, and criminal law. Roman law introduced the very concept of legislation as a primary source of lasting law. The state acquired the function of giving expression to the relationship of its subjects with each other in the institutions of private law (Berman 1983).

The overall reception of Roman law at the later stages was, however, ambivalent. The Renaissance and popularity of Roman law in Continental Western Europe from the thirteenth century was due to the adaptation of the Code of Justinian to the new socio-economic conditions. Roman law, under the Corpus Iuris Civilis, had entered the universities and, along with Canon law, had become the basis for legal studies and jurisprudence (Sojka-Zielinska 2000: 31).

In Poland, Roman law did not encounter an entirely positive reception, mainly for two reasons. Firstly, the new codified Roman law was associated with universal aspirations of the Holy Roman Emperors and was therefore perceived as dangerous to the position of any sovereign state. Secondly, the Polish nobility resisted Roman law, as it could be used as a medium to legitimize the ideas of absolute power. The ethos of freedom and equality of the nobility, which was deeply rooted in the local customary law and reflected by the political organization of the kingdom, did not accord with the strong legislative and executive prerogatives of the monarch. According to the Roman law (Continental) tradition, the monarch stood above the

2 The evidence of the chronicles of Thietmar shows that Bolesław the Brave was hard on those who committed adultery or broke their fast. Corporal punishment was the penalty in both cases (Michalowski 2005: 34).

law (*princes legibus solutus*) and his will constituted the law (*quod principi placuit legis habet vigorem*) (Sojka-Zielinska 2000: 39). Although Roman law was taught at the Kraków Academy, the Roman jurist Pedro Ruiz complained that 'to Poles, a Roman lawyer means as much as a fur seller from Ethiopia' (Sojka-Zielinska 2000: 39). Roman law was, however, widely applied in municipal jurisdictions based on German, Magdeburg law.

Why did the adoption of Roman law encounter such serious problems in early modern Poland? Kaminski (2000) offers one possible explanation: in Western Europe, the Code of Justinian gained popularity mainly due to the support of the aristocracy, who, tired of bloody religious conflicts, supported rulers who wanted to fight anarchy and promised to make the works of state administration more effective. This wide support enabled Western rulers to gain absolutist power and centralize the administration at the cost of privileges of the nobility and the role of local government (Kaminski 2000). Roman law made the will of the ruler – sanctioned by the authority of positive law – the prime source of legislation in the capitals of France and Spain.

The role of the aristocracy was limited to the execution of law at the local level (Kaminski 2000: 32). At the same time, certain areas of public and especially private law were to balance the monarch's strong executive power and protect the rights of the citizens (nobility) in case the monarch would take a turn towards more authoritarian methods of ruling.

Poland, on the contrary, was spared from both the anarchy following the Black Death (1348–1350) and the subsequent chaos caused by the religious wars as a result of the Reformation (1517–1555). Therefore, the increased power of the monarch could not be justified in the eyes of the nobility; what is more, it stood in clear conflict with the interests of the Polish nobility, who, by the sixteenth century, regarded themselves as the political nation. The increased importance of Roman law would enable the monarch to enter the fields of customary law and neglect the 'traditional and ancient' privileges of the nobility. The Code of Justinian clearly stated that the will of the ruler is equivalent to the law (Kaminski 2000: 46); therefore, Roman law was perceived as an obvious threat to the special position held by the Polish nobility which was preserved by local customary law, along with their influence on the political life of the kingdom.

Law as Freedom

Although the roots and origins of the Polish legal tradition rest firmly in the Continental West, the ambivalent reception of Roman law marks the distinctiveness of the Polish socio-legal history and its tradition of legal culture.

In contrast to the weakening influence of Western aristocracy on political life, the Polish nobility's personal and economic freedom – *Neminem Captivabimus* (equivalent to the English *habeas corpus*) and almost complete exemption from taxes after 1374 – was reflected in constitutional arrangements favouring the nobility. This resulted in the nobility's immense role in legislature, leaving the execution of law in the hands of the monarch. The main rule upon which the political order was based was the principle of the free election of the monarch by the whole of the nobility. Bicameral *Sejm* (since 1493) – General Assembly – which evolved from earlier regional and provincial meetings (*conventiones generales*) of the nobility and was granted extensive legislative prerogatives, was to balance the power of the monarch. According to the *Nihil Novi* constitution (1505),[3] no new laws could be introduced without the consent of both chambers of the *Sejm*. No proposal could become law and no decision was binding unless it received the full agreement of all those persons who were competent to consider it (Opalinski 2005: 241). As a result of these constitutional advancements, a nobleman was to conform only to the laws he himself constituted, passed and agreed upon. The *ius resistendi*[4] – right to Confederation – gave the nobility the right to militarily resist the monarch if he was to compromise any of the constitutional rights or privileges.

As a result, a different source of authority from the Western (Continental) model which was attributed to law – law as freedom from restrictions (of the monarch) rather than rights and obligations (towards the state) – resulted in the adoption of a specific model of governance: the Noble Democracy (1374–1795). The social base of this political regime was the politically and economically liberated nobility, constituting between 8 and 12 per cent of the population (Wandycz 1980).[5]

However, the ideal balance of competence and power of the Noble Democracy was, in practice, unattainable, as one side – the nobility – systematically grew stronger and became more influential. Their rights extended at the cost of other groups in society – the burghers and the peasants. Their freedom had justification in law, which gave them an unthreatened position in any conflict with the monarch. Therefore, whenever the monarch was trying to strengthen his position in the state (the attempts undertaken by the last two Jagiellons – Sigismund I (reigned 1506–1548) and Sigismund II Augustus (reigned 1548–1572) – were the direct echo of the popularity of Roman law in Western Europe), the nobility would oppose the king on the basis of the customary *ius resistendi*. The idea of the righteous execution of 'traditional and ancient' freedoms was at the core of the execution-of-rights movement established by the nobility in the form of a Confederation against the monarch's absolutist experiments and to 'remind' the king about his role. The movement strengthened the interpretation of laws as freedoms. It deepened the

---

3 In Poland all parliamentary legislation was called constitution(s) – *constitutiones*. Constitutions thus dealt with questions as diverse as taxation or war on the one hand and the fiscal immunity of certain lands or the obligations of peasant tenants on the other (Kaminski 1994).

4 *Ius resistendi* was a legal practice derived from local customary law, also known in the West. It gave the nobility the right to oppose the monarch. In Poland it gained a special role and was practised as the right to Confederation, the lawful act of disobedience to the king.

5 Compared to one to two per cent in the rest of Europe (Wandycz 1980).

nobility's conviction that it was in rulers' natures to ignore inconvenient laws; therefore, they should be distrusted and kept under control (Opalinski 2005: 245).

This understanding of law – strongly intersected with the notion of freedom – dominated the political writings in modern Poland and was very different from how the Western sources linked law with the notion of rights and obligations. The Polish nobility viewed the Polish nation as 'free', contrary to other 'non-free' nations in the era of early absolutism. The Polish Great Chancellor and Great Hetman, Jan Zamoyski (1542–1605), advocated that 'Poland was born to *Freedom* while Germany and Sweden had to bear strong monarchies' (Bahlcke 2005: 163. In his treatise *Quincunx*, Stanislaw Orzechowski reflected in 1564 on the rights and prerogatives that constituted the essence of the concept of 'a free Polish nobleman':

> A Pole wears a superb robe, freedom, which is equal to the freedom of the king; … he shares an ox with the king, his Master, that is, the common law which, in Poland, like an ox, serves equally both him and the king. (Starnawski 1972: 556)

The law also made the nobleman free and equal to the king in terms of legislative power. It was also the law that safeguarded the nobility's freedoms and privileges.

Free Election Principle

The origins of the free election principle go back to the fourteenth century and mark the establishment of a new ruling dynasty in Poland – the Jagiellon dynasty.[6] The selection of Jogalia (Władysław Jagiełło) by the Polish nobility as the successor to the throne in 1385 also marked the first documented election of a Polish king by the whole of the nobility.[7] From the reign of Władysław Jagiełło, the free election principle ossified, although it was formally limited to the selection of future heirs from the Jagiellon dynasty. In Poland the king was the executor of a sacred trust which was not inherited directly from God, but was carefully conferred on him by the clergy and acclaimed by the people (the nobility) (Davies 2005b: 105).

6 As the last king from the first Polish Piast dynasty, Casimir the Great (reigned 1333–1370), died without a legal heir, the Polish throne went to the Hungarian dynasty of Anjou. The daughter of Luis of Anjou (reigned 1370–1382)– Hedwig (Polish: Jadwiga (reigned 1384–1399)) – was the successor to the Polish throne. The Polish nobles selected the Lithuanian Prince Jogaila as Jadwiga's husband; through this marriage, a personal or dynastic union between Poland and Lithuania was created.

7 This alliance between Poland and Lithuania, signed in the town of Kreva on 14 August 1385, resulted in the Christianization of Lithuania and a personal union between the Kingdom of Poland and the Grand Duchy of Lithuania that lasted for a prolonged period of time and led to the creation of a Polish-Lithuanian federation – the 'Republic of the Two Nations' – in 1569 and eventually to the creation of a short-lived unitary state in 1791 (Davies 2005: 163).

The ritual of the coronation ceremony showed that the Polish king was explicitly bound by the consent of the people. After the elector's oath, the Lord Metropolitan would address the people gathered at the ceremony with these words:

> Will you submit yourselves to such a prince and rector, to confirm his rule and put your trust in him: will you obey his laws according to the apostles, and given that his whole be subordinated to the higher powers, will you submit to this excellent king? (Kutrzeba 1910)

Then the surrounding clergy and the nobility would unanimously agree.[8]

The principle of free elections was modified after the death of the last king from the Jagiellon dynasty, as Sigismund II Augustus died with no heir whose rights to the throne could be accredited by the nobility. As a result, from the second half of the sixteenth century onwards, the principle of free election expanded in scope: every nobleman (not necessarily of Polish origin) theoretically had the right to be elected as the king of Poland.[9]

The Constitutional Contract between the Monarch and the Nobility

To ensure that the nobility's freedom and laws would be respected by all future elected kings, the first *viritim* election of 1573 – following from the Union of Lublin (1569) and establishment of the Republic (the Commonwealth of Poland-Lithuania) – introduced a legal contract between the king and the nobility, a set of conditions on which they would agree to his coronation. The 'Henrician Articles' (assembled by Henry of Valois (reigned 1574–1575)) ensured the nobility's right to elect their king freely in the future, their right to approve declarations of war, the imposition of taxes and all summons of the *levée en masse*; they insisted on regular meetings of the *Sejm* and on the principle of religious tolerance.[10] The final article secured the nobility's right to resistance and to disobey the king if he contravened his oath – the article *de non praestanda oboedientia* allowed the noblemen to deny allegiance to the king if he had failed to observe the law (Jedruch 1982: 88).

---

8 This particular text, which survived as Codex 17 in Półkowski's Catalogue to the MSS of Krakow Cathedral, was drawn up for the coronation of Władysław III (reigned 1434–1444) in 1434 and was used as the basis for all subsequent coronation oaths during the Jagiellonian period. A slightly modified version was also used for the coronations of the elected kings of the Polish-Lithuanian Republic from 1574 to 1767 (Davies 2005: 417).

9 The election of 1573 saw the representatives of four influential European dynasties running for the title of the king of Poland–Lithuania: Henry of Valois, who was the brother of the King of France, Charles IX, the Russian Tsar Ivan IV 'the Terrible', Archduke Ernest from the Austrian Habsburg dynasty and the King of Sweden, John III.

10 Agreed upon by the Polish and Lithuanian nobility at the Warsaw Confederation (1573).

During the second election in 1576, additional conditions, known as the *Pacta Conventa* (agreed points), were made regarding the conduct of foreign policy and the management of the royal debt. Both the Henrician Articles and the *Pacta Conventa* defined the future role of the king in the state and his practical subordination to the nobility (Jedruch 1982).

Although these contracts were along the lines later advocated by Jean Jacques Rousseau and Thomas Paine, they had, nevertheless, a destabilizing effect. They seriously restricted the traditional role of the monarch as the creator and executor of law. The idea of law unrestrained by any authority put the monarch under the strict control of the nobility. A series of legislative initiatives to introduce reforms such as new taxes (which could support the army or royal officials – an important branch of the executive authority) were perceived by the nobility as an attack on their 'ancient' laws, ultimately leading towards the increased authority of the ruler. This situation resulted in poor law enforcement. And since laws which could not be executed were eventually neither binding nor respected, the position and regard of the state law seriously deteriorated.

Law without Authority

Włodzimierz Łozinski, in his study of the legal culture of the seventeenth-century Polish and Lithuanian nobility, concluded that it was not the lack of law that destroyed the good customs but a lack of authority; not the lack of legal sanctions but the lack of their execution (Łozinski 1960: 7).

It is not particularly difficult to observe that the concept of law strongly intersected with freedom, as understood by the majority of the Polish nobility, was not far from the notion of anarchy. Neither the legislation passed by the *Sejm* nor court sentences were righteously enforced or executed. As a result, alternative extra-legal methods of social ordering to state authority intensified and became more vivid.

One of these was the colonization of the public domain by the private interests of the nobility. Over time, the increase of magnate influences posed an insoluble problem for the Republic. Each member of the oligarchy ruled in his own domain like a princeling in his own 'private state within a state'; he maintained his own clientele of nobles who defended his interests in the dietines or the courts, and who staffed his own private army. To spite the king was, in the seventeenth century, the most infallible way of winning popularity among the gentry, as well as a way of extorting new grants from the monarch (Gasiorowski 1984).

The institution of free elections had become the playground for foreign diplomacy. The leading noble families, sympathizing with the French, Russian, Spanish or Habsburg courts, could command far greater respect and obedience than the state itself (Davies 2005). Thus, non-unanimous royal elections frequently resulted in civil wars (in 1704–1706 and 1733–1735), which, in addition, profoundly transformed the legal culture with regard to state authority, property law and religion. By the eighteenth century, the direction of politics and the selection of candidates seemed to be motivated either by the promise of French gold or Russian coercion (Davies 2005).

The legislature did not command respect either. The growth of large numbers of quarrelsome, peacock-minded clients, sworn to uphold the honour and interests of their patron and dependent for promotions and livelihood on the successful prosecution of his whims and feuds, gradually undermined the workings of legislative authority at both the central and provincial levels (Davies 2005). Corruption, as an alternative mean of social ordering, spread from top to bottom (Davies 2005). Between the seventeenth and eighteenth centuries, 73 *Sejms* had been obstructed by *liberum veto* (unanimity principle) and suspended without passing any legislation (Jasienica 1988). The state lacked 'healthy' mechanisms; therefore, venality, debt and dependence sapped the noblemen's ability to change with the times (Davies 2005: 176). In his 'Remarks on the Government of Poland', Rousseau expressed this point forcefully by observing that nobody controlled the *Sejm* and nobody obeyed its decisions either (Jedruch 1982: 362).

Justice iure et gladio

One immediate consequence of the legislatiive anarchy was the severe crisis of the justice system. The Latin formula *iure et gladio* – by law and sword – rightly captures the climate of customary legal practices, lawsuits and private vendettas pursued by the Polish and Lithuanian nobility in response to an ineffective justice system (Łozinski 1960).

The lawsuits and court trials in which the nobility were engaged were numerous and endless. Incorrigible litigiousness, complex and formalized legal procedures combined with the lack of strong executive power made law enforcement very inconsistent and chaotic. The haphazard execution of court sentences enabled alternative strategies of law avoidance and private justice to emerge.

Zajazd was the most popular extra-legal form of sentence execution illustrating the deterioration of 'good customs'. Originally it was an institution derived from customary law that was designed to obtain compensation. It was usually performed by a royal officer – usher – accompanied by two other noblemen and sometimes also the representatives of the aggrieved party. Faced with ineffective law enforcement, the nobility transformed the institution of *zajazd* into a private vendetta. In the seventeenth century, in the name of the *zajazd* a whole noble clan supported by other fellow noblemen would not hesitate to violently invade the premises of an opposing party in order to settle a conflict (Łozinski 1960).

Poor law enforcement, internal power struggles between the nobility and their elected kings, and the general tendency to seek private justice outside the court system, combined with military calamities of the seventeenth and eighteenth centuries (most notably the Khmelnytsky Uprising (1648–1655) and the Swedish Deluge (1644–1660)), resulted in political anarchy and compromised the government beyond repair. By the beginning of the eighteenth century, the

Polish-Lithuanian Commonwealth, the largest European state, was dependent upon its neighbours (the Russian Empire, Prussia and Austria) who interfered in its domestic politics almost at will.

Attempts to introduce reforms, launched in 1788 by the Four-Year *Sejm*, resulted in a constitution which, although it abolished the practices of the old Republic – *Liberum Veto*, the right of resistance, the Confederations and the 'free elections' – had no practical means to enforce the new legislation. Weak executive authority, no law-enforcement agencies, an empty treasury and a small army, combined with the colonial plans of Russian and Prussian officialdoms, resulted in the partition of Poland between the neighbouring powers.[11]

The widespread and simple belief among the Polish nobility that the law – as the 'ideal' – should remain beyond the influence of authorities (the government and the monarch) actually resulted in a system which justified and legitimized the law without authority. This conservative attitude – opposing any plans or reforms aimed at strengthening the government, which was perceived as a threat to the nobility's freedom – paralysed the executive branch and left the law without enforcement, without authority and vulnerable to the infringement of rights and abuses of competence and power. The law functioned as a form, not as an executive.

As a consequence, this led to a historical paradox where a country so frantically scared of an absolutist rule found itself under a colonial-like rule of three absolutist monarchies – Russia, Austria and Prussia – for more than a century.[12]

The Civil Law Tradition

The colonial-like period of the partitions (1795–1918) was parallel to the strengthening of the civil law tradition in Continental Europe (especially in Austria and Prussia) and for Poland resulted in the pluralism of socio-legal traditions and a specific relationship between the citizens and the state.

The tradition of law-making in civil law, with its written laws, rules and regulations, puts stress on the strict phrasing of the laws to pre-condition and ensure that the relations between the citizens and the governors are determined

11 According to Norman Davies, the partitions of Poland had a clearly observable blueprint. During 1773, 1793 and 1795 the same scenario was re-enacted with only minor variations; a pattern of subsequent events was clearly observable. The Polish reformers, supported by the last king, Stanisław August Poniatowski (reigned 1764–1795), obstructed in their plans to remedy their country's ills by legal means would turn to an illegal adventure which had to be forcibly suppressed by Russian arms. Russia, in order to maintain 'the balance of power' in Europe, would ask its neighbours – Prussia and Austria – to join and re-instate order in the Republic. They, in return for military help, demanded slices of Polish territory each time (Davies 2005: 398).

12 Russia annexed around 62 per cent of the land and 45 per cent of the population. Prussia took 20 per cent of the land and 23 per cent of the people. The respective figures for the Austrian share were 18 and 32 per cent (Wandycz 1974: 11).

from above (Staskiewicz 2007: 70). The far-reaching developments in the civil law tradition took place at the time of the Enlightenment, with great reforms making a system of laws where all was set forth precisely. According to the philosophy of rationalism, the relations between the citizens and the state were to be predetermined in advance, and the natural order in government was to resemble the order that philosophers of the Enlightenment thought they had found in nature (Fisher 2002).

For the Poles, however, this time of legal rationalization and civil law reforms was parallel to foreign rule. As a result, this 'modernization' towards civil law was perceived by the Poles as imposed through the barrel of the gun and without consideration for their cultural identity, religious beliefs, political autonomy or national sovereignty. The state, the source of law, in the hands of three absolutist rulers moved away from its earlier vulnerability and incapacity. The fact that Polish society, traditionally having little regard for the strong authority of the state, had to conform to a foreign state's authority of an absolutist (or enlightened absolutist) character as the source of state law (for one and a half centuries), was pregnant with many important consequences. The state law had to be obeyed because of severe sanctions; nevertheless, it was considered foreign and imposed by the colonizers, hence it did not command much respect among the Polish people. Like other colonial countries, the state law was distrusted and perceived as an imposed, 'alien' system (Benton 2002).

It is therefore during the period of the partitions when disregard for the state authority and a particular attachment to the idea of law as freedom intensified. This idea of freedom, combined with a strong nationalist movement of a stateless Polish nation in the nineteenth century, resulted in four national insurrections[13] and dedicated, although often irrational, fights for independence. Reading the national literature of those times, one is struck by the strong, clear division between the state (Austrian, Russian or Prussian governors and legislators) and the Polish stateless people (cf. the works of Adam Mickiewicz, Juliusz Słowacki and Cyprian Kamil Norwid). The latter either openly fought for freedom from the foreign rulers or operated within the official borders of the law, but with the intention of challenging the order imposed by the state (Gadowska and Majcherkiewicz 2005).

At the international level, foreign rule apologists from Berlin, St Petersburg and Vienna expatiated on the Poles' good fortune in receiving the blessings of absolutist rule, as the faults of the Polish anarchy were universally recognized (Serejski 1970). In the Russian literature there were a number of references to Poles as rebels.[14] Among the Poles, this resulted in the rather low legal expectations of never being too 'comfortable', 'at home' and content with the prevailing state

13 The Kościuszko Uprising of 1794, the November Uprising of 1830, the Spring of Nations 1848–1849 and the January Uprising of 1863–1864.

14 E.g. Dostoyevsky ridiculed Poles in *The Brothers Karamazov* and branded them as rebels and conspirators in *The Diary of a Writer* (Lewitter 1984).

law, as well as in the popularly held national myth of Poles as the law breakers and rule evaders that was strongly preserved in the national imagination.

Adapting Legal Tradition: Relationships with the State

The period of partitions therefore also revealed the adaptive qualities of the Polish socio-legal tradition, how it was able to accommodate different (from the Republican) sources of legal authority and the relationship between law and authority respectively from the conditions prevalent under various colonial rules. These adaptive strategies to colonial-like rule often took the shape of – alternative to state law – practices of social ordering prevalent among close-knit circles of friends and family networks.

The Austrian partition was distinctive, not only because it contained a plurality of legal orders, but also because the structure of its plural legal orders was the most explicit. The Habsburgs' political attempts to pass rules relating to the various legal authorities and forums acknowledged the existence of different forms of social ordering, including those outside the Austrian civil law books.

Local customary and 'living' laws (Ehrlich 1912) amongst Poles, Armenians, Germans, Gypsies, Jews, Poles, Hungarians, Romanians, Russians, Ruthenians and Slovaks existed parallel to Austrian court rulings and state legislation. Designing, announcing and fighting for rules, and the interaction of various legal authorities, fashioned a place for the state as an instrument and a forum for the production of such rules (Benton 2002: 10). The ascendancy of state law was, however, matched by policies of cultural and political autonomy. As a result, the Habsburgs succeeded in achieving the relative acceptance of their rule.

In the Russian partition, the state law constituted by the will of a Russian tsar had to be, and was, obeyed under threat of severe sanctions. Russian emperors ruled by their personal power and authority, and merely used legal devices (which they created) to assist them, discarding these devices at will (Berman 1963: 203). Russia allowed almost no political representation for the nations under its governance, either at the local or at the central level. Personal and constitutional freedoms were non-existent; instead, Muscovite social traditions required a total submission of the citizen to the ruler and the total effacement of the individual to the interest of the collective. Surveillance and harassment could not be objected to, since every loyal citizen's duty was to cooperate with the authorities (Davies 2005).

Russian autocracy therefore ran completely contrary to Poland's traditions, and the perception of the state law as foreign and imposed, combined with strong nationalist sentiments, could not result in the internalization of the state law or the incorporation of its cultural values, mores, motives, etc. Therefore, unsurprisingly, the Polish adaptation to Russian autocracy took an ambivalent turn. The state law was observed and conformed to where necessary, through fear of severe sanctions, but in everyday social relations, alternative and informal structures of social ordering emerged. These were founded on what Petrażycki calls 'intuitive law' (Petrażycki 1955). The concept of intuitive law was:

> associated with the broad generic concept of law ... embracing incomparably more than does law as jurists use the term, and comprising imperative-attributive experiences which contain no references to outside authorities. (Petrażycki 1955: 221)

Intuitive law embraced patterns of interactions to which moral obligations were attached in a form of unwritten – intuitive – codes of conduct. They could, of course, vary as the content of intuitive law was defined by each person's individual conditions and life circumstances (one's character, upbringing, education, social position, professional occupations, personal acquaintances and relationships, etc.). However, certain factors – common historical experience, for example – allowed the morality of intuitive law to be more or less congruous for a certain number of individuals.

Yet, the intuitive law should not be confused with the desired or ideal law, as its content – due to the different cultural as well as personal circumstances of individuals – could have been (and often was) extremely barbarous, more laggard and often irrational (Petrażycki 1955: 255).[15] For example, since the state law was perceived as 'alien' and imposed, tricks that outfoxed the law and its apparatus were sanctioned by the norms of intuitive law and were regarded as virtuous rather than illegitimate behaviour (Podgórecki 1994). The intuitive law, developed in Polish Russia as an adaptive strategy to foreign rule, 'married ill' with Western-rational methods of administering justice and emphasized the need to understand, on its own terms, the authority that the Poles attributed to law, their relations with freedom and the role of the state.

Poles living on the lands annexed by Prussia also found themselves under a regime that was different from that of the Commonwealth. Initially, Polish law survived, but in the long run it became restricted to matters of inheritance and marital contracts. In 1794–1797 the *Allgemeines Landrecht* brought Prussian codes of law into the former Polish territories (Wandycz 1974: 14) and the Prussian bureaucracy took over effective control. The sound administration was, however, equally used for the proper functioning of the state as well as for the suppression of opposition and minorities, for the Prussian state authorities seemed to restrict themselves to legal methods of harassment.

Modern Prussia was an *Obrigkeitsstaat* (Davies 2005: 85); it operated on the principle that the will of the ruler and his government was supreme. However, Prussia, in contrast to Russia, was also a *Rechtsstaat* – a political community which functioned within the framework of law (Skapska 2002). It operated through legal means and regular procedures enforced by largely uncorrupted and efficient

15 Cf. Banakar's (2008) discussion on Ehrlich's *living law* as not necessarily being more humane and democratic (Banakar 2008: 57).

bureaucracy. In the Prussian tradition of *Rechtsstaat*, the colonial-like rule made the structure of legal authority even more intertwined with the structure of cultural hierarchies. In other words, contests over cultural and religious boundaries and their representations in law became struggles over the nature and structure of political authority (Benton 2002: 2). These conflicts took various forms and revealed how the legal tradition was able to adapt.

In response to the *Rechtsstaat* tradition, another form of adaptation emerged. Polish resistance to the cultural contests of the colonization campaign and *Kulturkampf* confined itself to legal methods of seeking loopholes and inconsistencies in the Prussian legal system. The legendary case of Michał Drzymała set an example for outwitting the law and its apparatus within the boundaries of the legal system. Due to the operation of the Colonization Commission, Poles were not allowed to buy new land or build permanent dwelling-houses in Prussia. Although Drzymała succeeded in legally purchasing land in the district of Wollstein, he found that, as a Pole, he was not allowed to build any permanent property on his land. In response, he set himself up in a wooden caravan and for more than a decade tenaciously resisted all attempts in the courts to remove him (Davies 2005: 96).[16]

The adaptive qualities of the Polish legal tradition not only advanced the plurality of legal tradition but also revealed its potential to accommodate different sources of law and authority. These in turn affected the subsequent attempts to integrate society around the law after the re-emergence of an independent state.

Integrationist Dilemmas of the Second Republic

The end of the First World War in 1918 marked the re-establishment of the independent Poland. The fundamental issue the Polish state faced during the early days of independence, which affected the subsequent legal and political character of the state, was the problem of integration: six different currencies were in circulation, five different regions (Posnania, Silesia, Cieszyn, East Galicia and Central Lithuania) maintained separate administrations, there were four languages of command in the army and two different railway gauges (Davies 2005: 298). The population of Poland was very diverse in terms of ethnic origin, tradition and social relations. In the first years of the Republic there was no integrated economic infrastructure, no common currency and no established financial institutions or government agencies (Davies 2005: 307).

In different provinces, different legal codes and legal systems, encompassing German and Prussian law, Austrian law, Hungarian law, French law and Russian

16 Drzymała lived for 10 years in a wooden caravan on wheels, because, as a Pole, he was forbidden to own a permanent dwelling-house. Each night he would move the caravan 10 or 20 cm within his plot of land. As his caravan was mobile, the Colonization Commission officials could not prove that he lived in a permanent dwelling-house. According to the law, that was the only ground on which Drzymała could have been removed from his land.

law, were in force. Although similar in their content concerning social rights, they reflected different political and legal regimes prevalent under Russian, Prussian and Austrian rule (Bardach et al. 2000: 552).

In order to avoid initial anarchy, the different legal codes and laws remained in force until the unification and codification of Polish law. In 1919 the Codification Commission was set up to integrate different legal systems and to create Polish civil and criminal law. Work on the codification of criminal law took 13 years; the Criminal Law Code was completed in 1931. Codification of the civil law, which required overcoming serious differences in the family, private, property and inheritance laws (prevailing in different provinces of the Republic), took even longer. Work and discussions on the various projects were impeded by the outbreak of the Second World War.

However, no Commission could be established to reconcile different understandings of legal norms and principles and different relationships with the state, which resulted from diverse adaptive strategies towards foreign rule. Although rules can change even overnight, it takes much longer for the law to reach the social tissue. The integration of different traditions and legal *mentâlities* (Legrand 1999) could only take place through everyday interaction between the citizens, their 'new' neighbours and newly introduced institutions.

The integration attempts were additionally hindered by mutual prejudices and stereotypes. Each legal culture tradition represented a different mode of understanding reality; each legal culture purported to formulate an original world-view. Prussian '*Ordnung muss sein*' was very difficult to reconcile with legal mores that Poles under Russian bureaucracy were accustomed to. The differences not only concerned diverse histories, legal orders or judicial texts but also different identities (Legrand 1999: 6).

Perhaps unsurprisingly, the independence of Poland after more than a century of colonial rule resulted once again in freedom exceeding the authority of the law. The Constitution of 1921 produced unstable governments due to the lack of a balance of power between the legislative and executive branches of the government. As a result, a similar problem to that which turned the Noble Democracy into a noble anarchy emerged – the Constitution gave the *Sejm* complete control over the executive (government). The total effect of this constitutional arrangement was an almost complete crippling of the executive branch, as well as political clientelism and corruption in the legislature (Jedruch 1982: 351).[17]

The Great Depression (1929–1935) left Poland's economy in a shambles. Hyperinflation fuelled public unrest and the government was unable to find a quick solution to the mounting unemployment and economic depression. The 20

17 The relations between the *Sejm* and the government under the 1921 Constitution enabled the party leaders in the *Sejm* to use the threat of removing ministers from office to force on them the appointment of political favourites not only to positions in the administration but also to state-run companies under the control of a given ministry (Jedruch 1982: 352).

years of independence saw attempts by the state to take control, but it proved a relatively short period for the quickly changing governments to be in a position to command the authority of law and to restore it. The difficult yet delicate balance between law's legitimacy and authority slipped towards the latter with the May 1926 *coup d'état* and authoritarian means of government, which served Poland until the outbreak of the Second World War.

The last inter-war Constitution of 1935 transformed the Polish parliamentary system into a presidential system, giving the president wide discretionary powers over the executive branch of government and the legislature (parliament) (Jedruch 1982). In the area of civil rights, the social and political rights of citizens became severely restricted and civil duties were stressed over freedoms. The Constitution insisted on ambiguous 'public good' as the borderline for personal freedoms (freedom of conscience, speech and assembly), which resulted in serious limitations to them (Bardach et al. 2000: 506).

The Adaptive Strategies to Socialism

The socialist period saw the development of further adaptive qualities of Polish socio-legal tradition. It was a colonial-like rule with a new legal system and law-enforcement mechanisms. These resulted in further changes of people's relationship with the state (deepening the alienation from the times of the partitions) and produced an economic response in the form of increased reliance on networks and informal economy, which, in turn, amplified people's skills in avoiding and manipulating the law.

The Stalinist times (1945–1953) saw the introduction of new legal statutes, even where many pre-war statutes remained on the books, which created a legal muddle. In the area of criminal law, the so-called Abridged Legal Code introduced new classes of offences: sabotage, organizing or leading a criminal conspiracy and a new crime of 'non-public dissemination' of 'false' information. The state determined what constituted 'false' (Morzol and Ogórek 1992: 63). Each legal fiat covered a wider area and the areas of life not subject to any punishment became ever fewer. 'The rules of the game' were changed unpredictably, being subject to no formal procedures of consequence. At different times, different 'extra-legal' administrative measures, invisible sentencing boards and secret informers took the place of law (Krygier 1990). Laws were drawn up ambiguously and imprecisely in relation to any set purpose – all the better to apply arbitrarily.

With the thaw of October 1956, mobilization became the essential tool of the state in integrating the people around centralized organizational structures. However, due to the almost complete subordination of social relations (political parties, voluntary organizations, trade unions, professional associations and local community associations) to the state, the side-effect was a growing social isolation and atomization of groups and individuals (Wnuk-Lipinski 1991: 5) at the intermediary level of civil society.

Over time, the centrally generated mobilization gradually gave way to connections based on the *do ut des* principle revealed in studies on mechanisms of corruption (Kojder 1995). Within formal state-controlled organizations, micro-structures emerged and provided a forum for the *behind-closed-doors* articulation and mediation of interests. These processes also brought about sharp splits between the public and private spheres of life, known as 'social dimorphism' (Wnuk-Lipinski 1991), 'amoral familism' (Tarkowska and Tarkowski 1988) or the 'society of families' (Wenzel 2009).

The social structures were juxtaposed with the operation of the legal system. The discretionary use of the law in a system in which extra-legal factors often determined the outcome of judicial decisions made people see the communist authorities and the state as the all-powerful *Other*. Among ordinary people, this led to the development of informal networks operating contrary to existing 'official law' (Marody 1987), breaches of law which followed it (Staniszkis 1984) or invocations of legality legitimized by the popular feeling of justice.

The adaptive strategies and changing relationship with the state were also visible in the sphere of the informal economy. Networks that connected individuals and groups to the state economy and bureaucracy also pervaded these institutions. As a result, legality and illegality overlapped in almost every sphere of the lives of the citizens, starting from the state-controlled, centrally planned economy through the government-sponsored system of hard currency bank accounts to the private sector that often, via *spekulacja* (the informal economy), helped the country meet its basic food production and distribution needs.

The informal economy was not a 'second system' but to a greater extent simply a constituent part of the first, that is, the official economy, to which its relationship bore a parallel character. The monopolistic control of the state – and its interlocking economic, political and legal domains – encouraged the blurring of law, politics and criminality. It also encouraged the development of systems of nuanced, albeit informal rules and regulations at the workplace, very often exercised via the network of relationships and practices, which penetrated and stood apart from the state while at the same time being circumscribed by it. In an article entitled 'When Theft is Not Theft', Elżbieta Firlit and Jerzy Chłopecki (1992) detailed the nuances of internal workplace regulations among Polish factory workers under late communism. Their accounts of the informal economy at the workplace revealed that a situation of a worker setting aside goods belonging to the state-owned factory – and therefore belonging to everyone and no one – to take home with him to use in his own *side job* was considered merely *lifting*. On the other hand, another scenario of a worker taking from his fellow worker that which had already been set aside for personal use (sic!) was considered *stealing* and morally wrong (Firlit and Chłopecki 1992: 97).

Although many were engaged in semi-legal activities, people concealed them as they themselves were vulnerable. At any point, a case could be made against them, as practically no one would come away clean from a close investigation. Although *spekulacja* and corruption were social evils for most people, almost everyone in day-to-day life was involved in it on a small scale and considered such activity as normal and acceptable (Wedel 1986: 51). In a society in which people found it necessary to slight the system, the boundaries between legal and illegal were understandably fuzzy – legal and illegal activities operated alongside and in conjunction with one another. What was legal was often considered immoral and what was illegal was often considered moral:

> A lawyer summed up the Polish predicament: 'Everything is so impossible that we have to avoid the law. We have to be more intelligent.' The profound disregard for the legal system is expressed in some of the Polish proverbs: 'Laws exist only to be tested.' Some situations demand dishonesty with authorities; others demand a mixture of truth and fiction. One does not always lie blatantly or tell the uncomfortable truth. Poles have learned to mix the two into credible stories to resolve bureaucratic problems or talk their way out of trouble. (Wedel 1986: 17)

Under the economics of shortage (Kornai 1980), the category 'to arrange' (in Polish: *załatwić*) claimed its place in life and language at the expense of the term 'to buy' (Firlit and Chłopecki 1992: 96). The elaborate etiquette of *załatwić* enabled people to sound one another out and proceed subtly in the making of informal economic arrangements – undertakings that were indeed semi-legal (Wedel 1986: 52). People have become so accustomed to using informal channels that they tended to think of the difference between informal and formal as a technical one:

> during the crisis years of [the] 1980s people became accustomed to asking their friends and relatives to załatwić goods for them. Even after the market situation improved, they still asked their friends and family for help, even with goods that could be obtained through legal and official channels, directly from stores. (Wedel 1986: 78)

This reveals the inertia of earlier adaptations and mentalities, as a result of which an official channel was therefore 'just another one'.

These practices and modes of behaviour, along with the corresponding attitudes, and patterns of thinking have also been visible in the adaptive strategies to the new socio-political conditions after 1989. Buchowski (2001) from a perspective of an anthropologist points to the prevalence of culture and mindsets inherited from the communist past in the context of the employment situation and the local economy of the 1990s. He considers instrumentalism persistent well into the decade, especially in the state-owned companies (Buchowski 2001). As a result of the economic transformation in the 1990s, a substantive group of the population still participated or preferred to participate in the grey economy, as this involvement often brought more profits than regular employment. In the 1990s 'unauthorised services and trade were flourishing. Law breaking too could be viewed as a flexible adaptation to the new situation' (Buchowski 2001: 92).

Although it has been over 20 years since the first elections of 1989, the recent transformation with its extremist politics, volatile economics and bewildering legislation did not inspire much confidence in the state law either. In the public media, the press, academic discourse and literature, the pre-1989 period is continuously referred to. In Poland, as in all former socialist countries, prefixes such as 'pre-' and 'post-' seem to be constantly present. Socialism is visible not only via people's memories but also in contemporary social reality, and, as Elster et al. observe:

> the shadow of the past can be visible at many levels: (1) the past may form the values, ideas, customs and attitudes of the people in Central-Eastern Europe, (2) past choices might serve as a limitation of various actors' political behaviour, (3) old systems may be treated as a model or reference point while shaping the new political and economic institutions, (4) the past offers a repertoire of arguments, which can be used in the political discourse. (Elster et al. 1998: 60)

From Legal Tradition to Legal Culture

From the insights into Polish history across the last millennium, we see that the socio-legal tradition is extremely rich and multi-faceted. Nevertheless, certain themes of the relationship with the law emerge and could be repetitively recalled.

In Polish socio-legal tradition, like other legal traditions, the development of the law was intertwined with the general development of society. However, while in the West the law was synonymous with order and balance between the rights and responsibilities (Bierbrauer 1994), in Poland it was associated with freedom. The law was to protect the nobility from their monarch's absolutist ambitions, and yet to participate in law meant to enjoy its freedoms rather than its responsibilities. This understanding of law among the Polish nobility was, however, subversive to the functioning of the legal system – the law was supposed to be imposed upon 'others' rather than on 'us'. Depending on the various contexts, the borderline between 'us' and 'others' was perceived and appropriated differently. In the event of a tax imposition or summons of the *levée en masse*, it was the king who should be reminded about his role by the whole of the nobility: 'the Polish Kingdom was not for the kings, the Polish kings were for the Kingdom' (Opalinski 1983: 791). In the event of a dispute with one's neighbour, *zajazd* was used to ensure that the other party did not escape 'the law'.

The view of law as freedom rather than rights stipulated that it should not be compromised by any authority. This undermined the role of the monarch, as the traditional creator and executor of law, and resulted in poor law enforcement. Laws which were 'infringing' on the nobility's freedom were often resisted. However, laws which were not executed were not obeyed either. This led to the development of an image of law which does not command authority – the law which could be ignored and dismissed at will.

The third characteristic that strongly emerges in the Polish socio-legal tradition is its adaptive qualities. The times of political dependence and the alienating character of the state law saw the development of various adaptive strategies to different state rules. However, these were often subversive to the state law and reinforced the alienation. The often extra-legal methods of organizing everyday life, demonstrating the transformative qualities of the Polish socio-legal tradition, could be observed during the Noble Republic, the partitions, the Second Republic and under socialism.

It is therefore possible to propose a conclusion that legal tradition, understood as legal principles and institutions that have been developed and applied through a significant run of history, is shaping the contemporary thinking of people belonging to that tradition (Kurkchiyan 2010). In order to understand how people relate themselves to law today, it is necessary to examine how the perception of law was produced and understood within the specific legal tradition and then to draw out its social implications, such as how people interpret the law, what expectations they have and how they behave towards it in their everyday lives (Kurkchiyan 2010). However, the influence of the legal tradition on the formation of the collective legal culture is only part of the story. The next chapter therefore turns to contemporary values, attitudes to law and patterns of legal behaviour. The comparative data suggests that although the legal tradition of Poland is clearly significant, it is not the only factor responsible for constituting the mass perception of what law is and how it should be implemented.

Chapter 7
Polish Contemporary Legal Culture in Comparative Perspective

The previous chapter provided an insight into Polish socio-legal traditions, and although the past might still have an impact on people's attitudes to law and behaviour towards it, it is not safe to assume that history or tradition alone determine the present. While the socio-legal tradition provides interesting insights into how the current relationship with law might have developed over the past years, it does not necessarily convey much about the character of the relationship with law now. Hence, further sociological analysis is needed to supplement the picture and trace the links (if any) between the past and the present.

Therefore, using the tools of sociological analysis – focus groups, surveys and interviews – this chapter turns to the values, attitudes and interpretations of law currently prevalent in Poland to see how different (or coherent) they are with the historical narrative. It also voices the agency of the Polish migrants themselves in tracing their pre-migratory experiences of workplace regulations, employment law and labour arrangements expressed in their recollections of the relationship between employer and employee, labour contracts and health and safety provisions.

One of the well-established and fruitful ways of characterization – making it possible to capture the distinctive nuances and subtleties – is putting the subject in question in a comparative perspective (Nelken 2004b). This chapter therefore provides insights into the Polish contemporary values, attitudes and experiences of law with reference to British legal culture in order to understand their contribution to the shape and characteristics of Polish post-2004 EU enlargement migrants' relationship with law in the UK.

The Image of Law: Law as Rules versus Law as Structure

What does law mean? What is meant by law? I posed these questions to see how law is embedded in larger frameworks of social structure and what is meant by law (what the law is 'for'), with the aim of providing a 'thick description' of law as a 'local knowledge' (Geertz 1983).

Although both Polish and British respondents agree that the law is important – 'Without the law there would be a mayhem' (Sylwia, Focus Group (FG) 2) or 'Law gives structure to everyday life' (Nick, FG 4) – the attribution of importance embedded in peoples' interpretations seems to be different.

To the majority of Polish people, law is seen as a collection of texts, paragraphs and written rules. This is because the law is synonymous with black letter law, the 'law in the books' (Pound 1910). As can be seen from Table 7.1, for just over 43 per cent of the Polish respondents, the law corresponds to written laws, rules and regulations, followed by the concepts of order and discipline (39.7 per cent).

Table 7.1 The Image of Law

When I say the word 'law', what images come to your mind?	Poland (%)	UK (%)
Written laws, rules and regulations	43.2	30.9
Order and discipline	39.7	30.9
People involved in making or applying the law	13.2	27.4
Mixed	2.4	7.2
None	0.4	1.3
Other/don't know/NA	1.1	2.3
Total	100.0	100.0

Source: 'Legal Cultures in Transition' survey 2008

In addition to its written and regulative qualities, the law as a text creates an image of 'special knowledge' that can only be learned, understood and legislated by professionally trained people. Therefore, law for the Polish respondents is a sphere reserved for professionals. Law in the form of written rules and regulations is complicated, rigid and better if created and applied by qualified people. As expressed by the focus group participants:

> To me, it makes me think of paragraphs, ordinances, I'm not going to use that professional language because I have nothing to do with it, luckily. (Iga, FG 2)

> I think the law should be made by professionals, not lay people. That's why we have universities and some kinds of schools that should educate good lawyers who would make good laws. It would be appropriate to ask: what is 'good law'? [It's] professional law. (Mirek, FG 2)

> I am not a lawyer. The law is created by educated people, who mix things up so that I will never know what it is all about. (Andrzej, FG 3)

> The law should be created by experts and they would then invite members of parliament and tell them why this law is good. (Grazyna, FG 3)

The image of law as a professional activity – the professionalization of law – is another aspect of 'the law in the books' characteristic, making it a discipline within the specialization of lawyers and experts. The highly professional character of the law suggests a particular, almost exclusive place for it in society. Due to its expert origins, it figures as if on a pedestal – it may command respect, dignity or admiration. When asked about the use and purpose of law at the normative level, many Polish people expected the law to regulate relationships between people:

> The law is important, because it regulates the relations between people. (Janina, FG 3)

> Laws regulate how people interact in a society. It has to be regulated somehow, in a society, in a group. (Zdzislaw, FG 5)

> The law regulates everything in life. The law says what is less important, what is more important, what should be the reference point, quite simply, what should be obeyed. The reference is to tell us if we are doing the right thing or not, as people. (Ania, FG 7)

Therefore, at the level of social expectations, society as a whole should be based on highly regarded and professional legal rules and codes. These are the rules that are expected to go deep through the social tissue and regulate relationships and the organization of people themselves. The expert origins of the rules, although external to 'true' social relations, nevertheless demand conformity. As one of the respondents put it: 'We must adapt. There always used to be some law' (Sylwia, FG 4). This view was expanded upon as follows:

> To be able to function in a social group, one has to observe certain rules, the rules accepted by the society, *not the ones we set for ourselves*. When we follow our own set of rules *it may not go along with the rules of the group*. Besides, it seems to me that all kinds of codes, collections of laws, such as school code – [they all tell you] what to do and what not to do. (Danuta, FG 8, emphasis added)

What emerges from this discussion is a dual image of law based on at least two different sets of rules. There is an image of socially desired and highly regarded law – certain rules, written codes and regulations at the level of society, which are expected to regulate relationships and the organization of individuals. Yet – perhaps due to their professional origins and character – this image of law appears to be in opposition or at least external to the second set of rules – 'rules we set for ourselves' (Danuta, FG 8). This inevitably creates another tension, when the rigid, written and complex rules are expected to be applied to a flexible, ever-changing and interpretative area such as everyday life. Perhaps unsurprisingly, such an exercise leads to confusion, a perceived ineffectiveness of law and stimulates behavioural strategies of 'keeping clear of the law altogether' (Zbigniew, FG 2).

Therefore, whenever the relationship between the law and everyday life is invoked, the experience of law seems rather complicated and perhaps inconvenient for people to use. As one of the focus group participants summarized: 'I think we've all been in many situations when we wanted to use that law and there were some hurdles' (Maria, FG 3). Others stressed the alienation of law from everyday life:

> Now in general, the law is only there for the state. The people don't benefit from it. The state gets all the advantages of all this. God forbid you have a number of income sources and you have to get square with the Revenue Office. One lady at the office tells you to do it this way, another calls you back and says it's not like that. And all this for this little money that you happened to earn. (Sylwin, FG 4)

In contrast, the British respondents saw the law more as a component of everyday life, as a communication process and as people involved in making and applying the law (cf. Table 7.1). The distribution of answers seems to indicate that the images of law as rules, regulations (30.9 per cent), order and discipline (30.9 per cent) are followed very closely by the image of law associated with the people involved in the legislation and law-making process (27.4 per cent). In the experiences of the British focus group participants, the law had more to do with everyday life and what is now seen as law had actually originated from the 'common practice, the way it's been for hundreds of years' (Nick, FG 4), with 'common sense' as the basis for regulations.

The consensus seemed to relate to the observation that although the details of legal rules might be complicated and technical, 'the operations of the mind in the domain of law seem to be based on common sense' (Vinogradoff 1913: 9):

> [Law should be based on] Common sense. Decency as well. (Alex, FG 1)

> Common sense should prevail and the law should have some kind of common sense to it. (Martin, FG 8)

> There's common sense. You know what's right, and you know what's wrong. (Keira, FG 3)

> A normal person is going to be within the law. You wouldn't make it so strict that 99 per cent of people fall outside the law. It has to be that 99 per cent of people are within the law and the people on the extremes at either end then are falling outside of it. Otherwise its unenforceable, everybody would be in prison. (Martin FG 6)

> If the common sense approach is not taken in law, then there are going to be individuals who are going to be discriminated against. It's got to be the common sense theme. (Wayne, FG 2)

The law was often perceived by the British people as the structure, the very general overarching skeleton of guidelines to everyday life, agreed upon and embedded in actions and reasoning:

> [The law] is what gives structure. Structure and order. It does teach a code of conduct. (Nick, FG 3)

> Because of our law and the structure of the law, we now have respect, hopefully, most of the time for one another. And there is an order, a way we conduct ourselves in society. (Nick, FG 3)

> [Without law] well society would sort of fall apart without it, if there's no structure. (Claire, FG 5)

> [Law is] sticking to guidelines, what's right and what's wrong, basically. (Michael, FG 8)

> It's never black and white, so I think they should have their guidelines and then work within that. Common sense. (Dorothy, FG 3)

This nuanced distribution of accents in voicing their image of law (i.e. what people mean by law) between the Polish and British respondents could partially be attributed to the historical differences in the origins of law in the civil and common tradition, respectively. In Poland, the civil law tradition, with the existence of strict, rationally derived written rules, codes of law that pre-conditioned and reinforced order and discipline, was preceded by years of consensual decision making and privileges for the nobility as derived from Polish customary law. Therefore, the civil law in Poland developed mostly during the colonial-like rule during the partitions (cf. Chapter 6), when the state as the source of law was represented either by the Austrian Emperor, the Prussian Kaiser or the Russian Tsar. All three of them – to different degrees – were considered to be foreign rulers and 'their' laws, although respected, were not regarded by the Polish people as integral to their ways of life. The majority of the Poles did not identify themselves with the colonial-like rule of the state-law.

The civil law tradition which developed particularly in the Austrian and Prussian partitions (and was briefly introduced to the Russian partition with the Napoleonic Code and the Duchy of Warsaw (1807–1815)) brought with it written codes, rules, codices and legal professionalism that were nonetheless quite distant from the earlier legal custom. The image of law as formalistic, written rules very much dates back to the period of Partitions, yet the popular, ambivalent attitude to it – due to the alienating character of the state and state law reinforced during the communist period – seemed to prevail for generations. As a result the law as 'special knowledge reserved for professionals', as originating from this tradition, is therefore quite distant from 'the rules we set for ourselves' (Danuta, FG 8).

British law, on the other hand, has its origins in common law and, as a result, the British respondents in their experiences pointed more to the process-oriented character of the legislation and stressed the human factor and influence of the lawmakers in creating social order and discipline. For both groups the law is important, yet in the Polish case perhaps a rather close normative reliance on laws to regulate relationships among the people, when their rigidity and strictness are widely recognized, makes it rather difficult for people to live up to their high expectations of law and reinforces the general feeling of 'never being too comfortable with the laws' (Sylwin, FG 4). In the British case, the law is the overarching structure enabling the flexibility of interpretations and behaviours.

The insights into the current research on the nature of the state law and the legal system in Poland seem to reinforce the rather rigid, complicated and confusing nature of 'professional' law. During the times of transition from the socialist regime to democracy, it was perhaps not surprising to observe the provisional, tentative and changeable character of laws rather than their desired certainty and permanency. The passing of a number of acts by parliament since 1989[1] was not necessarily followed by their clarity and intelligibility. The normative acts were formulated in a lengthy and descriptive language; they mixed notions from different branches of law and, as a result, they were lacking uniformity in terminology. This, among other issues, led to the incompleteness of patterns of procedures which were subject to regulation. As Zirk-Sadowski observed, in many cases the legal acts did not even contain the definitions of the notions used in them, which made it possible to use the legal text to omit the law and to apply acts that were even contradictory to the aims of regulation (Zirk-Sadowski 2006: 304).

The lack of cohesion in the system of law is also reflected by the workings of the Constitutional Tribunal in Poland. As the report on the workings of the Constitutional Tribunal prepared by Stawecki et al. (2008) observed, between 1997 and 2008, the majority of the regulations declared by the Tribunal as contrary to the Polish Constitution were of public (state) law origin (Stawecki et al. 2008: 82).

More recent research by Bukowski et al. (2008) revealed that the interpretation of EU regulations in Polish secondary legislation, taking the form of ever-changing, rigid, unstable and complicated legal procedures, posed serious barriers and obstacles in the process of the awarding and implementation of EU funds in Poland (Bukowski et al. 2008). The elaborate path of using European funds as expressed in the Polish legislation and procedures – which, it should be noted, were more complicated than Slovakian or Czech requirements (Bukowski et al. 2008: 446) – caused extensive delays during the project selection, fund transfer and expenditure control phases..

1 During the third term of office, legislators adopted 640 acts, while during the second term of office 473 acts were adopted. The average number of acts adopted at each of the meetings of parliament between the third and the fourth terms of office rose from five to nine (Zirk-Sadowski 2006: 302).

Freedom from Law versus Freedom within the Law

Law and freedom seem to continue to figure together in peoples' interpretation and experiences of law. However, the distribution of accents in this relationship has changed. In the case of Polish contemporary attitudes to law, one finds that while law was originally synonymous and strongly intersected with freedom, it currently contradicts it. The Polish interviewees saw law as a collection of rules and regulations. In their experiences, the law flowing from these written rules is often rigid and restrictive, limiting their freedom of activities and undertakings:

> Well, I think that if there is more law then the situation gets worse because there are more restrictions. The law never goes towards tolerance but always towards restrictions and that's the truth. Someone comes up with something, 99 per cent of our laws ban something, so to speak. They regulate things. These are all regulations which impose things on us. (Mirek, FG 2)

Generally, most of the Polish respondents agreed that law does not make people feel free but, due to its restrictive qualities, usually limits their personal freedom and scope for action. The key to unlock this understanding is to have a closer look at what, exactly, is meant by freedom? The discourse of law as freedom and the restrictions on it begs the question: whose freedoms and whose restrictions do the respondents refer to? The association of law with freedom rather than with rights and responsibilities is deeply embedded in the Polish socio-legal tradition (cf. Chapter 6). The image of law as 'freedom for myself and restrictions for others' nevertheless suggests that it perhaps has more in common with an 'anarchic' freedom (Davies 2005), a freedom that comes without responsibility and without restrictions. As summarized by one of the focus group participants:

> The non-smoking regulations in private cars – to me it's a paranoia. If I want to poison myself in my own car, I should be free to do it! (Tadeusz, FG 2)

The restrictions are defined with reference to others, who should be kept at bay from impinging on one's freedom. The law is therefore required to restrict others from limiting one's freedom rather than to allow the same scope of freedom to others. From the times of the Noble Republic, the idea of freedom seems to be preserved closely in the national imagination and reflected in the educational curricula. This tradition is often referred to in popular conversations and Polish people still display it to a considerable extent:

> This is a nation, this is special to our nation. Poles are difficult, everyone is, so to speak, individualistic. (Przemek, FG 2)

> We have the heart of a knight, the heart of a vigorous noblemen. (Grazyna, FG 2)

> We have it in our blood. Hitler didn't defeat us, Stalin didn't defeat us so who will? Ziobro [the former Minister of Justice] didn't defeat us and Kaczynski [the former president] didn't. We have it in our blood. No system will help us. (Robert, FG 1)

The deeply embedded intuition toward the law as protecting 'my freedoms' means that, in practice, whenever the law imposes limitations by the way of regulations, it is met by resistance and alienation, as intuitively it should not restrict one's freedom. In Poland, people display a high value and regard for law because they acknowledge that without it there would be no orderly society. Nevertheless, this is accompanied by deeply embedded animosity and resistance towards anything that restricts them. As illustrated by one of the focus group participants:

> In Germany when there is a ban, for instance a speed limit of 50 something kilometres then perhaps one citizen in 100,000 will break it. And in this country one citizen in 100,000 will not break it if the police was not around. Nobody will stick to the speed limit knowing there is no police. It's hard with Poles. (Przemek, FG 2)

Therefore, when the current, shared image of law as written laws, rules and regulations comes together with the image of law as restricting one's freedom, it results in an ambivalent relationship with law. In people's interpretations and intuitions this is not what the law should stand for. Therefore, perhaps unsurprisingly, in the case of restrictive laws, laws that impose certain conditions: 'Poles would obey the laws only when they feel a whip on their bottom. Otherwise they would dodge it' (Janina, FG 2).

The current image of restrictive, complicated and often contradictory laws has therefore, in the course of historic events and experiences, drifted far from the old and imagined idea of law as freedom. This suggests an interesting evolution in Polish socio-legal tradition from 'law *as* a superb robe, freedom' (Starnawski 1972: 556) in the times of the Noble Republic to the current, largely preferred attitude of being free *from* law in the sense of 'not having to do anything with it at all' (Sylwin, FG 4):

> To me [the law] is important but I wanted to say that it's best not to have any dealings with it in everyday life. In general, the law is to tell us what we can and what we can not do, and we should move around in our daily life so as to *keep clear of the law*. It is important not to expose oneself to it. (Zbigniew, FG 7, emphasis added)

When faced with limiting and restricting laws, Polish people admit to by-passing the law in order to 'get things done' (Grazyna, FG 5) or simply 'keep clear of the law' (Marysia, FG 2) altogether.

In contrast, the dominant image of law among the British respondents is an overarching structure of guidelines that are close to everyday life as it is based on the common sense and process-oriented law-making tradition of the common law. Such law is set for a certain purpose – it comes with rights but also obligations. The latter are accepted as part of the deal, the other side of the coin. Perhaps due to the consensual and overarching common sense approach in characterizing the nature of the law, the order that emerges is neither strict nor too rigid – it allows for the flexibility of legal behaviour and experiences. The structure of law then becomes filled in with the flesh of people's subjective interpretations, ideas and goals of how to use it in everyday life:

> This is the law, but then you have human beings carrying out that law and you can't pre-empt people's personalities or what side of the bed they got off on the wrong day, their ambitions and stuff … So you have *a template* which is within the best intentions and we as human beings have to do our best to live within that template. (Karen, FG 2, emphasis added)

> The law can only do so much and it's a guideline and then you as a person or a member of your community have to take on board your own responsibilities. (Karen, FG 2)

British respondents were more or less content with the legal system, as they saw the purpose of the rules derived from common sense and at the same time felt free to exercise the latter in taking responsibility for the application of the law in everyday life. The flexibility and freedom of interpretations *within* the template, *within* the structure of the law figured prominently as one of the dominant characteristics of experience of the law in everyday life:

> Well actually I think there is a core set of laws which I think the majority will follow and then I think there are some laws which *people make their own risk assessment* on like breaking the speed limit. (Duncan, FG 2, emphasis added)

The degree of freedom in taking responsibilities for one's actions within the overarching structure of the law as an inseparable feature of the British 'ways of law' was also observed by some of my Polish interviewees in the UK:

> In the UK, you have these yellow lights. Everybody knows that this is the passage and the car stops. But it is up to you which way you cross the street, you can cross it between the lights, you can cross 20 meters on each side. There will not be a policeman waiting for you around the corner asking for your ID and questioning the mode you chose to cross the street. (Interview No. 18)

I do not intend to say, however, that the British people obey all the rules down to the last letter. Some of them openly expressed instances when either they themselves or people they knew broke the law:

> However, I bet every one of us in the room speeds at times and that's a very interesting debate. (Nick, FG 2)

> Smoking. I don't think anybody obeys that law. The amount of people I still see smoking in their car and company vehicle and such like that. (Gemma, FG 3)

> Drunk and disorderly, or centres of towns. Mass law breaking at the weekends. That's people who would normally be law abiding during the week. (Lee, FG 8)

The British respondents generally acknowledged that there *are* laws and rules in the UK that are broken. At the same time, the examples of breaking the law that the respondents recalled were not considered subversive to the legal system as a whole. They encompassed mostly small, petty traffic offences such as 'crossing the street at a red light', speeding (by far the most popular), parking a car in non-designated areas or parking in disabled parking slots to save time. In the opinion of the respondents, these were 'small things that did not harm anyone' (FG 8):

> All those [speeding] laws are set up for benefiting the Council or its coffers. It's got nothing to do with whether you're doing 30 or 34 [mph]. It bears no relevance really on what is going to happen. (Alex, FG 4)

> You probably feel that there are a lot more important things that they [the police] should be going to pursue and we would probably all agree with you. (Arlene, FG 7)

> If it's not going to harm somebody else or something like that … that's the majority of it [motivation to break the law]. (Ryan, FG 8)

At the same time, these instances of law-breaking did not point to the dynamics of social acceptance of the very act of 'breaking the law' among the focus group participants. People reflected on law-breaking as a reality, yet not a socially accepted reality, and generally displayed the attitude of obeying the law:

> So I think there are some laws like that [that people break] but I think broadly, most people abide by the law. (Duncan, FG 2)

> You can do it [break the speed limit] by accident, yes, but it's 40, so you've got to set the limit at 40. As far as the roads are concerned, where kids, where anybody can be killed, I think you've got to stick by those guidelines. (Anne, FG 5)

Law without Authority versus Binding Law

In Poland the view of law as strict rules and regulations, as an area reserved for professional specialists, reinforces the image of law as detached from the notion of freedom not only due to its restrictive nature and complexity of written codes, but also due to the values and attitudes towards the legislators themselves. The image of 'unprofessional' and 'corrupt' legislators who pass and apply the law 'depending on who is in power' (Przemek, FG 2) in turn results in the general notion of law as not commanding authority.

The analysis of the relationship between the citizens and officials brings to the forefront the issues of trust, lack of trust and distrust in their reciprocal relations, questions relating to the legal competence of the legislators, whether the product of their work reflects the general public interest and translates the interests of different social groups into the legal categories or – on the contrary – conceals the 'privatization' of the public interest (Zirk-Sadowski 2006). The importance of trust has long been emphasized by social and political theorists from Locke and De Tocqueville to Putnam (2000) and civil society theorists. In Galligan's opinion, the relationship of trust between the people and officials, as one of the defining qualities of modern legal order, is necessary for the law to function in modern society (Galligan 2007: 131) and therefore has consequences for the analysis of the legal culture.

For the British respondents, the strong intersection of law with the people that use, make and apply it – the government, public officials and local MPs – is reflected in the situations where the local representatives of the law are recalled as the first point of contact, when there are problems with the law or when the law needs changing:

> If there are some troublesome laws that need changing, then turn to your MP. (Megan, FG 3)

> Well I think that in the case [of an unreasonable and unjust law] you should tell your local MP because they're the ones that speak for us, that's why we elect them to do those things and they go and speak for all of us. That's the only thing you can do. (Rachel, FG 4)

This is not to say that the British general public is not critical of its legislators, public servants and MPs. The MPs are considered to be accountable for the laws they produce and are not perceived as standing above the law. As a result, there seemed to be a general consensus among the British respondents that law, as the general structure, stands above everybody in society and everyone has to abide by its rules:

> We live in a country where everybody has to abide by the laws of the state and the government and nobody is above it. I don't think we'd function correctly if somebody was above the law. (Wayne FG 3)

This reveals the general consensus around the functioning of the legal system and helps to draw references about the social attitudes towards the institutional capacity of the courts and the institutional processes as a whole. If the governors happen to break the law or put themselves above it, there is the general trust in the public institutions to make them accountable for their actions:

> We've had government ministers who have fallen foul to the law, they've disobeyed the law, and even with their high position and all the money that they've acquired, they've not been able to get out of a prison sentence. (Nick, FG 4)

> People that set laws should never break them. So they lose their moral right to set laws once they've broken them. (Sarah, FG 5)

> It's really comforting to see that it [law] applies to them too. If he broke the law he's got to be subject to the same [law] that you and I are subject to. (Nick, FG 4)

Despite the criticism of the legislators as individuals, there was the general trust in the legislature (as an institution) to draft clear and effective laws. It was not over-enthusiastic but rather consolidated around the consensus of democracy being the 'only game in town' (Linz and Stephan 1996):

> Who else is going to do it if the government don't? They look as if they do [are capable of drafting good laws], don't they? I mean they're not perfect, nobody is perfect. You've got to, really, trust somebody. (Margaret, FG 8)

> Whichever political party is in power, at the end of the day, to get a law passed and put through … I think that it's still the best place to do it, even if it's not perfect. (Lee, FG 8)

> But I suppose you've got to rely on the professionalism of, the know-how of civil servants, really. (Phil, FG 2)

In Poland, on the other hand, the government and the MPs were not considered professional enough to deal with the law or to apply it effectively. Their competence to pass effective laws was consequently largely distrusted:[2]

---

2 The lack of identification between the Polish citizens and their state officials was also reflected by the most recent opinion poll by the Centre for Public Opinion Research (CBOS) in Poland (2006) on the *Prestige of Professions, Professional Honesty and Integrity.*

> To me the law means the makers of the law. And my attitude towards their mandate is very negative because I think the law should be made by professionals, not lay people. (Mirek, FG 1)

According to a 2008 survey,[3] 51.2 per cent of the Polish general public, as reflected in Table 7.2, did not trust the government to draft clear and effective laws. By comparison, the same question asked to members of the British public revealed that 62.2 per cent of the respondents did trust the government to draft good laws.

Table 7.2 Trust in the Government and Parliament

The government and parliament can be trusted to draft clear and effective laws	Poland (%)	UK (%)
Agree	37.9	62.2
Disagree	51.2	35.6
Both Agree and disagree	3.1	0.4
Neither agree nor disagree	3.2	0.5
Other/don't know/NA	4.6	1.3
Total	100.0	100.0

Source: 'Legal Cultures in Transition' survey 2008

The relationship between the Polish people and their governors is best described as a sceptical one. What could explain this ambiguity? The sense of inequality before the law – Polish respondents often doubted whether in Poland people were treated fairly and considered equal before the law:

> The law is not just and equal for everyone, so to say. (Grazyna, FG 4)

> If only the law were equal and treated every thief the same. But in Poland it depends who you're dealing with, and with some they look the other way. (Grazyna, FG 4)

The feelings and impressions of inequality before the law were mainly recalled when describing relations between citizens and state officials in a situation of unequal power bargaining. The state representatives were often perceived as

Polish legislators – MPs – scored the lowest of all, only 7 per cent of positive opinions, high state officials scored 14 per cent and local officials 21 per cent, in comparison to academics (68 per cent), nurses (60 per cent) and teachers (50 per cent) (CBOS 2006b).

3 This survey was conducted as part of the 'Legal Cultures in Transition' project.

people with higher economic status, affluence and position in society who would not hesitate to use it for their own benefit:

> As a little chap I get frustrated. Because we are daily inundated with messages that ordinary people have to comply with the law, whereas there are people who are above the law. (Andrzej, FG 2)

> I share the group's opinions because the law protects people who hold important positions, who have money. And the ordinary citizen gets kicked onto [sic] a certain part of the body, excuse me. It ruins people. We can't afford to hire some super-great lawyers who will protect us against sanctions. And a member of parliament or a businessman is well connected and will wriggle out of it. We see new examples every day, on television. Sadly, this is our Polish reality. (Marcin, FG 5)

> The law is not enforced equally. When one has committed a crime, an offence, one was driving under the influence of alcohol; it should not matter whether it was John Doe or [the] prime minister. They all should be treated equally and convicted equally. But they aren't treated equally, because the prime minister has connections. (Interview No. 26)

> I have the impression that rich people in Poland have different rights than poorer ones, if we're talking about this. For instance, someone who is rich might stray from the straight and narrow but I think he won't be punished as severely as someone who is poorer. (Ewa, FG 6)

At the surface level, the responses reveal an active dislike of people with extraordinary positions and profits. Some researchers in Poland try to explain this attitude. In her insights into discourses of 'normal life' in contemporary Poland and among the post-2004 EU enlargement Polish migrants in the UK, Galasinska invoked the theme of 'moderation', which has been influential both in communist and post-communist Poland. Arguably, the discourse of moderation originated from communist propaganda, where it was marked by strong anti-materialistic tendencies that aimed to promote post-materialistic values and an aversion towards growing rich (Galasinska and Kozłowska 2009: 100).

Prior to 1989, 'emotion was valued over pragmatism, and people who could afford commodities were perceived as having excessive needs. However, those who could only provide for their own basic needs were also frustrated with their position' (Galasinska and Kozłowska 2009: 100). And yet the continuation of this phenomenon was still very much present in the reality of the post-communist era, where the displayed ownership of middle-class status symbols tended to evoke appreciation but also envy among those who could not 'keep up'. Social scientists named this phenomenon 'envious egalitarianism' (Machonin 1997).

However, at a deeper level, the negative image of those in favourable economic positions within Polish society does not necessarily refer to the economic difference as such but to the fact that this difference was very often translated into inequality before the law. In public evaluations during the post-communist transformation, 'individuals grabbing money (speculators, middlemen, corrupt government officials) were deemed to be morally reprehensible' (Galasinska and Kozłowska 2009: 100) and were perceived as trying to 'work the system' to obtain scarce resources, goods and benefits (not always of a direct material value). A total of 75.2 per cent of the Polish general public agreed with the statement that the government and parliament in Poland were 'too favourable towards the rich and powerful'. However, this negative sentiment was not directed against the differences in earnings as such, but the fact that they were translated into privileges, perquisites and fringe benefits when dealing with law.

Table 7.3 The Government and Parliament's Goals for Drafting New Laws

The government and parliament draft laws for their own personal advantage or business interests rather than for the good of the country	Poland (%)	UK (%)
Agree	62.6	45.2
Disagree	25.2	50.3
Both agree and disagree	3.2	1.0
Neither agree nor disagree	2.9	0.7
Other/don't know/NA	6.1	2.8
Total	100.0	100.0

Source: 'Legal Cultures in Transition' survey 2008

A total of 62.6 per cent of the Polish public regarded the laws passed by parliament as being drafted for the government and parliament's personal advantage or business interests rather than for the good of the country (cf. Table 7.3). Only 25.2 per cent of the respondents disagreed with this statement. The tendency to respond to the influence and lobby on the side of the legislators when drafting new laws was perceived as compromising to the law as a method of social ordering and reinforced distrust in political and state institutions, deepening the alienation between the general public and the government.

Alongside the perceived inequality before the law, another related problem that may be helpful in explaining the lack of legitimacy of law is the rather widely acknowledged corruption among the Polish political class. Table 7.4 demonstrates that 53.8 per cent of the Polish respondents considered that the Polish government and the state officials were willing to take bribes. In contrast, 60.2 per cent of the British general public disagreed when asked about potential corrupt practices among their MPs.

Table 7.4 The Government and Parliament's Corruption

The government and parliament are willing to take bribes	Poland (%)	UK (%)
Agree	53.8	31.4
Disagree	20	60.2
Both agree and disagree	4.3	0.2
Neither agree nor disagree	6.0	1.5
Other/don't know/NA	15.9	6.7
Total	100.0	100.0

Source: 'Legal Cultures in Transition' survey 2008

What the survey results suggest is that in Poland, the lack of authority on the side of the law is attributed to the legislators themselves. The strict, limiting yet vague legal rules result, on the one hand, from the haste and unprofessional preparation of legal acts, but, on the other hand, are frequently perceived as attempts to manipulate or water down the effects of regulation by legislators (who are prone to bribery and lobbying). As a result, the structure and the body of law are often instrumentally used to disguise private interest as a public one.

Consequences for Law Enforcement

The law's ability to command authority has important consequences for its enforcement. In the UK, among the focus group respondents, trust in the government to pass effective laws very often translated into trust in the laws themselves:

> But the law is there to help you. So if you have an accident and you crash into me and my car is written off, the law has helped me in some way by making it the law that you have insurance … whatever the government is doing now they are passing the laws that going to help somebody so yes, I guess they are there to help us. (Sarah, FG 2)

> Respect the law no matter what it is because it's being enforced and it's there for a reason … I'm trying to say they've got [the laws] in place for a reason. They just have to let people know what the reason is, the structure, the outcome

> is going to be this in five years' time because we're doing this now. You know, I think if you make people more aware they're more than likely to follow in line with the law. You have to trust it. (Debbie, FG 4)

The general consensus around the law as binding in the UK makes it easier and takes less effort to enforce it. The majority of the British focus group participants considered themselves and other people in society as law abiding:

> If the laws being passed, it stands, you've got to abide by it. (Lee, FG 8)

> Most people [obey the law]. I think most people. (Lyn, FG 6)

> I think people see there is a benefit in it [abiding by the laws] in the long run. When explained in the long run they [people] know it's better. And everyone else is doing it anyway so you accept it. (Jeff, FG 5)

In Poland, on the other hand, the image of law as not commanding authority was reflected by the frequent recollections of breaking the law. For the Polish respondents, when they talked about their relationship with law, their responses would often be intertwined with anecdotes, examples or reasoning for breaking the law:

> And sometimes the law makes no sense. Then we break it consciously. Because it's set up in this way so we need to break it. (Marysia, FG 1)

> In many cases you can get more things done if you break the law. (Grazna, FG 1)

> You know, there is this old saying, 'the law exists so that people could test it'. (Stefan, FG 5)

> I bet none of us have always lived by the book. Everybody breaks the law to some extent. Even if you jaywalk. But the thing is you cannot live strictly by the law. (Sylwia, FG 4)

These open, sometimes rather bold statements regarding the act of breaking the law (for whatever purpose) observable in the Polish focus groups point to a rather ambivalent relationship between the Polish people and their law. They suggest that in Poland, although the image of the law – as the ideal regulator of the relationships between people – is highly regarded, it is nevertheless quite disengaged from everyday life.

Therefore, what concerns people in their everyday dealings with the law is not necessarily the written rules, codes and regulations that are problematic, but their lack of authority and therefore enforcement by the public officers, courts, state officials and the Polish people themselves:

> I mean, the law doesn't cause problems perhaps but it makes things difficult if you want to enforce your rights or some other things. There's excessive bureaucracy, a multitude of laws that contradict one another. An ordinary citizen is not able to grasp … (Jacek, FG 8)

> Personally I prefer to break the law and get things done. If I need to follow the fully legal path, that would cost me so much nerves. (Grazyna, FG 1)

> Things are just different in our country. It's not bad, I think. The problem lies in enforcement and in our nature. We, Polish people, we don't obey anything. (Beata, FG 6)

The examples which the respondents gave to support their attitudes towards law enforcement in Poland were mainly informed by their dealings with laws and regulations concerned with the their common day-to-day actions and matters of importance – social security provisions, benefits and TV and radio licenses:

> If there is a law [what is the point of changing it?]. Because it is impossible to enforce it. It spoils people and everybody thinks that a law has been introduced. For example, I have to pay public radio and TV fees. Collectability is zero. I pay because I like to. Let's say I feel bad when I don't pay. And nobody else pays. (Kasia, FG 3)

The respondents' experiences of tax officers, local bureaucracy or social security officials who 'represent the law' and are responsible for its application at the grassroots level informed their opinions of inconsistent law enforcement and execution in Poland. According to the Polish Public Opinion Research Centre survey of 2007, more than a third of the people (37 per cent) did not agree with the statement that the 'local administration offices are focused on serving their function to the public and proper customer service' (CBOS 2007: 3). Almost half of the respondents (48 per cent) admitted that they were not familiar with the rules of the decision making concerning their applications pending with the administration. This could lead to a twofold conclusion – either the applicants' legal knowledge concerning their rights was low or the decision-making process in question lacks transparency and accountability (CBOS 2007).

The functioning of local bureaucracy, the excessive red tape and formal requirements do not inspire much confidence in the quality of the law or encourage dealings with the local offices. Talking about his legal expectations upon arrival in the UK, an owner of a small business in Poland, when interviewed in the UK, did not regard them as particularly high. Drawing upon his personal experiences with the tax officers in Poland, he considered the state law to be too harsh, too complicated, overloaded and inconsistently applied:

> And the Polish institutions, tax offices were chasing only the people who operated legally. It was easier to track them, and, due to the proper documentation, point out that this and that tax has not been paid. They completely did not care about the people from the black market, as of course, they had no way of tracking them in the first place. The officers and inspectors had the right to close your business for any reason. Very often, if they did not receive a tribute from the local businessman, they would openly say: 'We will destroy you.' It happened to me. If you gave them a bribe you were safe for some time at least. If you did not give them a bribe, then it did not matter whether your business was legal and you had all the regulations in order. They would find something for you anyway. (Interview No. 4)

The absurdity and arbitrariness presented in this 'bottom-up' perspective of the functioning of the Polish local bureaucracy – as expressed by the interviewees and focus group participants – is supported by several sociological and anthropological studies which stress the importance of connections and the prevalence of dishonest procedures (Dunn 1999; Laciak 2005; Miszalska 1996) rooted in ubiquitous informal networks from communist times (Kula 2006; Wedel 1992).

Other interviewees representing the small and medium-sized business sectors supported these views of legal overload and lack of consistency, drawing from their personal experiences and dealings with the social security officers:

> There is such [a] concept that unfamiliarity with the law does not release you from liability. So I would have to sit down all the time and know everything. I run my own business and I have problems with ZUS [social security]. So silly sometimes. I would have to just sit down [to familiarize myself with their new laws] and do nothing else. They change the law all the time. I would have to be on the phone all the time. They do not inform [me] about this. Once I got ill and took a sick leave. And then I learnt that two years before I had a contribution underpayment of 12 zlotys or so [equivalent to £2.5]. They didn't pay me for the sick leave. I had to go to court, appeal. So silly, isn't it? But nobody informed me that I had to pay these 12 zlotys. Interest was growing. So I ask who the law is for? I would be satisfied if I got a letter earlier. You owe us this and that amount, please pay, and this is it. Such small, tiny things. (Olek, FG 3)

In reading these experiences as expressed by the interviewees or focus group participants, it should not be assumed that this is nothing more than just a way of thinking. The research into the institutional sphere confirms these attitudes. The relationship between the citizens and their local administration was recently investigated by Bukowski et al. (2008) in their insight into the process of awarding and implementation of EU funds in Poland. Aside from the complicated rules (and their various interpretations) and public procurement procedures (as discussed earlier in this chapter), the other main barrier to the awarding of funds was the applicants' experiences of law enforcement by the local bureaucracy officers. The authors pointed to the excessive red tape – complicated formal requirements for the project applications, numerous certificates and excessive paperwork – which was also revealed in the attitudes of the administration officers towards the applicants. Requirements enforced by the officers obstinately and inflexibly precluded any amendments even in the case of 'minor miscalculations, the use of the incorrect ink colour or the lack of some attachments' (Bukowski et al. 2008: 447).

Perhaps as a result of these rather negative experiences when dealing with law in everyday life (at the level of law enforcement) on the whole, 49.6 per cent of the Polish general public in the 2008 survey did not consider the law to be fair. As can be seen in Table 7.5, in contrast to the Polish attitudes, the law was considered to be fair by 66.3 per cent of the British respondents.

Table 7.5 Is the Law Fair?

On the whole, do you feel the law in your country	Poland (%)	UK (%)
Is fair	32.4	66.3
Is unfair	49.6	23.4
Both/depends	13.1	7.9
Neither	1.3	0.6
Other/don't know/NA	3.6	1.8
Total	100.0	100.0

Source: 'Legal Cultures in Transition' survey 2008

The Normative Gap in Polish Experiences of Law

In the discussion relating to the image of law in Poland, certain thematic oppositions can easily be distinguished. On the one hand, law is highly regarded and expected to regulate relationships between the people, while on the other, it is perceived as a complicated set of written rules and regulations limiting one's freedoms and scope for action. In addition, there is a consensus that the law should be created and applied by professionals, yet almost everybody in Poland agrees that it is passed and enforced by socially distrusted politicians and state officials. Moreover, the professional law is expected to be enforced and consistently applied, yet people's experiences show problems with enforcement not only at the level of dealing with state officials and bureaucracy, but also among the respondents themselves, who openly spoke of their preference of 'getting things done' (Grazyna, FG 1) even outside of the law. This, in turn, reinforces the image of law as not commanding authority.

This analysis points to a rather ambivalent relationship with law, when people's experiences of law are additionally complicated by their prevailing *normative* expectations of how the law *should* work and *be applied* in society:

> The law is important, because it regulates the relations between people. And there would be no order without the law. (Norbert, FG 4)

> There always used to be some law. One cannot live without law, because there would be mayhem. It's simply impossible. What if there were no law? (Sylwia, FG 8)

This results in a gap, a cognitive dissonance between what people expect of the law at the normative level and their daily experiences. When brought together, they reveal a very mixed, complicated set of social expectations towards the law:

> The law means different things for different people. Even if it exists people find ways to evade it. (Waldek, FG 3)

> The example with [the] TV and radio license fee is a very good one. Only 30 per cent of people pay it. You can't have a situation where 30 per cent of people pay the licence fee and they rest pretend they don't know. That's ridiculous. And we're supposed to have the rule of law in this country ... We can't have laws that nobody obeys. (Krzysztof, FG 6)

Although the divergence between what people think and what people do is a well-documented paradox in social science, this gap between the normative expectations and experiences holds its purpose for the analysis of the role of law in Polish society.

Firstly, it points to a conclusion that the situation with the Polish expectations towards the law is not so straightforward as could be judged by only looking at the declining quality of the parliament' legislated law (Zirk-Sadowski 2006), or people's experiences of low levels of law enforcement and its complicated application by the public administration. In Poland these day-to-day experiences of law are accompanied by the very high normative regard for *the law* – considered as 'justice, fairness and legal rights' by 74.7 per cent of the respondents in the 2008 survey.

Very helpful insights supporting (albeit not explicitly) the normative gap interpretation – as suggested in the interviews and focus groups – can be found in Galasinska and Kozłowska's analysis of the discourses of normality among the Polish people and Polish post-2004 EU enlargement migrants in the UK (Galasinska and Kozłowska 2009). What the authors defines as normality is the desire for a 'normal' life in the context of post-communist transformation. Polish people justify their decision to migrate by offering arguments focused on the need to migrate for the sake of having a 'normal' life (Galasinska and Kozłowska 2009: 88). In response to the authors' analysis, one is struck with a question: 'Where does the desire for a "normal life" originate from?' Surely, as the Polish migrants (young people) lived and worked in Poland most (or all) of their lives, they should primarily perceive that reality as the 'natural' or 'normal' one.

From Galasinska and Kozłowska's work, however, one can learn that the reality of the Polish employment market and earnings are considered far from 'normal' by the interviewed migrants (Galasinska and Kozłowska 2009: 99). Their research suggests that there must be an internal and strong normative gap between people's ideas of 'normality' (almost an ideal, which the author refers to as 'a lived definition': Galasinska and Kozłowska 2009: 99) and their everyday life experiences. Similarly, in terms of their social expectations towards the law, there is a deeply embedded 'lived definition' of *law* as justice, fairness and legal rights that is not met by the day-to-day experiences of law, law enforcement and legality.

As the normative standards are not necessarily met by people's experiences of law, this results in contrasting attitudes. On the one hand, the law is more likely to be bypassed or ignored – when convenient – by some, as the obedience towards law brings with it the internal, normative incoherence: 'If you feel the law is wrong, try to change the law; if you cannot do this, follow the law that is there and that's it' (Marta, FG 7). This is down to the socialization and the historically embedded feeling of being *uncomfortable* with the prevailing laws as the source of the internalized legality.

On the other hand, as the discussion over the TV and radio licence fees reveals, people want the laws which are not adhered to to be changed and therefore reduce the normative gap. All this points to a conclusion that the general attitude to law is a more sophisticated (albeit an ambivalent) one.

Secondly, the normative gap between legal expectations and practical experiences has consequences for the binding force of the law and legal norms in society. The phenomenon of semi-legality and semi-compliance, as revealed in Polish post-2004 EU enlargement migrants' experiences of the immigration and workplace regulations in the UK, suggests that, in spite of the law being perceived as paramount and a source of certain goods, it is not necessarily integrated within the social fabric as an everyday life duty. This makes the law external to the 'true' and actual social relations:

> I don't think about whether the law is necessary or not. In everyday life [we often go by] quite different rules, not legal rules. (Malgorzata, FG 2)

Thirdly, over time, the prevailing normative gap blunts social sensitivity towards the law as a value and sharpens the instrumental attitude towards it. Although law in general could be considered as a tool to achieve certain social goals and aspirations, in Poland it is the narrow interpretation of the instrumental quality of law, especially the manipulative character of enacting and using law in a political game by state officials, that seemed to be dominant (Stawecki 2000: 39). As Kurczewski observes, the most common social expectation towards the law is the interest in claiming 'one's own' right to obtain a certain goal, no matter whether the pursuit of 'one's own' right takes place through legal or illegal means, or somewhere in-between (Kurczewski 2007: 33–60). 'One's own' rights are evoked to justify the achievement of instrumental needs. This behaviour is socially tolerated as long as the similar behaviour of others does not interfere with the fulfillment of one's own aims. In the event of such conflict, the law is treated more as a constraint to a preferred action than as a means of resolving such a conflict.

When asked about popular associations with law among the Polish people in London, the image of the colour red – *stop, you cannot do this* – prevailed among the interviewees:

> To me law means red, as red means warning. It's something you have to do, you must do. That's my first association.
>
> – Do you feel that the law can protect you? [A.K.]
>
> No, not really. It usually tells me what to do. Maybe if I was pregnant, maybe I would look differently at law, maybe I could see that it protects me. Now, I am single so the law usually tells me what to do, do this, don't do that, this sort of thing. OK, I can go to see a doctor on the NHS for free, but it's because I pay taxes. So I pay for it, and am not sure whether it has much to do with the law. (Interview No. 12)

The image of law as a red colour very often also symbolized risks associated with law: 'be careful, it could be dangerous'. Engaging with the law for many of the Poles meant embarking on some rather murky waters – unforeseen, due to complex rules and regulations which often contradicted each other. Hence, well before the law's instrumental capacities were discovered, in a given context or situation, all these attitudes – low expectations of the law as fair, low expectations of an equal treatment before the law and mixed experiences of how the state's law officials operate – produced rather low social expectations towards the law, strategies of law avoidance and keeping a low profile among the Polish people.

Polish Experiences of Workplace Regulations

Although the above analysis gives a general understanding of the socio-legal climate and culture in Poland, it nevertheless runs the risk of forgetting the narration and agency of the particular group of Polish post-2004 EU enlargement migrants in question. Only by looking at the Polish relationship with the law through the lens of their experiences can we see how the interpretations, values and attitudes towards the law correspond with the wider, legal culture context. Therefore, the following part of this chapter is based on Polish migrants' experiences of law before their arrival in the UK.

As Polish migrants mainly come to the UK as workers (only between 8 and 9 per cent of those registered under the WRS actually have dependants with them), the relationship they form with the workplace rules and regulations is an inseparable part of their socio-legal integration process. In order to understand the variety of their legal expectations towards this social sphere (Galligan 2007), this section looks into migrants' personal recollections of the workplace regulations, employment law and labour arrangements in Poland, of how these experiences were built up in the legal environment and how they were expressed.

Work Contracts

The majority of interviewed migrants – young people (in their twenties or early thirties) who arrived in the UK after having worked for a couple of years in Poland – had no experience of long-term, stable employment and contracts. Prior to their arrival in the UK, most of the people I interviewed were either employed on short-term contracts or had unwritten agreements with their employers giving them basic or no job security:

> All these jobs I had were either not financially rewarding, e.g. telemarketing – I was just working for the commission, around 100 Zl per month (approximately £20), or short-term, unstable. I did not have a written contract, but it was more a pyramid type of business – someone was in charge of a group of telemarketers and paying a percentage of his commission to his workers, there was another person on top of him, etc. We were not signing a short-term agreement with the company, but with the person directly on top of us. (Interview No. 14)

> Everything was short-term, unstable: contract-order, contract for work, or even without that. (Interview No. 34)

The beginning of the 1990s saw the introduction of the freedom of contract – the fundamental principle of private law. However, this situation led to legal interpreters raising various doubts and queries as to whether the scale of private law autonomy is helping to achieve goals often considered against or contrary to state law or the public interest (Stawecki 2003: 88). Although a written contract is an inseparable part of registered (i.e. legal) work, in Polish law it could take the form of a contract of employment, a contract-order, a contract for work or any other written agreement between the employer and the employee regardless of the economy sector (including those employed on farms in agriculture). The employment relationship is considered to be a registered one regardless of whether it has been established according to the Polish Labour Code (*Kodeks Pracy*) or civil law.

To clarify, registered labour contracts in Poland can either be based on the Labour Code or civil law regulations. The crucial difference is that the contracts derived from civil law do not give rise to an employment relationship between the employer and the employee. In contrast to the contracts derived from the Labour Code, those based on civil law are not bound by the workplace and employment regulations which normally regulate the relationship between the employer and the employee (e.g. maximum working time regulations, overtime payments, leave entitlements, public holidays or breaks at work). They are therefore more popular and are considered freer and more flexible.

In practice, however, the heavy reliance on civil law-derived work contracts often leads to appointments on the basis of personal choice (it is not necessarily the better qualified worker who receives the position but the one who is willing to accept the conditions of the contract) and constitutes the main protection from social insurance contributions on the side of both employers and workers.

What worries Stawecki (2003) and probably other legal interpreters (Boni 2004; Portet 2007) is that this flexible working relationship – registered work established according to civil law – actually takes place at the margins of the Polish Labour Code. The workers and the employers enter into their contracts as 'free' individuals with fewer rights but also fewer obligations towards the state and each other.

As a result, the Polish employment law, being a mixture of labour law and civil law provisions, provides effective structural conditions for semi-legality at the workplace. Portet (2007) claims that the Polish private sector is a place of de-standardization of the employment relationship and its increased flexibility, which, however, usually takes place at the borderline between legal and illegal (Portet 2007: 123). In 'Uncovering the Flexibility of the Polish Labour Market', he demonstrates various ways popularly used to bypass the labour law and 'contribution chock-a-block' resulting from the labour contract.

The first is the popularity of contracts of employment for a definite period of time, with fewer obligations and duties on the side of the employer than those conferred by a permanent contract (e.g. no or a very short notice period). The contract of employment for a definite period also serves as a particular method of personnel management (Portet 2007: 122), where the employers use the contract's 'uncertainty' to motivate the productivity of labour. This was also revealed in the interviews:

> You will hardly ever start a job in Poland with the normal contract for employment. The employer wants always to probe you first, see whether you deserve a contract. (Interview No. 27)

According to Article 25 of the Polish Labour Code, a third subsequent contract for a definite period of time signed between the employer and the employee transforms the employment relationship into a permanent one. However, the typical way to get around this regulation – as observed by Portet (2007) – was to wait more than 31 days on the side of the employer in signing the third contract. Polish law says that when the third contract is signed in a period of time longer than 31 days, it automatically ceases to be perceived as an extension of the existing employment relationship. Yet the 31-day gap does not necessarily mean that the worker becomes unemployed. His or her contract *of employment* (for a definite period) either becomes transformed into a one-month-long contract *for services* (derived from civil law) or he or she receives remuneration as 'cash in hand' (Portet 2007: 121).

Another popular strategy to get around the labour law regulations is the self-employment option. Signing contracts for services with one-man firms enables employers to avoid National Insurance contributions (constituting on average 36 per cent of one's salary) as well as not to conform with the workplace regulations as specified in the Polish Labour Code.

Such employees in practice (and service-providers in the light of the law) are also released from paying the full amount of National Insurance; instead, their contributions are calculated from 75 per cent of their income (Portet 2007: 123). Although since 2002 the Polish Labour Code provides a tool to test whether the contract for services is a genuine one or actually disguises an employment relationship (Article 22, para. 1), it is not used much. Many employees, forced by their employers to resign from a permanent contract *of employment* in favour of a contract *for* services or to undertake overtime work on legal bases different from those specified in the labour law (e.g. derived from civil law), agree to do so either fearing unemployment or due to the fact that such a relationship is beneficial for them in the short-term. This was confirmed by many of the interviewees:

> I was working in a shop with agricultural tools in Poland, but as the taxes and social security were quite high, the owners wanted me to be self-employed. It would mean that I had to pay my own insurance contribution[s], but it was really difficult to do so from the money they were paying me every month. But I was working for them as self-employed. Thanks God my parents had a small farm, so I could be insured with them and pay a really low premium. (Interview No. 2)

The popular practices of replacing labour contracts with contracts derived from civil law (e.g. a contract-for-work or a contract-order) are not necessarily rooted only in the particular form of capitalism that emerged in Poland after 1989 ('capitalism without capitalists' (Eyal et al. 1998) or 'hybrid capitalism' (Morawski 2000)). Portet (2007) observes that these practices could be traced as far back as the socialist period in Poland, where they were used to enable the part-time employment of people who already had other sources of income (e.g. students, retired persons and farmers); to get around the working time regulations with regard to overtime (avoid payments for overtime); or – paradoxically – to give pay rises to workers without having to pay the subsequent social security contributions (and therefore reducing labour costs) (Portet 2007: 132).

This demonstrates that – like the UK (cf. Chapter 4) – the flexibility of work contracts in Poland was moved to the margins of labour law and was left to the competence of private arrangements in the 'grey' area of regulation.

National Insurance and Tax Regulations

The short-term, unstable employment relationships as experienced by the interviewees result from the fact that the employment law in Poland favours the workers but puts high obligations on the employers for paying National Insurance contributions:

> The National Insurance contributions were disproportionate to what I actually could pay my workers. With my revenue they would be taking approximately 70 per cent of a worker's salary. (Interview No. 26)

The high National Insurance contributions were also recalled as disproportionately high by the owners of small and medium-sized businesses:

> No matter what you started doing, you had to pay the National Insurance contributions within a one month's time from setting up a business. Of course it was higher than any possible capital gains you could earn during the first month of being in business. (Interview No. 32)

> When the health insurance was introduced in Poland I had to pay 300 Zlotys, since I had a shop and a farm, and insurance business – I had to pay 100 Zlotys for each and every of businesses. But since they all belonged to me, to one person, I was considered by [the] NHS as a single patient and was treated as anyone else who paid only 100 Zlotys. (Interview No. 9)

The high National Insurance contributions attached to permanent, standard labour contracts were reflected in the interviews and recalled as the main causes of losing or resigning from a current job:

> It was a job that did not allow me to start a life on my own. It was 25 hours per week and I got 700 Zl per month [approximately £145] on a short-term contract. Initially, I was promised a long-term contract, but because it would imply higher taxes, they did not want to upgrade it. Before me there were five project assistants doing the same job. I was the 6th one. None of us was kept for longer than a year, as [a] permanent contract would imply high insurance contributions. (Interview No. 14)

The owner of a small business in Poland actually admitted that the bureaucratic inefficiency in terms of tax collection was one of the reasons that made him close his business and come to the UK:

> The decision was immediate after one of the discussions with the Polish officers in the tax office. I submitted all the required documents; I came home and received a telephone from the lady in the tax office, that she could not locate our documents. It was the same lady who received my documents and confirmed the receipt. I locked my office and decided to come to the UK. (Interview No. 9)

Alternatively, going around the National Insurance or tax requirements, or turning to less secure employment relationships was often recalled as the way to adapt – to ensure that the job brought sufficient income:

> I worked in a hotel, and I was happy not having the normal contract. It was a part-time job, and I much rather had more cash coming in, rather than having to pay all the insurance contributions. (Interview No. 39)

The variety of experiences of the interviewees reveals that a significant group of them, before coming to the UK, did not experience regular National Insurance contributions or tax payments:

> I worked in a cafe and I was still a student in Poland. So I did not have to pay National Insurance. As per the taxes, well, I got paid cash in hand at the beginning of every month depending on the hours I worked. (Interview No. 27)

> My only experience of work in Poland was at the petrol station, in the shop. I found this job after my A levels. But I had to pay my own National Insurance. (Interview No. 12)

> Before I came to the UK I worked as a florist assistant at our local shop. It was a small, private business – only the owner and myself – hence I got paid depending on how the business was doing. In cash. (Interview No. 34)

Other respondents admitted working in the grey area in Poland as their first choice, as the risks usually attached to unregistered work were often cushioned by existing family or close-knit connections between the parties:

> My husband and I were working for my father-in-law, who had a car hire company. At that time I could not even register as an unemployed, as I did not have any previous work record. But it was at least something. (Interview No. 37)

> When I got married, my father-in-law took me as his shadow helper to run with him the garage he owned. (Interview No. 4)

These experiences, although expressed by individuals from the interviewed group of Polish post-2004 EU enlargement migrants in the UK, seemed to be largely shared in the Polish population. According to the CBOS 2006 survey into *Collective Bargaining, Employees' Rights and the 'Grey Sphere' in Employment*, more than one-third of skilled workers (36 per cent) and 26 per cent of unskilled workers admitted having National Insurance contributions deducted only from part of their earnings, with the remainder being paid 'cash in hand' (CBOS 2006a). With regard to the occupational groups, the above phenomena were mostly observed among construction workers: 33 per cent of them were not having National Insurance contributions deducted fully, while for people employed in services sector, the figure was 19 per cent (CBOS 2006a: 10).

With regard to the experiences of workplace regulations while actually at work – concerning safety or working hours – some of the interviewees reflected upon the prevailing casual attitude towards health and safety regulations or unpaid overtime work:

> There was one guy working before me in the factory on the machine and he was some sort of a Stakhanov fan [Alexei Stakhanov – the Russian working-class leader from the 1950s], then he had left and I became the main operator. That guy was crazy about money. He made all the norms too high, and I could not cope with it. Not even mentioning the health and safety that English people here are so crazy about. I had to stay overtime. I tried to speak to the manager to get paid for it or to negotiate reducing the norms, but we had a production manager – a paper man rather, with completely no experience to manage [sic] a big production team of 70 people. This guy liked games, cliques, 'circles of trusts', informal arrangements that was sick in my opinion. I had enough. (Interview, No. 18)

The CBOS 2003 survey (a year before the enlargement of the EU) placed the experiences of workplace regulations whilst at work (regarding health and safety enforcement and overtime) in the wider, Polish context; it revealed that 21 per cent of the interviewed workers in Poland happened – or were forced – to work in conditions contravening health and safety regulations. Just under one-third (30 per cent) of the workers admitted doing overtime work without receiving remuneration for the longer hours (CBOS 2003). These surveys demonstrate that the phenomenon of non-compliance or semi-compliance with the workplace regulations – as initially pointed out by the interviewees reflecting on their work arrangements in Poland – could concern up to one-third of the workers employed in the Polish economy before the 2004 enlargement of the EU.

As far as the attitudes towards semi-legality at the workplace were concerned, those expressed by my interviewees did not seem very different from the views of the Polish general public. In 2009 the CBOS conducted a survey in which respondents were given a couple of scenarios of 'workplace arrangements' to grade according to their own judgment on a scale from appropriateness to non-appropriateness.

When confronted with a situation of a person taking up a weekend, part-time job (aside from the primary, registered employment) for which he or she receives the payment 'cash in hand' and does not intend to declare this as an additional income to the Tax Office, 38 per cent of the respondents considered this behaviour inappropriate (with 27 per cent stating it was '*rather* inappropriate' and 11 per cent 'completely inappropriate'), while 26 per cent remained indifferent towards it. The complete results can be found in Table 7.6. A total of 29 per cent considered it quite likely that they would behave in the same manner as the person in question (the last figure not reported in Table 7.6).

Among all the people that considered such alternative employment as 'rather appropriate' (19 per cent), the highest support was expressed by unskilled workers (50 per cent) and young people aged between 18 and 24 (37 per cent) (CBOS 2009).

Table 7.6 Attitudes Towards Unregistered Employment

A person takes up a weekend, part-time job (aside from a main job), for which he or she receives the payment 'cash in hand' and does not intend to declare this additional income to the Tax Office. In your opinion, is the person's behaviour:	**Responses (%)**
Completely inappropriate	11
Rather inappropriate	27
Neither inappropriate nor appropriate	26
Rather appropriate	19
Completely appropriate	9
Difficult to say	8

Source: CBOS 2009

When presented with the scenario of a handyman and a home owner agreeing on a payment for a particular service bypassing the relevant tax regulations (VAT), 48 per cent of the surveyed people have found it inappropriate (32 per cent found it '*rather* inappropriate' and 16 per cent 'completely inappropriate'), while 25 per cent remained indifferent, finding it neither appropriate nor inappropriate (CBOS 2009: 6). What is interesting is that at the declaration level, 34 per cent of Polish people surveyed by the CBOS admitted that they would have done the same as the home owner in question (the last figure not reported in Table 7.7).

Table 7.7 Attitudes Towards Tax Evasion

A handyman and a home owner agree on a payment for a particular service bypassing the relevant tax regulations (VAT). In your opinion is their behaviour:	**Responses (%)**
Completely inappropriate	16
Rather inappropriate	32
Neither inappropriate nor appropriate	25
Rather appropriate	14
Completely appropriate	5
Difficult to say	8

Source: CBOS 2009

The research reveals that strong judgments (acceptance vs. non-acceptance), although theoretically safe to choose as they were measured anonymously and at the level of a declaration, were not very popular among the respondents. Instead, the most preferred response was 'rather inappropriate', pointing towards a general non-acceptance, although equivocally. This first choice was usually followed by indifference ('neither appropriate nor inappropriate'), with these two figures quite often being very close. Declared strong non-acceptance was usually the third or fourth most popular response, albeit rather distant from the first two (in terms of the figure).

What the survey's results suggest is that the attitudes to employment and fiscal regulations among the Polish people are far from extreme but reflect a rather complex and ambiguous relationship with law and legality instead. The general disagreement with morally doubtful acts is closely followed by indifference or simply lack of judgment. This view is supported by Miszalska (1998) in research into the more general 'Social Reactions Toward the Transformation' in Poland. She observed that the 'particular quality of the social consciousness in the era of systemic change was characterised by amorphism, lack of inner cohesion of people's attitudes and beliefs' (Miszalska 1998: 88). The socio-legal consequences of the transformation in the 1990s were the state of anomie, often accompanied by axiological chaos (Miszalska 1998). This is also true with regard to the legal socialization and expectations towards the law, where the knowledge of rights and wrongs is often confronted and potentially challenged by situations, various engagements or distribution of loyalties in everyday life:

> The way we act in our life is somehow governed from above. Parents set an example for their children and then the children act like that. This is coded somewhere and stays there. So that we act this way and not that way, don't we? Just like crossing the street. If Dad used to drive around, breaking traffic regulations, and it was normal, the child looks at these things in a different way. It is very likely that he or she will do the same thing. And so we grow up with this. (Ula, FG 3)

The Choice of Semi-Legality over Legality

The interviewees' experiences of the labour market, workplace regulations and employment arrangements back in Poland demonstrate that the choice (although the term 'choice' vastly over-simplifies the highly complex relation between structure and agency which has given rise to a considerable body of literature: Emirbayer and Mische 1998) is hardly ever between compliance versus non-compliance with the labour law regulations. Effectively, the choice takes place between compliance and semi-compliance.

As used earlier in this book, the category of semi-compliance – encompassing a wide range of violations with varying degrees of severity (Anderson and Ruhs

2010) – reveals that the experience of semi-legality of Polish post-2004 EU enlargement migrants in the UK is not that different from the experience of a group of Polish workers with the employment law and workplace regulations before their decision to migrate. In the context of the Polish labour market, semi-compliance with labour laws was invoked and relied upon to ensure that the workers and employers themselves benefit most in a situation where full compliance incurs expensive labour costs and the heavy burden of National Insurance contributions.

The common experience, as indicated by the interviews, hardly ever rested on the 'ideal type' of unregistered work (in the Weberian sense). Instead, it embraced a variety of experiences, ranging from:

1. working with no employment contract or a contract that did not reflect the actual working arrangements (a contract-for-work or a contract-order derived from civil law provisions);
2. receiving the wages 'cash in hand' (fully or partially, e.g. for overtime work);
3. using part-time engagement to disguise a full-time work (resulting in receiving registered payslips with partial deduction of taxes and National Insurance contributions);

In other words, the aim was to ensure the maximization of economic benefits from employment while minimizing the threat of state sanctions for violations of labour laws. In practice, different workers attach different weights to stability of employment, economic improvement and social security, while employers make different decisions regarding the cost of employing legally and the potential cost arising from state sanctions towards employers who violate employment law. The latter will, of course, depend on the probability of detection (a function of state enforcement) and the actual level of sanctions such as fines, imprisonment, the possibility of being barred from participation in professional organizations (if they exist), 'bad' reputation, etc. (Anderson and Ruhs 2010).

In investigating Polish workers' experiences of semi-legal work, the research conducted in the year of Poland's accession to the EU (2004) commissioned by the Main Statistical Office (GUS), casts more light on the choices of semi-compliance over compliance with workplace regulations and employment law. Due to the illicit nature of the unregistered or semi-registered work (the latter being treated as a derivative of the semi-legality with the employment law regulations), it is, of course, very difficult to estimate the scale of the phenomenon. According to the GUS research into the 'Grey Sphere of Employment' (thus encompassing both unregistered and semi-registered work), the number of persons employed in the national economy in Poland in 2004 was 12,720,200; out of this number, approximately 1,317,000 (10.4 per cent) were employed in work other than registered work (that is, with one or more characteristics of unregistered employment) (GUS 2005: 11).

The research demonstrates that the main reasons for choosing unregistered over formal (legal) employment were: the lack of opportunities in finding alternative employment (63.9 per cent); difficult financial situation (insufficient income from regular employment – 46.7 per cent); and high premiums for National Insurance contributions which reduced the attractiveness of regular employment (21.3 per cent) (GUS 2005: 11).[4]

These responses might well have resulted from the structural changes to the Polish labour market after 1989 (its 'marketization'), which brought about greater competition and recognition of the role of skills and educational qualifications. The side-effect of the labour market transformation was reduced demand for and thus an increase in the pool of available workforce. This led to unemployment which, in turn – as an objective factor – brought about a socially constructed phenomenon of 'fear for jobs' (especially in the public sector, which was still quite prominent in Poland from the late 1990s to the early 2000s: Marody 2000: 82). This, in turn, reduced the bargaining power of workers when negotiating terms and conditions of employment with their employers or managers. These arguments suggest structural roots to the problem of informal employment lying in the condition of the Polish economy in the run-up to Poland's accession to the EU.

However, the initial reasons for semi-legality, resulting from 'objective', market-generated factors, were followed in the GUS 2004 survey by the following responses: 'the employer offering higher wages if the contract of employment is not registered' (18.2 per cent) or 'the possibility of losing certain social benefits upon undertaking registered employment' (7.6 per cent). These point to the reflexive nature of the phenomenon and suggest that both employers and employees take the law as their framework and make choices ensuring that they themselves benefit more.[5]

Unregistered or semi-registered work was most popular among so-called *handymen*: plumbers, electricians and gas specialists at 44 per cent, followed by builders in the construction industry (39.9 per cent), care workers (24.5 per cent), cleaners (20 per cent) and people offering gardening services (17.3 per cent) (GUS 2005).[6] The survey results broken down into occupational groups seem to resemble the range of occupations in which the majority of Polish migrants find work upon their arrival in the UK (UK Border Agency et al. 2009).

There are also other observable similarities between the Polish people performing unregistered or semi-registered work (as reported by the GUS in 2004) and the metric group characteristics of a substantive number of Polish migrants

4 The unemployment rate in Poland in 2004 was 19 per cent (GUS 2005). The total figures show more than 100 per cent as the respondents were asked to choose more than just one reason (GUS 2005).

5 The total number of responses is more than 100 per cent as the respondents were asked to choose more than just one reason (GUS 2005).

6 The total number of responses is more than 100 per cent as the respondents were asked to choose more than just one reason (GUS 2005).

in the UK. It should be noted that undeclared work in Poland was, in a large number of cases, characteristic of casual, short-term, seasonal employment. This is illustrated by the fact that over 96 per cent of the people working in the informal economy were doing so only once a month. For 29 per cent of workers within the grey area of the economy, the period of informal employment lasted between one and two months. Only 19 per cent of those performing unregistered or semi-registered work admitted to continuing their work for five months or more (GUS 2005: 16).

The short-term character of the employment was also declared by the majority of Polish post-2004 EU enlargement migrants in the UK (approximately 43 per cent between May 2006 and December 2010) with their intended length of stay being less than five months (UK Border Agency et al. 2009; Office for National Statistics 2011).[7]

From all the people surveyed by the GUS in Poland who declared being engaged in unregistered or semi-registered work in 2004, 20 per cent were between 15 and 24 years old and 24 per cent were between 25 and 34 years old (GUS 2005: 35). According to the Office for National Statistics (ONS) data, the vast majority of workers arriving in the UK between May 2004 and March 2011 were young: 81 per cent aged between 18 and 34 (UK Border Agency et al. 2009; Office for National Statistics 2011).

This comparison does not intend to imply that all Polish migrants who had similar employment experiences and socio-economic characteristics to those Polish people engaged in semi-registered or unregistered work in Poland simply continued to do so upon their arrival in the UK. However, comparison of the data can suggest that this excess (surplus) of workers in the Polish economy – young people without dependants, engaged in casual, temporary labour in Poland or elsewhere – who did not have a stable employment relationship or contract could potentially be the most interested in migration. Upon arrival in the UK, with the aim of short-term economic gain rather than settlement, they could have either continued to apply the same arrangements under which they were working in Poland or find it appropriate when such arrangements were suggested to them by either new British employers or employment businesses/agencies.

Personal characteristics and aspirations, when set within certain broader economic and social contexts, can create inverse relationships ('trade-offs') between the host country's policy objectives (e.g. integration) and migrants' goals. As Anderson and Ruhs (2010) observe, migrants intending a short-term stay abroad may be much more concerned with maximizing economic benefits from employment abroad than with social integration, potentially even at the cost of insecurity of residence and employment (Anderson and Ruhs 2010: 4). The Polish migrants' priority of short-term economic gains over longer term settlement

7 This was derived from applicants' responses to the following question on the WRS application form: 'How long do you think you will stay in the UK?' This question was not asked until March 2005. The Home Office did not verify these responses.

could be found in the Home Office data and is also indicated in other research into the contemporary post-2004 EU enlargement Polish migration trends to the UK (Clarke and Drinkwater 2008; Garapich 2008; Portes and French 2005; Salt and Rees 2006).[8]

As a result, this group of Polish migrants in question, with previous experience of semi-legal work or common-sense knowledge of conditions under which semi-legal work largely functioned in Poland ('it wasn't anything new – it wasn't anything surprising' (Interview No. 33)), could have been less interested in legalizing their work or fully complying with employment law in the UK. They did not necessarily see the National Insurance and tax regulations as an 'investment' or 'protection', but rather as a constraint to employment, and 'could make their peace with working without them' (Interview No. 34). As the registration of employment with the Home Office or obtaining a National Insurance Number would accrue additional costs and liabilities in the UK, some preferred to avoid it and keep a low profile following the common truth of 'better to keep clear of the law' (Zbigniew, FG 7).

Migrants' experiences of work in the UK mainly in the services sector, as handymen, plumbers, builders, construction workers, cleaners or care workers (UK Border Agency et al. 2009), bear close resemblance to the 'types' of work that in Poland were not closely associated with a stable employment relationship, but were rather derived from the experience of an 'on the side', casual and often semi-registered work (GUS 2005). Drawing from their experiences back in Poland, many migrant workers were not alarmed or particularly inspired to follow the law too closely if they found themselves in the UK performing a similar types of job. Therefore, for many, the initial path of semi-legality was the 'safe', 'familiar' and 'known' choice.

Recognizing the Role of Legal Culture

This chapter aimed to analyse the nature of current values, attitudes, interpretations, experiences and social expectations towards *the law* that Polish migrants arrive with in the UK. They were considered as both resulting from and reflected by the socio-legal history of the complex relationship between the Polish people and their state law and state officials, as well as contemporary observations on the role of the law in Polish society.

8 Another methodological remark worth making at this point is that the Home Office data gives only approximate characteristics of migrants and talks mainly about those people who actually registered their employment. However, due to the nature of the enforcement of the WRS, the registration does not exclude former unregistered or semi-registered work. Moreover, the Home Office data says nothing about National Insurance contributions by Polish migrants or tax matters.

The role that legal culture plays in affecting migrants' initial responses to the British immigration and workplace regulations is rather nuanced and subtle; it goes beyond the well-established stereotype of 'Polish people as law evaders' (Robert, FG 1). It takes into consideration the changing role of the law in society and how it both shaped and was shaped by the different models of relationship between the people and their governors. In Poland the law seems to be treated more as an aspiration rather than a blueprint for guiding behaviour. The traditionally embedded image of 'law as freedom' – freedom for oneself and restrictions for others – over generations of an ambivalent, often alienating relationship between the people and their state law (embodied in governors and local bureaucracy) has been transformed into the currently prevailing 'freedom from law' and strategies of keeping a low profile and dislike of interacting with the law.

This, in turn, has consequences for law enforcement and ideas of the authority of law that lie behind this behaviour. A high regard for the law is considered more as an ideal ('law on a pedestal') than emulated more closely after what is already considered reasonable behaviour within the wider culture. This has resulted in the normative gap between the image of law, expectations towards it and practice – the experience of law 'on the ground'.

This general socio-legal climate very much corresponded to the experiences of law as reflected in the interviews of the group of Polish post-2004 EU enlargement migrants. Their experiences of the workplace prior to migrating to the UK largely resonate with the questions of semi-legality. Semi-legality is experienced either through the contracts of employment – seemingly within the boundaries and yet on the outskirts of employment law – or a range of more or less severe violations of employment regulations (partial deductions of taxes, non-payment of National Insurance, less protection and an ambivalent attitude towards health and safety).

From the analytical point of view, Polish contemporary legal culture therefore provides both an insight into and an explanation of Polish migrants' responses to the British state law and workplace regulations. As such, the findings of this chapter complement the analysis of the impact of the British legal environment on the socio-legal integration of Polish post-2004 EU enlargement migrants. They point to the conclusion that in order to obtain a more comprehensive picture of the formation of Polish migrants' relationship with law in the UK, it is necessary to look beyond the structural determinants of institutional arrangements and legal architecture. One should recognize migrants as active agents, reflectively taking into account (as a framework for their actions) both the legal environment and their own experiences and expectations towards how the law works and is enforced in society as derived from their legal culture.

Chapter 8
Gradual Legality: Changing Behaviour, Changing Attitudes

Chapters 6 and 7 demonstrated that Polish legal culture is not resistant to change and adaptation. Although certain patterns and themes could be detected over the generations, the legal culture largely reflected the adaptation of society to the socio-legal environment of a particular time. Taking this feature of the Polish values, attitudes and behaviour towards the law under scrutiny, this chapter investigates further responses of the initially semi-legal post-2004 EU enlargement migrants in the UK towards the British rules and regulations. Is the semi-legality static and ascribed or is it fluid and changing? How do the migrants go about their semi-legal status? How and to what extent does the British legal environment and Polish social expectations towards the law continue to influence the steps that migrants take in terms of changing their status? And, finally, how does the legal status of Polish migrants influence their attitudes and values towards legality?

Behaviour and Attitudes in the Cultural Context

The behavioural formation of legality, together with migrants' attitudes and values towards legality, bring to the forefront the long-standing relationship between behaviour and attitudes. The analysis has so far been largely undertaken within – and limited to – the domain of social psychology research (Aronson 1973; Festinger 1957).

Festinger's (1957) theory of 'cognitive dissonance' was first developed to explain the processes that determine how people resolve important discrepancies between their behaviour and attitudes (beliefs). Festinger observed that when at least one of the cognitive elements (attitudes or beliefs) is inconsistent with one or more of the other cognitive elements of one's behaviour, people become motivated to restore the consistency. Festinger's conclusion, which is particularly meaningful for this study, was that the process by which people restore consistency among conditions can lead to enduring and meaningful changes in their view of the social world (Stone and Fernandez 2008). Subsequent research has shown that dissonance between behaviour and attitude can cause attitude change following a wide variety of decisions (Crano and Messe 1970; Harmon-Jones and Harmon-Jones 2002; Johnson and Rusbult 1987; Stone 1999; Stone and Fernandez 2008; Walster 1964). As a result, people will go to great lengths and will make substantial changes in their attitudes and beliefs to restore consistency following discrepant behaviour.

However, what presents a considerable shortcoming in the social psychology approach to the attitude–behaviour relations is that the cultural context is seen only as a background factor rather than as a fundamental component of attitudes. Although Festinger (1957) noted that prevailing 'cultural mores and norms' can determine whether or not the relations between attitudes and behaviour are inconsistent, and stressed the role of culture in influencing the choice of dissonance reduction, the topic of culture did not receive widespread attention from social psychology researchers.

Smith's and Hogg's (2008) explanation for the historical treatment and neglect of the socio-cultural context in attitude research points to the early individualist definitions of attitudes and a clear focus on individuals, rather than groups, as the units of analysis (Allport 1920; Allport 1935). In their paper on 'Social Identity and Attitudes', Smith and Hogg (2008) call for a 'reconceptualization of attitudes as fundamentally entwined with the social environment and inherently social, rather than simply reducing the social context to the inclusion of norms' (Smith and Hogg 2008). After all, attitudes are indeed socio-culturally learned, socio-culturally changed and socio-culturally expressed.

The empirical insights into the responses of the Polish post-2004 EU enlargement migrants towards the law and regulations in the UK contribute to the recognition of the socio-legal cultural contexts as critical for the attitudinal phenomena and change. Behaviour and attitudes operate within cultural conditioning. That is how the prior development of ideas (from earlier interaction) conditions the current context for action, confronting people with clusters of beliefs, theories and ideas that both enable and constrain their behaviour (Archer 1996). Both past and future are living in the present: 'for we are all born into and can only live embedded in an ideational context which is not of our own making' (Archer 1996). Whatever human beings do in the present is decisively influenced by the past and by the future. The repertoire ('cultural toolkit') of basic signposts – general principles and strategies of action – are informed by past experience and memories adjusted to present situations and projected outcomes in the future (Morawska 2001).

The specific patterns or regularities detectable in the diversity of the responses of Polish migrants to the British legal system are the products of the interplay between immigrants' cultural resources and the goals they pursue on the one hand, and, on the other, the 'limits of the possible' set by the structural conditions of their lives (cf. Morawska 2011: 7). Although this perspective admits that the attitudes are pre-eminently social (Terry and Hogg 2000), at the same time it does not base its analysis on the concept of cultural determination. The agency responds to this inherited cultural context, and in responding, actors can exploit their degrees of cultural freedom.

This chapter therefore explores this new dimension of Polish post-2004 EU enlargement migrants' responses to the law in the UK: when actors – from initial semi–legality and 'keeping clear of the law' – become actively engaged with the environment and when they actively interact with it. The active behavioural responses to the socio-legal environment – challenging and contesting the clear-cut divisions between legal and illegal categories – bring with them subtle changes which constitute the underlying conditions in which new normative categories suddenly become foregrounded in practice, new self-definitions are crystallized and gradual changes in the 'cultural substratum' occur.

My research therefore finds new application for the behaviour–attitudes, actor–structure categories in the socio-legal setting. The analysis of the interaction of Polish post-2004 EU enlargement migrants with the British legal environment and the strategies which they employ in order to engage with the law and its institutions focuses on migrants as active agents, while placing their attitudes and behaviour in the context of the interplay between legal architecture, law enforcement and the legal culture.

Gradual Legality

The fieldwork demonstrated that the semi-legal status shared by a large number of Polish post-2004 EU enlargement migrants was not necessarily static and ascribed. Initially, for the majority of my respondents, it was acceptable to take up employment without registering under the WRS and without a NIN, although they were aware that these documents were required. They would agree on 'cash in hand' payments with no tax deducted.

Gradually, however, and over time, migrants negotiated changes in their status and developed a new quality of behavioural responses towards the British immigration and workplace law and regulations. A wide variety of strategies were adopted as migrants turned to different means (repertoires and 'toolkits': Swidler 1986) in shaping their responses. When and how did the Polish, semi-legal migrants decide to turn to law? Recognizing law's instrumental power (as linked with the features of Polish legal culture) was encapsulated by one of the interviewees:

> I think, from my experience, the law becomes important for the Poles in the UK, when they actually get into some sort of trouble and need help, need legal advice. I think we are a nation, that we start caring, we start complaining, we start making a fuss when something is taken away from us, or when someone does not want to give us something, we believe that should be ours. Then we say: 'oh law is this and that, law is unfair'. (Interview No. 38)

Although potentially stereotypical and detrimental in form, this opinion also revealed a shared perception that affected the quality of Polish migrants' responses to law. A 'problem', 'trouble' or a situational dilemma concerning a workplace or immigration matter (mainly relating to the issue of access to benefits) were the main factors which 'triggered' a new type of response towards the law on the part of migrants. In other words for many of the interviewees, a low-profile job that brought in the money with no 'major problems' and yet without the WRS registration or a NIN, was a sufficient condition that enabled many migrants to take the legality of their actions for granted:

> It made me thinking [sic] only now, how could I not have all these documents and registrations and still feel that I had a legal job. (Interview No. 9)

It was only later – usually after a major turning point: 'a legal trouble' – that migrants gradually started questioning their earlier behavioural responses and interpretations of legality.

Gradual Legality: Solving Problems

The initial indifference towards the law – drawn from migrants' past experiences from Poland – pushed the workplace regulations and Home Office registration requirements down the scale of importance. When the situation became serious, the conditions deteriorated and other, extra-legal options did not seem readily available, the same law came to be recognized as a tool to tackle people's problems. In other words, legality was not necessarily the first option many of the semi-legal migrants turned to upon arriving in the UK and it was not their priority – nevertheless, its potential became recognized in a situation of desperation and trouble.

Marek[1] came to the UK in March 2005 and initially worked via an employment agency as a vegetable packer for a company that supplied the main UK supermarkets. In terms of the legal situation, he worked without Home Office registration, with weekly wages paid 'cash in hand'. He was aware of this; in trying to make sense of his behaviour in relation to his status, he said:

> To be honest I worked there rather illegally. I realized it only after some time, though. But one had to do something; one had to have money. I also wasn't asked by anybody about the insurance number or Home Office registration. (Interview No. 25)

After three months, Marek had to leave his job, as all the workers who were working on that particular shift were made redundant. At this time, he could speak a little English and he looked for jobs via the Job Centre. In November 2005 he found a job on a farm. There was no written contract proposed, but the farmer offered to pay him monthly. The farmer also told Marek that he would 'sort out the papers'. After four weeks, however, when the payment was due, the farmer did not want to speak to any of the workers employed:

> I realized that there will be no contract, there will be no papers and, what was worse, there will be no payment. (Interview No. 25)

1 The name has been changed.

Marek reported the incident to the local police. He received an interpreter, his testimony was taken down and he was given a case number. However, as he revealed, nothing was done and the case went cold. In a Polish newspaper, Marek found an advertisement for a Polish lawyer who was operating on a 'no win no fee' basis. The Polish lawyer took on Marek's case. He wrote several letters to the farmer on Marek's behalf, requesting payment in accordance with the modified grievance procedure. As the farmer did not respond, the case went to the Employment Tribunal, which awarded Marek the wages and compensation. Soon afterwards, he found a job via an employment agency, which helped him to formalize his working situation by supporting his registration with the WRS.

Marek's life is now much less on the margins than it used to be; nevertheless, it took him three jobs and a case in front of an Employment Tribunal to finally legalize his employment and immigration status in the UK. His story relates a rather dramatic way of coming to terms with the law's instrumental capacities.

Realizing the law's potential to solve problems was, for many of the Polish (initially semi-legal) migrants, also the first incentive that triggered thoughts and considerations of their own immigration and legal status in the UK (arguably a motivating factor towards legalization). This was well expressed by the following quote:

> The case went to the Employment Tribunal and after that the farmer did pay the money. Quite promptly to be honest. So the conclusion is that you can stand and fight for your rights even if you work illegally here [the UK]. It takes time but you can do it! (Interview No. 25)

Nevertheless, this experience stood in conflict with the doctrine of illegality (Ryan 2005). During the fieldwork at the legal NGO, I observed that Polish as well as other A8 migrants seeking help in their conflicts with employers or problems with various administrative agencies were first asked about their immigration status in the UK, that is, their position with regard to the WRS. The inquiries relating to their WRS certification were not necessarily motivated by the drive to disclose migrants' illegality, but – more importantly – by the fact that regularized immigration status was the first condition required to start any legal action directed at helping them.

Under UK law, A8 workers (and therefore also Polish workers) who fail to comply with their obligations risk being prevented by the doctrine of illegality from enforcing their employment contract and related rights (Ryan 2005, 2008).[2]

2 The doctrine of illegality states that unauthorized work (for A8 workers who had not registered under the WRS) is likely to involve the commission of a criminal offence by both the employee and the employer. Ryan, in his analysis of the evolving legal regime on unauthorized work by migrants in Britain, sees the established doctrine of illegality as the main obstacle to enforcing the contract of employment, or statutory rights, against the employer in front of Employment Tribunals. While many unauthorized workers are

Therefore, in the majority of cases, the law's instrumental capability of 'solving problems' could be fully utilized only in a situation when one's legal status was regularized. This realization – often learnt the 'hard way' – in turn led many Polish respondents to legalize their immigration and work position in the UK.

Małgorzata,[3] upon arriving in the UK to work as a care worker for B, initially did not register her employment with the WRS, nor did she apply for a NIN. She had been working for B for five months when certain irregularities at her workplace – which, at the beginning, she tolerated – started becoming more and more acute. During the first month of her employment, when she officially remained 'on training', she received a working roster like every other experienced employee and was asked to do the same work, for which she was never paid. Even later on, after her 'training' officially ended, she still did not get paid for all the hours she worked for B. She started looking for help on Polish websites and forums and came across the Citizens Advice Bureau. Three months later, she started a formal grievance procedure against her employer for unauthorized deductions from her wages and unpaid working hours.

After submitting the official grievance letter, she received an email from her employer, where the issue of her late registration with the Home Office was stressed as a potential problem:

> I would also mention the topic – not contained in your grievance letter – concerning the Worker Registration System [sic]. It was your responsibility to apply for registration. You failed to do this. I tried to assist you. You then make untrue allegations about your passport and fees. (Exchange of emails, author's archive)

Małgorzata had delayed her Home Office registration. For her, as was the case for many other migrants, registration and the legalization of status was initiated well beyond the 30 days required by the 2004 Accession Regulations. The effect was her vulnerable position in a situation of conflict with her employer. She could not fully rely on the law's instrumental capacities to solve problems as her situation was an ambivalent one. She sought help to 'right the wrongs' that she believed she experienced; nevertheless, she had to be cautious in her demands for compensation, as her bargaining power was seriously undermined by her lack of WRS registration and claims regarding the illegality of her employment which could follow from it.

---

indeed reluctant to draw attention to themselves through employment litigation, some may wish to do so, particularly where they cannot be removed from the jurisdiction, they have already left it or have been removed from it (Ryan 2005). The cases on tax and National Insurance evasion show the seriousness with which the doctrine of illegality is taken within employment law (Ryan 2005).

3 The name has been changed.

Gradual Legality: Changing Status

Although other Polish migrants interviewed for the study were more fortunate, they shared with Marek and Małgorzata the time factor of legalizing their immigration status, encompassing rather slow, intermittent, gradual changes:

> I came to the UK with the plan that I wanted to stay there for longer, I wanted to earn money for my pension. *Therefore, I had to make all my papers in order sooner or later*. (Interview No. 25, emphasis added)

An interesting question is why did so many of the interviewed Polish migrants decide to do it later rather than sooner? Szymon,[4] upon arrival in the UK, was at first working via an employment agency. He worked without registering with the Home Office and without a NIN; he had been sent to various short-term assignments:

> First I worked for H: I worked there couple of days. Then [a] couple of days I worked for someone else. I worked for P, another agency, I was packing cosmetics, two days maybe. (Interview No. 18)

The longest job he was offered lasted a month. Then he went back to short-term positions. At one point, one of the companies for which he had been working on behalf of the agency contacted him to work for them. He worked (via an agency) for that company for another couple of months. Then the company offered him a contract of employment. Soon afterwards he also applied for a NIN and – later on – registered with Home Office under the WRS. His WRS registration was initiated well beyond the 30-day grace period.

Szymon's employment history in the UK nevertheless casts some light on his choices for semi-legality and late registration. In the short-term assignments he performed for various agencies, he did not consider WRS registration important or helpful, and therefore it was not worth applying for in his situation. He could not see how the WRS or a NIN could change anything in his status – there were days when he was working and days when he was not. The chances of accumulating a continuous 12-month period of employment were rather slim.

Registration was therefore viewed as a burden and trouble, perhaps even restricting his choices of employment: 'the common knowledge had it that one needed to re-register with every new job' (Interview No. 18). This was considered pointless and not worth the trouble by many respondents. To them, this resembled the formalistic, confusing and avoidable bureaucratic practices they were all too familiar with from their experiences in Poland (cf. Chapter 7). Therefore, unsurprisingly, it was 'better to stay out of it altogether' (Interview, No. 18).

4 The name has been changed.

As a consequence, Szymon decided to register when his work situation stabilized. Therefore, on the one hand, the uncertain situation in the low-skilled, low-wage sector of the labour market did not encourage WRS registration and legalization of employment; on the other hand, migrants' reluctance to enter into formal dealings with the bureaucracy and institutions – as supported by their earlier experience ('It took them absolutely ages to process my application form to register with the agency. I was waiting and waiting' (Interview No. 18)) – fostered the practice of keeping clear of the law.

It was only after Szymon had secured permanent employment that he first applied for a NIN and then for WRS registration. Although according to the Accession Regulations, Polish post-2004 EU enlargement migrants had one month to find employment and apply to join the WRS, Szymon's story nevertheless exemplifies that – especially in the case of the low-skilled, low-wage sector of the labour market – it hardly ever happened.

Due to the fact that Szymon's registration was also long overdue, he encountered some administrative problems when it finally came to filling in the application for the WRS. The application was supposed to be dated within 30 days of starting his engagement at the employment agency, while in fact he stayed with the employment agency for more than a year before applying for his WRS certificate. A member of staff at the agency – who was also Polish – helped Szymon to overcome this problem by forward-dating the letter from the employer supporting the WRS application:

> So in the letter of support from the employer, Agnieszka, who was working at reception in X, changed my date of first registration with the agency, so it could be less than one month between the start of my employment and the time I sent my application to join the scheme. So she changed the date on the letter so that everything looked OK. (Interview No. 18)

Szymon was a semi-legal worker in the UK for almost a year. It also meant that due to his late WRS registration, he missed out on about a year's worth of registered work, which, in reality, would mean a complete exemption from further registration. This is to vividly illustrate that Szymon's initial priorities were far removed from the legalization of his immigration status. In Szymon's story, one can see how he gradually climbed up the 'legality' ladder.

The Polish migrants' uncertain situation in the conditions of the flexible labour market, as well as the fact that the WRS was perceived more as a formalistic requirement than as a law that 'could help' (its instrumental capacities in terms of access to benefits were extended in time to 12 months), stimulated the strategies undertaken by the majority of Polish, initially semi-legal migrants of avoiding the law.

Gradually, generally following the same order, other migrants would also first take care of finding secure employment, or at least one that would ensure that wages were paid regularly. Due to the fact that the majority of migrants interviewed came to the UK without a job offer, this first stage of their immigration experience was particularly uncertain and for some extended in time as far as 8 to 12 months:

> In my first job, the salary was irregular, but now, with my second job I was finally receiving the wages in cash, weekly. Every week, every Thursday, if I remember correctly, I would go to the office, there was a cash box with money, and they would pay me my wages, along with the payslip. (Interview No. 10)

The second step that migrants took was to apply for their NIN. Here the main motivation was an instrumental consideration in the form of immediate financial consequences – reduction of the tax rate. A permanent, individual NIN reduces one's tax obligations from the tax deducted at the basic rate to the tax code in accordance with one's level of earnings. Most of the migrants interviewed knew about National Insurance and pointed to it as the one of the first 'things to do' in regularizing their status:

> In my first job, I did not have National Insurance Number. The number belonged to the employer [it was a temporary NIN]. Now everywhere you go, you have to have your own National Insurance Number. (Interview No. 12)

When applying for a NIN, A8 nationals (including Polish nationals) were required to present their WRS certificate at the interview in order to qualify for a NIN. Therefore, many of the migrants who had not (yet) joined the scheme had to skilfully come up with good enough reasons for their non-registration to convince the clerk to accept their NIN application. Some of the migrants prepared justifications about starting their WRS application process, but not yet receiving notification about the outcome from the Home Office:

> During the interview for [the] NIN I had a story prepared that I sent the documents, and I hoped they would believe me. I did not go round to registering, cash is short, I really don't have time to think of it now. (Interview No. 25)

All the interviewed migrants had been – at some stage – awarded their NINs. For the majority of them, the application process for the NIN went off smoothly. Many of them did not even recall the situation of being asked about their Home Office registration during the NIN interview:[5]

> The NIN interview went off very fast and OK. I actually needed only passport, letter of employment, and address confirmation from the bank. It all went very smoothly. (Interview No. 13)

---

5 This shared experience once again brings back the issue of inconsistent enforcement of WRS registration by the British authorities, as discussed in Chapter 4.

> When I went to the Job Centre for my NIN interview, I was served so politely, a gentleman told me where to go, where to wait, then the whole interview took 10 minutes of my time. I was worried as I did not have WRS at that time, but now I know I should not have. Couple of weeks later I received my NIN card in the post. (Interview No. 16)

The third step for the initially semi-legal Polish post-2004 EU enlargement migrants was to register with the WRS. For many of the migrants, WRS appeared as a voluntary scheme (cf. Chapter 5), because, due to the lack of immediate legal consequences, non-compliance did not actually feel as if one was breaking the law. Registering under the WRS was usually postponed until it became absolutely necessary or practical. 'The necessity' for many of the migrants meant either direct pressure from their employers or the practical advantages of the Scheme interpreted as the right to apply for welfare support and means-tested benefits:

> After the first year I have [sic] been working for the cafe, they wanted me to have it done, to register. They were sending me strong signals to do it. So I did it. (Interview No. 12)

> I know I have to do it. WRS is the only *thing that is left*, I have the insurance number, I pay the taxes. I only need to register. I will do it, when I'll get round applying for benefits for my son. (Interview No. 25, emphasis added)

By registering with the WRS, the migrants' formal regularization would be completed. They would join the scheme and work towards the 12 months of being exempt from the Scheme and gaining full residence rights as EU citizens. However, it would be too easy and too simplistic to assume that migrants' behavioural choices towards gradual legality were only unidirectional. Migrants, for various reasons, might have dropped out of the WRS or – in the event of changing their job – might not have re-registered their employment. As a result, some of them would have returned to their previous semi-legal status. This would delay (sometimes indefinitely) the legalization of their work and residence in the UK, and thus their full inclusion into the welfare system. However, the majority of the migrants, generally motivated by instrumental gains, would at some stage continue in their move towards legality.

Changing Attitudes: Legality as a Value

The legal status of migrants impinges on many vital spheres of their existence and shapes who they are, how they relate to each other and to the law in the host country, their participation in local communities and their continued relationship with their homeland (Menjivar 2000). Legal status also affects how migrants interpret the world around them and judge their actions. Those Polish migrants who shared, or at some point in life used to share, semi-legal status also developed a particular interpretation of law and legality in their everyday life in the host country. The behavioural strategies of 'legalizing one's status' were accompanied by changes in migrants' perceptions of and attitudes towards legality.

The way in which interviewees made sense of how they related their experiences to the concept of legality revealed that semi-legality itself was dynamic and changing, and could be placed on a continuum between the poles of legality and illegality. As far as the immigration status and work situations were concerned, in the view of the interviewed migrants, someone could be more legal than someone else or less legal than someone else, or *less-semi and more-legal* or *more-semi and less-legal*.

From the accounts of the interviewees, I managed to gather in which sequence of importance the certain steps of moving status were placed on the continuum between legal and illegal.

Firstly, legality seemed to be associated with weekly wages that were paid regularly. If the employer was not paying the wages or was delaying the weekly payments, then the job automatically became illegal in the opinion of the Poles. Receiving a payslip and having the wages paid into a bank account (instead of 'cash in hand') would make the job look more legal:

> In my first job, I was receiving wages in cash, at the end of every working week. I was working night shifts and was usually getting my wages on Thursday, around 10 am, in an envelope with my surname. My second job was with a different agency, it was also a packing job, but it was *all normal*. I received payslips and the wages were paid in cheques. I had to open a bank account too. (Interview No. 2, emphasis added)

The next step that would make a job look more legal in the opinions of the respondents was to obtain their NIN, as a permanent, individual NIN would help lower the amount of tax and National Insurance contributions, bringing these into line with their actual earnings and reflecting their annual tax allowances.

Further along in the scale of legality were paid holiday entitlements. Some of the migrants – driven by their experiences from Poland, where their employment on, for instance, a contract-order would leave them with no paid holiday rights – initially understood that all their holidays in the UK were also to be taken in the form of unpaid leave:

> My manager was employing people in such a way that you were paid all the hours you worked, everything was legal, you received payslips … the only difference was that when it says holiday on the payslip, you did not have written how much holiday you've earned, as – according to him – all his workers were all part-time and casual and he did not have to pay the holiday, or give paid holiday to his employees. In this respect, my next job was *more legal*, as I received both holiday pay and the contract. (Interview No. 21, emphasis added)

Then came a written contract – it might have been very general and short, but it was a written one, with terms and conditions stated. The former agency workers in particular were very much looking forward to receiving a written contract with their direct employer for whom they had so far been working via an agency. As their engagements with the agency were short and unstable, these workers valued the permanent contracts most – they were hoping to obtain greater job security and upgrade their working status:

> Everyone was waiting for contract, like for some sort of revelation. It would mean an end to temporary job, when they could say bye to you anytime. After nine months, when I finally got my contract, I was happy. I received it all well and clear, my manager explained to me everything I needed to know. He allowed me to take the contract home before actually signing it. (Interview No. 18)

The more of these elements an individual accumulated (sometimes in different combinations, depending, of course, on the individual circumstances), the more legal his or her stay and work in the UK *was perceived.* At the very end of the illegality–legality continuum was the WRS. For many of my respondents, joining the WRS in the pursuit of legal status was considered optional and dependent on whether one wished to claim benefits in the UK at a later stage or not.

Gradual legality – moving status between different stages of semi-legality and eventually legalizing one's stay – was therefore, in a majority of the cases, inspired by instrumental needs and attracted by prospective gains (better job security and working conditions, and access to benefits and welfare support). The different interpretations attached to the particular stages of legality – gradual legality being considered as a process – also revealed migrants' changing attitudes to legality: legality perceived as a value.

The subsequent stages on the scale of moving status – National Insurance, work contracts and Home Office registration – were combined with a greater appreciation of legality. Migrants gradually assigned a more important role to law; the law might still have been perceived quite distant, but more often than not it was associated with the sense of comfort and order:

> Here [in the UK] it's much more relaxed, people are much more relaxed about the law. OK, for example there is a street crossing, there are these yellow lights, but you can cross the street from one side, you can cross it from the other side of the lights. Here you just have some general rules, but you can go around them, or take your own responsibility for yourself, for what you find reasonable or not, then you learn the value of it, and start appreciating it. (Interview No. 18)

> It's true people here do whatever they like. It's more freedom here than in Poland. The law is simple and understandable by a simple man. At the same time one still has more freedom here than one had when one was living in Poland.

> The law is more effective, because people understand it, and they don't have to seek how to go around it. (Interview No. 26)

This prompts me to suggest that legality, as a social construct, could be discussed at two levels: the behavioural level and the value level. At the behavioural level, it relates to an objective status of acting in accordance with the law (changing or legalizing status) or turning to law as a tool for solving people's concrete problems (seeking help from the Citizens Advice Bureau or engaging in litigation). At the value level, it is appreciated as a quality of social life; nevertheless, it still may incorporate multiple, sometimes contradictory, normative claims, meanings, sources of authority and cultural practices that are recognized as legal and legitimate regardless of who employs them and to what end (Ewick and Silbey 1998).

Polish post-2004 EU enlargement migrants' experiences of law in the UK inspired their gradual behavioural choices with respect to the legality of their immigration and work status: engagements with the legal institutions when seeking help with problems, applications for NINs, contributions of tax and tax returns and finally joining the WRS. This is because once people behave in a certain fashion, their behaviour becomes a part of the totality upon which they can reflect (Hill 1981). The law and the legal infrastructure might have proved helpful in the event of a dispute with an employer in cases of exploitation, non-payment or discrimination or – due to the particular nature of the Accession Regulations – crucial for the access to welfare support and security of residence in the UK. Discovering the law's instrumental capacities triggered gradual changes in the immigration status of migrants.

The behavioural changes usually followed a similar pattern across three most distinguishable stages: firstly, securing the stability of employment; secondly, applying for a NIN; and, thirdly, registering under the WRS. This is not to say that all the interviewed Polish migrants who applied to register under the WRS continued their journeys until legal residence and exemption from the WRS. Some of them did not register their subsequently held jobs and therefore dropped out of the scheme, slipping back towards semi-legality. However, the majority of my respondents – perhaps paradoxically, due to late and very overdue registrations – realized the value and importance of joining the Scheme and continued towards the uninterrupted completion of 12 months and lawful residence.

The moves on the behavioural scale of legality towards regular immigration status and residence in turn brought with them a greater appreciation of legality as a value. Respondents started appreciating legality – acting in accordance with the law – as a quality of everyday life. The image of law might still be quite distant and rather different from how the British public perceived it; however, more often than not, it raised positive associations and was associated with comfort and order.

The ways in which people place themselves as legal subjects in turn affect how they relate themselves to the law and legality. Through the everyday actions of changing status, people experience new qualities of being 'legal' (in the sense of lawful and authorized), which then brings about the internalization and appreciation of the value of legality. The behavioural changes towards greater legality inspire and subsequently result in attitudinal changes regarding the evaluations of legality. From understandings and interpretations of law as a complicated matrix of rigid rules and regulations that were unevenly enforced and constituted a constraint to action, the law has turned to be appreciated as a value and quality of everyday life.

The observation that the behavioural changes inspire subsequent attitudinal changes, just as the move on the behavioural scale of legality brings with it a greater appreciation of legality as a value, places the current social psychology literature engaged in the cognitive dissonance theory in a new socio-legal context. My research presents a strong argument that the relationship between behaviour and attitudes could be meaningfully investigated not only in controlled laboratory settings but also in an applied domain, investigating migrants' responses to their new socio-legal environment.

This conclusion of gradual, intermittent changes at the level of behaviour and attitudes has important consequences regarding the meaningful focus of any future research on migrants' socio-legal integration. Directing the sole attention at the host country's laws (migration policies), legal institutions and law enforcement is insufficient, as migrants not only respond to the socio-legal environment but, in exercising their agency, also actively engage with it, which in turn may lead to changes at the normative level.

Conclusions: Towards an Improved Understanding of Migrants' Socio-Legal Integration

This book has addressed the question of how Polish post-2004 EU enlargement migrants in the UK form their relationship with British law – with the immigration and workplace regulations in particular – and which factors affected the formation of this relationship.

Answering the research question, the socio-legal literature on migrants' responses to the host country suggested focusing on the host country's laws, rules and regulations as the main factors that decided the form and characteristics of migrants' legal assimilation and integration. It followed the traditional approach to socio-legal research representing the 'law-first' perspective (Cowan 2004), where the primary concern is the study of law per se and its effects in society. Indeed, states' legal frameworks and political discourses are integral to immigration, as without law and migration policies (applicable within and across national state boundaries), what is termed immigration would only be the movement of people with no legal consequences (Coutin 2000).

As frameworks for researching migrants' incorporation, migration literature and transnationalism particularly exposed the 'double-edged sword' characteristics of the host country's changing immigration laws and policies. The latter, encouraging assimilation in civic and legal matters, have now turned out to be the main tool preventing migrants from settling, differentiating foreigners from those who can claim the right to belong. Borders are under surveillance, access to visas and work permits are restricted, and sharp lines are drawn between citizens and denizens (Glick Schiller 2007). As a result, many contemporary migrants decide to lead their transnational lives while maintaining strong links with both the societies of the host country and their country of origin.

American legalization literature introduced another important factor influencing migrants' responses to law in the new socio-legal environment. Aside from focusing solely on the host country's immigration laws, it brought to the forefront the role of agency – migrants' engagement in strategies aimed at securing legal status and residence. The research looked at how migrants responded to the law of the host country, actively engaged with it and sometimes even contested the state law frameworks in order to win their 'battles over permanent residency' (Coutin 2000).

Culture, as an additional factor, has been widely acknowledged in the migration scholarship as influencing migrants' responses to the new, host country environment. Researchers consider legal culture – as a part of general culture – to play an important role as a factor influencing people's relationship to law and responses to newly introduced legal institutions. However, legal culture – values and attitudes to law, as well as certain patterns of legal behaviour – has not received much attention in migration studies as a factor influencing the form and character of migrants' relationship with law upon their arrival in the host country.

My research with the Polish post-2004 EU enlargement migrants in the UK was therefore an attempt to better explore their values, attitudes to law and legal behaviour as 'luggage, repertoire of habits' they brought with them from home, which was a factor in their socio-legal integration. Legal culture was viewed not as a deterministic force but was expressed through migrants' choices (and reasoning) of following, avoiding or contesting the law upon arrival in the host country. The theoretical goal was the 'proper' recognition of legal culture – as mediated through migrants' agency – in the socio-legal and migration scholarship.

The research has demonstrated that the socio-legal integration of Polish post-2004 EU enlargement migrants in the UK is a complex and gradual process caused by a number of factors. Addressing the research question, the chapters of this book have analysed the various factors that played a role in influencing migrants' relationship with law. The chapters looked not only into the role of the British legal environment but – interchangeably – also focused on migrants' choices, needs and their legal culture in addressing the research puzzle.

The Socio-Legal Environment as a Factor

The investigation of Polish migrants' relationship with law started with presenting the British requirements towards A8 migrants in the UK (Chapter 4). There were two sets of rules that were particularly relevant for analysis: the 2004 Accession Regulations, regulating migrants' access to the labour market and legal residence in the UK and – due to the fact that the majority of Polish migrants arrive in the UK as workers – the workplace regulations and arrangements.

Analysing the role of the British socio-legal environment as a factor contributing to the shape of Polish migrants' relationship with the law, the chapter looked into the rules and the political rationale behind the immigration regulations, as well as how the rules were enforced, particularly in the area of the low-skilled, low-wage sector of the labour market in which the majority of Polish post-2004 EU enlargement migrants found employment.

Evaluating the functioning of the transition provisions between 2004 and 2011, it became apparent that the immigration regulations were thought of originally as a compromise between the national economic interest of filling numerous job vacancies – very much corresponding to the EU principle of free movement – and the protection of the welfare system from 'benefit tourism'.

As a result, the rules that were put in place were not to limit the number of workers but to better administer their numbers and prevent wider access to the welfare system. The WRS legislation did not have the authority of a prohibition or possess the same severity as breaking a law. Non-compliance did not attract a general punishment – e.g. in form of a fine – but rather designated migrant workers to a sometimes indefinite exclusion from participation in the welfare system.

There was some confusion around who was and who was not required to register, as the law did not apply evenly to all Polish post-2004 EU enlargement migrants in the UK. With regard to law enforcement, a battery of bureaucracy was involved. Although the legislation devised fines for employers hiring unauthorized workers, law enforcement in this area remained rather low. The inconsistent and uneven law enforcement of the immigration regulations did not inspire much confidence in the law altogether.

With regard to the workplace regulations, the recent changes towards a more flexible labour market made many workers – including migrant workers – uncertain of their employment status, particularly in the low-wage, low-skilled sector of the labour market. This led to confusion relating to employment rights as well as responsibilities towards the state, which remain largely 'a grey area' in this particular sector. The low-road practices, especially in the '3D' ('dirty, dangerous, demanding') jobs niche, attracted a rather inconsistent application of the law and often semi-regular employment via various employment businesses and employment agencies.

This points to the conclusion that the British legal environment in the transition period after the enlargement of the EU towards the Polish as well as other A8 migrant workers did not encourage compliance with the law or – at least – did not effectively discourage non- or semi-compliance.

However, the analysis of the British legal environment, stressing the role of the law and its enforcement in the context of institutions and structural conditions, seems to give only a partial answer to the question of the shape of Polish post-2004 EU enlargement migrants' relationship with law and their socio-legal integration in the UK. The deficiency of such a one-sided analysis lies in the nature of the law itself. The advocates of the invincible role of the law in society and the 'law first' type of analysis – without taking into account migrants' values, attitudes and their agency towards the law – ultimately contribute little to explaining why some migrants register, others do not and some others delay their registration process or drop out of the registration scheme altogether.

Migrants' Agency as a Factor

In Chapter 5 I therefore turned to the migrants themselves and looked at their responses and reasons for complying, not complying or semi-complying with the law. The fieldwork demonstrated that Polish post-2004 EU enlargement migrants in the UK were not merely passive recipients of the opportunity structures available to them in the host society, but shaped their responses towards the law according to their own needs.

As EU citizens, they felt allowed to enter the UK without any restrictions at airports and ports, they felt free to take up various forms of employment and they experienced no fear of deportation for not complying with the immigration regulations. The fieldwork demonstrated that my interviewees thus felt that they had a higher degree of choice as to whether to comply with the law, not comply or comply selectively – an experience they made very active use of.

Many of the Polish migrants (workers in the labour market), in their responses to the British immigration and workplace regulations, prioritized certain rules that benefited them directly (e.g. National Insurance regulations) over those whose potential benefits could not be seen directly and were directed more at the long term (e.g. the WRS). They also developed their own understanding and interpretations of the legal requirements.

Due to its close connection to access to benefits and inconsistent enforcement, the WRS was considered by many migrants who did not have long-term settlement plans as optional and not compulsory to follow. Not surprisingly, such migrants very much linked their registration to their future plans for applying for benefits and making use of the welfare system.

Polish migrants' varied responses to the workplace regulations challenged the long-standing dichotomy of an irregular migrant either as a victim or a villain (Anderson 2008). The non-payment or partial payment of taxes did not necessarily mean that migrants were exploited by their employers or that they themselves wanted to outwit the system in place. The target-earner strategy of migrant workers, often combined with the particular needs of their employers in the low-skilled, low-wage sector of the labour market, could account for the fact that non-payment of taxes or partial National Insurance deductions were due to specific, usually orally agreed working conditions outside the work contract. For the same reasons, the statutory provisions regarding overtime work and National Minimum Wage payments were often ignored and bypassed.

In analysing Polish migrants' responses to the British socio-legal environment, Chapter 5 therefore concluded that there exists a rather prominent group of semi-legal Polish post-2004 EU enlargement migrants in the UK and attempted to contextualize their semi-legality with reference to the past research on semi-compliance (Anderson and Ruhs 2010) and twilight, liminal legality (Menjivar 2006).

The British socio-legal environment and migrants' agency – their responses towards this environment – are therefore two important sets of factors which influence the form and character of Polish post-2004 EU enlargement migrants' relationship with the law in the UK and – to a large extent – explain their semi-legality. However, migrants' agency does not operate in a vacuum or with sole reference to the newly encountered legal environment. Polish migrants arrive in the UK with certain 'luggage' – a set of values, attitudes and shared patterns of behaviour towards law – which they can draw upon in exercising their choices of responses towards the environment.

Legal Culture as a Factor

Chapters 6 and 7 addressed the integration puzzle from the perspective of legal culture. The chapter on the Polish socio-legal tradition looked at the interplay of values, attitudes and legal behaviour with the development of Polish state and legal institutions.

The past very often contributes to a better understanding of the present, and although the Polish socio-legal tradition is rich and multi-faceted, certain patterns could be distinguished. The association of law with freedom rather than rights continued to surface from the historical analysis; the restrictive nature of certain laws was therefore intuitively perceived as against the ideal image of law as freedom. This, in turn, resulted in the lack of the law's ability to command compliance and authority. In circumstances of colonial-like rule, the lack of the law's legitimacy was reinforced by the alienating, foreign character of the state law. As a result, the formal rules were obeyed but despised, and society organized itself by different – from the state – intuitive laws (Petrażycki 1955).

Although tradition in the form of myths, symbols and interpretations becomes settled over generations, it nevertheless undergoes a constant change and adaptation to the various historical conditions. Hence, assuming deterministic forces and the impact of tradition on contemporary understandings, interpretations and behaviour towards law in Poland would not lead this research very far. Therefore, the analysis of the Polish socio-legal tradition was followed by the sociological analysis of the contemporary, popularly held values, attitudes, images of law, and the accompanying forms of legal behaviour.

Whilst acknowledging the heterogeneity of legal culture, I was interested in detecting certain patterns and themes that would help me to understand the repertoires of values, attitudes and interpretations of law that are perhaps more dominant than others and are therefore drawn upon and recalled by Polish migrants in shaping their initial responses to law in the UK.

The comparative perspective on legal culture – with the UK – brought about the main differences in understandings of the role of law, its image in society as a self-image of the group, and law enforcement. Chapter 7 demonstrated that both in Poland and the UK the law is highly regarded, although for different reasons and with different consequences.

While in Poland the law continued to be associated with freedom for oneself and restrictions for others, the current, rather restrictive, nature of complex and complicated laws led to a popular consensus of 'freedom from law' and keeping clear of the law. The law is associated with special knowledge and is therefore perceived as a sphere that has little to do with everyday life and is more reserved for 'professionals', who should pass, apply and interpret the law. In Poland the normative gap between social expectations towards the law and its everyday life experiences fostered practices of avoiding the law and a general consensus of semi-compliance. People prefer to 'keep clear' of the law or admit breaking it 'to get things done'.

These interpretations of law and experiences of law enforcement that Polish migrants 'bring' with them tend to be different from what they encounter when they arrive in the UK. In the UK the law tends to be perceived as guidelines and something that gives structure to everyday life. People see the law as they see themselves – a rather orderly society, organized around some overarching principles based on common sense. British people think of themselves as generally law abiding; they might break the law, but usually only to commit petty offences. Breaking the law does not meet with social acceptance. As a result, the image of the law in the UK as the overarching, consensual structures gives enough freedom and flexibility in the application of the law, as people attribute different meanings, experiences and upbringings to interpreting those general principles for themselves in everyday life.

When exploring Polish legal culture, Chapter 7 also gave voice to the Polish post-2004 EU enlargement migrants in the UK reflecting on their experiences of workplace rules and regulations in Poland. It demonstrated that the choice of semi-legality over legality reflecting the rather ambivalent attitude to law is a long-standing one, and one that is often made.

The analysis of the Polish socio-legal tradition and contemporary legal culture demonstrated the experiences, values and attitudes towards the law that Polish migrants arrived with in the UK. They in turn – at least initially – were employed to help the Polish migrants navigate when shaping their relations with British state officials, immigration and workplace regulations. The values, attitudes and images of law – at the beginning of their migratory experience – continued to be relied upon as a familiar guide, as cultural codes are often linked to specific contexts and specific institutions regardless of their geographical position. They played a role in the migrants' choices of initial semi-legality, strategies of avoidance or indifference towards the law, its institutions and representatives in the UK.

Answering the broader research question on the form and character of migrants' relationship with the law in the host country and the factors that influence it, this book therefore concludes that it is not the institutional arrangements and legal architecture alone that decide the nature of migrants' semi-legal relationship with the law in the host society. A more comprehensive insight into the socio-legal integration of migrants is possible only when we combine in the analysis the interplay between the structural factors of the host country's legal environment, migrants' agency and the culturally derived values, attitudes and social expectations towards the law and its enforcement, and how these values and expectations are met – or mismatched – as migrants rebuild their new lives in the new surroundings.

When analysing the socio-legal integration of migrants, the legal environment, migrants' agency and their legal culture have to be taken into consideration together as (although they could be separated for the purpose of analysis) ontologically they are intertwined with each other in the complex social reality. As a result, the influence they exert could not be attributed to just one set of factors, but instead stems from the interaction and the complex interplay between them.

Legal Adaptation

The book also demonstrates that any discussion on the form and character of migrants' relationship with the law in the host country – their socio-legal integration – should take into account the fact that values, attitudes and patterns of behaviour do not continue unchanged, but, over time, adapt to specific conditions of the socio-legal environment.

As the American legalization literature looked at migrants' engagement in legalization programmes at a particular time in their immigration history – usually some time after their arrival – it reflected on their values and interpretations of law well after the migrants themselves became settled and exposed to different sets of attitudes and legal behaviour stemming from the new legal environment. Therefore, the values and attitudes to law of those migrants actively engaged in the legalization programmes – as depicted in the studies – more closely resembled the American civic engagement values usually found in discourses on rights and justice (Abrego 2008).

In the context of migrants' initial responses to the law of the host country, it is difficult to conclude that after troubled journeys of, for instance, being smuggled into the country, fleeing persecution, conflict or an unsettled political situation (as in the case of Mexican, Guatemalan and Salvadoran immigrants in the USA), migrants facing the complex legal environment of the US immigration laws would immediately organize themselves and 'stand up for their rights'. Migrants' experiences of leading illicit lives, working in the precarious sectors of the host country's labour market or confining their lives to spaces of 'non-existence' (Coutin 2000) seriously question their immediate and indisputable experiences of legality and the association of law as the source of social order.

Polish post-2004 EU enlargement migrants in the UK are similarly engaged in multi-layered frameworks which have both a constraining and an enabling effect on their behaviour and choices. Therefore, their attitudes and priorities might be more complex, ambiguous and less unidirectional than suggested by the current legalization literature. The empirical evidence reveals that many migrants – who, it should be noted, experienced no difficult journeys or problems being admitted to the country – initially drawing on their accustomed 'ways of dealing with law' when faced with the immigration and workplace regulations, displayed rather a ambivalent attitude towards the law, prioritizing any job over a 'legal job' and 'keeping clear of the law' (Zbigniew, FG 2) over WRS registration. They aimed at securing their existence and 'normality' – as they knew it – over meeting the requirements for legal residence.

The formal legality of their status was therefore extended over time, as migrants negotiated their new lives by initially semi-complying with the laws, then gradually approaching them with instrumental considerations and complying with some laws rather than others, moving closer towards legality as time progressed. Some migrants, of course, dropped away from the path towards lawful residence, while others – perhaps intermittently – continued towards formal legality.

This chapter also revealed the changes in Polish migrants' attitudes to law. Gradual, behavioural moves on the scale of legality (towards the formal legality of one's status) brought with them a greater appreciation of legality as a value. The study of Polish post-2004 EU enlargement migrants in the UK and their responses to British law and legal institutions therefore calls for a balanced approach in researching migrants' behaviour and attitudes to legality, and the factors that mediate between them.

The Internal Dynamics of Legal Culture

The behavioural formation of legality which accompanies the gradual process of changing status together with the subsequent attitudinal turn to legality as a value (as observed in the Polish migrants' gradual adaptation strategies) also makes it possible to theorize and draw conclusions about the change of legal culture.

Legal culture is not just an important explanation of Polish migrants' initial semi-legality, but as an intervening variable in migrants' socio-legal integration, it is not rigid and constant but rather adaptable and changing.

The example of Polish post-2004 EU enlargement migrants in the UK demonstrates that at the value level, the law becomes appreciated as a quality of social life; nevertheless, 'what is legal' may still incorporate multiple, sometimes contradictory, normative claims, meanings, sources of authority and cultural practices that are recognized as legal and legitimate regardless of who employs them and for what ends (Ewick and Silbey 2002). Such an interpretation of legal culture is particularly conducive to innovations, as the mutual reconstitution over time of structure (law) and agency (responses to law) allows for alterations in the pattern of this reciprocal engagement that spring from actor's innovations (gradual behavioural and formal legality) and from the cultural schemas and toolkits that inform such actions (Emirbayer and Mische 1998; Sewell 1992).

When talking about legal culture, as part of 'general' culture:

> [People] draw from a multiform repertoire of meanings to frame and re-frame experience in an open-ended way. In debate, they may be unselective, taking up any argument that seems handy. In other situations, they take up one cultural frame … until they run up against an unsolved problem. Undaunted, they usually simply escape the conundrum by jumping outside its boundaries, invoking another situation, another metaphor, another symbolic frame. This frequent shifting among multiple cultural realities is not some anomalous sleight of hand but the normal way in which ordinary mortals (as distinguished perhaps, from trained philosophers) operate. (Swidler 2001: 40)

Legal culture therefore constitutes a pool of different toolkits, repertoires of values, attitudes, interpretations of law and legal behaviour, and – while some of them might be stronger than others – these schemas are complex and often contradictory (Ewick and Silbey 1998). These inherent complexities and contradictions in turn provide spaces for the change of legal culture. If the only thing people knew about the law was its profane face of crafty lawyers and outrageous tort cases, it would be difficult to sustain the allegiance and support necessary for legal authority (Silbey 2005). Similarly, if the image of law among the interviewed Polish migrants reflected only the restrictive nature of many laws they faced in Poland, the scope for appreciation of legality as a value would be rather scant.

As the example of Polish post-2004 EU enlargement migrants in the UK demonstrates, the contradictory and complex nature of different repertoires, attitudes, values and schemas within legal culture results in a situation where, over time, certain schemas and attitudes become – in specific contexts – partially redundant, while others gain greater importance. The behavioural patterns, values and attitudes upon which the initially semi-legal migrants drew (from the available 'toolkit' of legal culture) when fashioning their responses to the new socio-legal environment gradually changed as a result of the complex interplay between the host society's laws and regulations and the migrants' day-to-day experiences with them, cultural diffusion and processes of acculturation.

The capacity of migrants to appropriate, adapt and, potentially, to innovate upon received cultural schemas, values and attitudes to law and conditions of action in accordance with their personal and collective ideas, interests and commitments allowed for alterations in the legal culture and the adaptation of legal culture to the new socio-legal environment. As a result, alongside the behavioural changes, Polish migrants gradually assigned a more important role to law. The law might still be perceived quite distant, but more often than not it was associated with the sense of comfort and order.

The legal culture is changing, yet its change could best be characterized by its attribute of inertia. This book concludes that the nature of legal culture change – constituted by the greater popularity of some cultural tools over others – yet still employed in a polysemous way – is characterized by initial resistance, moderation and intangibility. Polish migrants gradually and over time legalize their status and start appreciating legality as a value in their social life. However, their behavioural changes towards legality take place well beyond the timeframe of compliance as designed by law in the UK.

Although formal rules may change overnight – as a result of political or juridical decisions – informal constraints embodied in customs, traditions and codes of conduct are much more impervious to deliberate policies (North 1990). As the example of Polish post-2004 EU enlargement migrants in the UK demonstrates, in fashioning their responses to the new laws (or newly introduced institutions), compliance competes with pre-existing, culturally mediated experiences of complicated and troublesome laws, familiar strategies of bypassing the law or indifference towards it and choices of 'free rides' on the state due to the deeply entrenched distrust towards it.

These cultural constraints not only connect the past with the present and the future but also provide researchers with a key to explaining the nature and character of change in legal culture. Legal culture, being the product of accumulative historical experience, reflects the development of state institutions and popular attitudes towards law but also enables a certain predictability regarding the future development of a society – its response to socio-economic change and its compliance, non- or semi-compliance with newly introduced institutions. The ability to proactively use it can influence other aspects of socio-legal epistemology.

Appendix

Table A1 Focus Groups Locations and Timetable: The UK

Group number	Location	Target group	Date
1	London	Better educated	9.01.2008
2	London	Worse educated	9.01.2008
3	Bristol	Cross-section	10.01.2008
4	Yate	Cross-section	10.01.2008
5	Villages in south-west England (Almonsbury, Winterbourne, Coalpit, Old Sodbury)	Cross-section	11.01.2008
6	Sheffield	Cross-section	12.01.2008
7	Villages in north-west England (Eckington, Ben Rhydding, Dronfield Dore, Mosborough)	Cross-section	12.01.2008
8	Leeds	Cross-section	14.01.2008
9	London	Polish migrants; cross-section	15.01.2008

Table A2 Focus Groups Locations and Timetable: Poland

Group number	Location	Target group	Date
1	Warsaw	Better educated	22.02.2008
2	Warsaw	Worse educated	29.02.2008
3	Katowice	Cross-section	13.03.2008
4	Turosl Koscielna	Cross-section	13.03.2008
5	Mierzecice	Cross-section	13.03.2008
6	Lubliniec	Cross-section	11.03.2008
7	Zambkow	Cross-section	12.03.2008
8	Bialystok	Cross-section	11.03.2008

Bibliography

Abrego, L. 2008. Legitimacy, Social Identity, and the Mobilization of Law: The Effects of Assembly Bill 540 on Undocumented Students in California. *Law and Social Inquiry*, 33(3), 709–34.

Ackers, L. and Dwyer, P. 2002. Senior Citizenship? Retirement, Migration and Welfare in the European Union. Bristol: Policy Press.

Alba, R. and Nee, V. 1997. Rethinking Assimilation Theory for a New Era of Immigration. *International Migration Review*, 31(4), 826–74.

Alba, R. and Nee, V. 2003. Remaking the American Mainstream: Assimilation and Contemporary Immigration. Cambridge, MA: Harvard University Press.

Allport, F. 1920. Behaviour and Experiment in Social Psychology. *Psychological Bulletin*, 17, 75–6.

Allport, G. W. 1935. Attitudes, in *A Handbook of Social Psychology*, edited by F. Allport. Worcester, MA: Clark University Press, pp. 798–844.

Anderson, B. 2008 'Illegal Immigrant': Victim or Villain? *COMPAS Working Paper Series*. Available at: http://www.compas.ox.ac.uk/publications/working-papers/wp-08-64/ (date accessed 3 January 2012).

Anderson, B. and Rogaly, B. 2005. *Forced Labour and Migration to the UK*. Oxford: Centre for Migration Policy and Society (COMPAS) in association with the Trades Union Congress.

Anderson, B. and Ruhs, M. 2010. Semi-Compliance and Illegality in Migrant Labour Markets: An Analysis of Migrants, Employers and the State in the UK. *Population, Space and Place*, 16(3), 195–211.

Anderson, B., Ruhs M., Rogaly B., Spencer S., 2006. *Fair Enough? Central and Eastern European Migrants in low-wage employment in the UK*. Report written for the Joseph Rowntree Foundation, University of Oxford: COMPAS.

ANIMATE 2008. *Your Rights in Northern Ireland. A Guide for Migrant Workers*. Belfast: Northern Ireland Human Rights Commission.

Archer, M. 1982. Morphogenesis versus Structuration: On Combining Structure and Action. *British Journal of Sociology*, 33, 455–83.

Archer, M. 1996. Culture and Agency. The Place of Culture in Social Theory. Cambridge: Cambridge University Press.

Aronson, E. 1973. The Rationalizing Animal. *Psychology Today*, 6, 46–52.

Arrowsmith, J. 2006. Temporary Agency Work in an Enlarged European Union. Available at: http://www.eurofound.europa.eu/pubdocs/2005/139/en/1/ef05139en.pdf (date accessed 3 January 2012).

Arrowsmith, J. 2008. *UK: Temporary Agency Work and Collective Bargaining in the EU*. London: Institute for Labour and Family Research.

Babiński G., Chałupczak H. (eds) (2006), *Diaspora polska w procesach globalizacji: stan i perspektywy badań [Polish diaspora in the processes of globalisation: state of the art and the perspectives for further research]*. Kraków: Komitet Badania Polonii PAN.

Babiuch-Luxmoore, J. 2008. *Employers and Service Providers: Experiences and Views. Migrant Workers' Experiences.* Oxford: Report prepared for the Citizens Advice Bureaux network, unpublished. Access and reference permission obtained from the author.

Bahlcke, J. 2005. Perceptions of 'Libertas' in the Corporate Societies of Early Modern Poland, Bohemia and Hungary, in *Political Culture in Central Europe (10th–20th Century) Part I, Middle Ages and Early Modern Era*, edited by H. Manikowska, J. Pánek and M. Holý. Warsaw and Prague: Institute of History, Academy of Sciences of the Czech Republic; Institute of History, Polish Academy of Sciences.

Ballard, R. (ed.) 1994. *Desh Pradesh: The South Asians Presence in Britain.* London: C. Hurst & Co. Publishers.

Ballard, R. 2006. Ethnic Diversity and the Delivery of Justice: The Challenge of Plurality, in *Migration, Diasporas and Legal Systems in Europe*, edited by P. Shah and W. Menski. London: Routledge-Cavendish.

Ballard, R. 2007. *When, Why and How Far Should Legal Systems Take Cognisance of Cultural Diversity?* International Congress on Justice and Human Values in Europe, Karlsruhe, 9–11 May.

Ballard, R. 2010. Analytical Vocabularies in Anthropology, Law and Religion: Time for a Rethink? RELIGARE, Queen Mary University, London, 24 June.

Banakar, R. 2008. Politics of Legal Cultures. *Retfaerd Argang*, 31(4/123), 37–60.

Bardach, J. Leśnodorski B., Pietrzak M. 2000. *Historia Ustroju i Prawa Polskiego* [The History of Governance and Polish Law]. Warsaw: Wydawnictwa Prawnicze PWN.

Bauer, J. 1999. Speaking of Culture: Immigrants in the American Legal System, in *Immigrants in Courts*, edited by J. Moore, Seattle: University of Washington Press.

Bell, J. 2001. *French Legal Cultures.* Cambridge: Cambridge University Press.

Benton, L. 1994, 'Beyond Legal Pluralism: Towards a New Approach to Law in the Informal Sector', *Social and Legal Studies*, 3, 223–42.

Benton, L. 2002. Law and Colonial Cultures. Legal Regimes in World History 1400–1900. Cambridge: Cambridge University Press.

Berman, H. J. 1963. *Justice in the USSR. An Interpretation of Soviet Law.* Cambridge, MA: Harvard University Press.

Berman, H. J. 1983. *Law and Revolution: The Formation of the Western Legal Tradition.* Cambridge, MA: Harvard University Press.

Berry, J. W. 1980. Acculturation as Varieties of Adaptation, in *Acculturation: Theory, Models and Some New Findings*, edited by A.M. Padilla, Boulder, CO: Westview Press.

Berry, J. W. 1997. Immigration, Acculturation and Adaptation. *Applied Psychology: An International Review*, 46, 5–68.

Berry, J. W. 2002. Conceptual Approaches to Acculturation, in *Acculturation: Advances in Theory, Measurement, and Applied Research*, edited by K. M. Chun, P. B. Organista and G. Marin. Washington DC: APA Books.

Berry, J. W. 2005. Acculturation: Living Successfully in Two Cultures. *International Journal of Inter-cultural Relations*, 29(6), 697–712.

Berry, J. W. 2008. Globalisation and Acculturation. *International Journal of Inter-cultural Relations*, 32(4), 328–36.

Bhattacharya, G. 2008. Acculturating Indian Immigrant Men in New York City: Applying the Social Capital Construct to Understand their Experiences and Health. *Journal of Immigrant and Minority Health*, 10(2), 91–101.

Bierbrauer, G. 1994. Toward an Understanding of Legal Culture: Variations in Individualism and Collectivism between Kurds, Lebanese and Germans. *Law and Society Review*, 28(2), 243–64.

Blanchflower D and Lawton H. 2008. *The Impact of the Recent Expansion of the EU on the UK Labour Market*. Bonn: IZA discussion paper 3695. Available at: http://ftp.iza.org/dp3695.pdf (date accessed: 6 January 2011).

Blanke, T. and Bruinsma, F. 1994. *Dutch Legal Culture*. Dordrecht: Kluwer Law International.

Blankenburg, E. 1998. Patterns of Legal Culture: The Netherlands Compared to Neighboring Germany. *American Journal of Comparative Law*, 46, 1–41.

Blumer, H. 1949. An Appraisal of Thomas and Znaniecki's The Polish Peasant in Europe and America. New York: Social Science Research Council.

Boni, M. 2004. Elastyczny Rynek Pracy W Polsce: Jak Sprostac Temu Wyzwaniu? [The Flexible Labour Market in Poland: How to Address the Challenge?]. Poznań: Wydawnictwo Fundacji Humaniora.

Borrie, W. D. 1959. The Cultural Integration of Immigrants: A Survey Based Upon the Papers and Proceedings of the Unesco Conference. Paris: UNESCO.

Boswell, C. 2008. The Political Functions of Expert Knowledge: Knowledge and Legitimation in European Union Immigration Policy. *Journal of European Public Policy*, 15(4), 471–88.

Bourdieu, P. 1981. Men and Machines, in *Advances in Social Theory and Methodology: Toward and Integration of Micro and Macro Theories*, edited by K. Knorr-Cetina and A. V. Cicourel, Boston: Routledge & Kegan Paul.

Brelvi, F. S. 1997. News of the Weird: Specious Normativity and the Problem of the Cultural Defense. *Columbia Human Rights Law Review*, 28, 657–83.

Brislin, R. W., Landis, D., and Brandt, M. 1983. Conceptualisations of Intercultural Behaviour and Training, in *Handbook of Intercultural Training, Volume I: Issues in Theory and Design*, edited by D. Landis, J. Bennett and M. J. Bennett. New York: Pergamon Press.

Brubaker, R. 2001. The Return of Assimilation? Changing Perspectives on Immigration and its Sequels in France, Germany and the United States. *Ethnic and Racial Studies*, 24(4), 531–48.

Buchowski, M. 2001. Rethinking Transformation. An Anthropological Perspective. Poznań: Humaniora.

Bukowski, A., Gadowska, K, and Polak, P. 2008. Barriers and Obstacles in the Process of Awarding and Implementation of EU Funds in Poland. *Polish Sociological Review*, 4(164), 437–69.

Bumiller, K. 1988. *The Civil Rights Society: The Social Construction of Victims.* Baltimore, MD: Johns Hopkins University Press.

Burrell, K. 2009 (ed) Polish Migration to the UK in the `New' European Union. After 2004. Farnham: Ashgate.Calavita, K. 2005. *Immigrants at the Margins.* New York: Cambridge University Press.

Carby-Hall, J. 2007. *The Treatment of Polish and Other A8 Economic Migrants in the European Union Member States.* Warsaw: Commissioner for Civil Rights Protection of the Republic of Poland. Available at: http://www.rpo.gov.pl/index.php?md=8562&s=3 (date accessed: 12 February 2012).

Carter, R. and Charles, N. 2010. Conceptualizing Agency in Human–Animal Relations: A Sociological Approach, in *Human and Other Animals: Critical Perspectives*, edited by R. Carter and N. Charles. Basingstoke: Palgrave Macmillan.

Castles, S. 2002. Migration and Community Formation under Conditions of Globalization. *International Migration Review*, 36(4), 1143–68.

Castles, S. and Davidson, A. 2000. Citizenship and Migration: Globalization and the Politics of Belonging. New York: Routledge.

Castles, S. and Miller, M. 1998. The Age of Migration: International Population Movements in the Modern World. New York: Guilford Press.

CBOS. 2003. Research Report: Compliance with Workers' Rights and the role of Trades Unions as Rights' enforcers. BS/42/2003. Warsaw: Centre for Public Opinion Research (CBOS). Available at: http://www.cbos.pl/SPISKOM.POL/2003/K_042_03.PDF (date accessed: 11 March 2010).

CBOS. 2006a. Research Report: Collective Bargaining, Employees' Rights and the 'Grey Sphere' in Employment.Bs/167/2006. Warsaw: Centre for Public Opinion Research (CBOS).

CBOS. 2006b. Research Report: Prestige of Professions, Professional Honesty and Integrity. Bs/37/2006. Warsaw: Centre for Public Opinion Research (CBOS).

CBOS. 2007. Research Report: On the Administration and Administrative Officials in Poland. Bs/150/2007. Warsaw: Centre for Public Opinion Research (CBOS),

CBOS. 2009. Research Report: Public Morality and Attitudes toward Socially Reprehensible Behaviours. Bs/71/2009. Warsaw: Centre for Public Opinion Research (CBOS).

Chappell, L., Latorre M., Rutter J., and J. Shah. 2009. *Migration and Rural Economies: Assessing and Addressing Risks.* London: Institute for Public Policy Research.

Chavez, L. 1998. *Shadowed Lives: Undocumented Immigrants in American Society*, Fort Worth: Harcourt Brace College Publishers

Chiba, M. 1998. Other Phases of Legal Pluralism in Contemporary World. *Ratio Juris*, 11(3), 228–45.

Chłopocka, H. 1967. Procesy Polski Z Zakonem Krzyżackim W XIV wieku. Studium Źródłoznawcze [The Lawsuits between Poland and the Order of Teutonic Knights in the 14th Century]. Poznań: Panstwowe Wydawnictwo Naukowe.

Clarke, K. and Drinkwater, S. 2008. The Labour-Market Performance of Recent Immigrants. *Oxford Review of Economic Policy*, 24(3), 495–516.

Cobb, C. 2005. Not Quite Formal: Theorizing the Informal Labor Market Experiences of 'Documented' Immigrant Workers. *Online Journal 2004/05 of the Ronald E. McNair Scholars Program*. Available at: http://www.mcnair-program.pdx.edu/Online%20Journal%20200405/Carrie%20Cobb--FINAL.pdf (date accessed 3 January 2012).

Coe, N., Johns J., and Ward, K. 2007. Mapping the Globalization of the Temporary Staffing Industry. *The Globalization of the Temporary Staffing Industry Working Paper Series; No. 2*. Available at: http://www.eurociett.eu/fileadmin/templates/ciett/research/MU_Mapping_the_globalisation_of_staffin.pdf (date accessed 3 January 2012).

Cotterrell, R. 1997. The Concept of Legal Culture, in *Comparing Legal Cultures*, edited by D. Nelken. Aldershot: Ashgate.

Cotterrell, R. 2001. Is There a Logic of Legal Transplants?, in *Adapting Legal Cultures*, edited by D. Nelken, J. Feest. Oxford: Hart Publishing.

Cotterrell, R. 2009. Spectres of Transnationalism: Changing Terrains of Sociology of Law' *Journal of Law and Society*, 36, 481–500.

Coutin, S. B. 1998. From Refugees to Immigrants: The Legalization Strategies of Salvadoran Immigrants and Activists. *International Migration Review*, 32(4), 901–25.

Coutin, S. B. 2000. Legalizing Moves: Salvadoran Immigrants' Struggle for US Residency. Ann Arbor, MI: University of Michigan Press.

Cowan, D. 2004. Legal Consciousness: Some Observations. *Modern Law Review*, 67(6), 928–58.

Coyle, A. 2007. Resistance, Regulation and Rights: The Changing Status of Polish Women's Migration and Work in the 'New' Europe. *European Journal of Women's Studies*, 14(1), 37–50.

Craig, G., Gaus, A., Wilkinson, M., Skrivankova, K., and McQuad, A. 2007. *Contemporary Slavery in the UK. Overview and Key Issues.* York: Joseph Rowntree Foundation.

Crano, W. D. and Messe, L. A. 1970. When Does Dissonance Fail? The Time Dimension in Attitude Measurement. *Journal of Personality*, 38, 493–508.

Cronin, C. 1970. The Sting of Change – Sicilians in Sicily and Australia. Chicago: University of Chicago Press.

Cruickshank, J. 2011. The Positive and the Negative: Assessing Critical Realism and Social Constructionism as Post-Positivist Approaches to Empirical Research in the Social Sciences, IMI Working Paper WP-42-2011. Available at: http://www.imi.ox.ac.uk/publications/working_papers (date accessed 3 January 2012).

Currie, S. 2006. 'Free'-Movers? The Post-Accession Experience of Accession-8 Migrant Workers in the UK. *European Law Review*, 31(2), 207–29.

Currie, S. 2007a. *Citizenship in the Context of EU Enlargement: Post-Accession CEE Migrants as Union Citizens*. European Union Studies Association (EUSA) Biennial Conference, Montreal, Canada, 17–19 May.

Currie, S. 2007b. De-Skilled and Devalued: The Labour Market Experience of Polish Migrants in the UK Following EU Enlargement. *The International Journal of Comparative Labour Law and Industrial Relations*, 23(1), 83–116.

Currie, S. 2008a. Challenging the UK Rules on the Rights of EU8 Workers. *Journal of Social Welfare and Family Law*, 31(1), 47–58.

Currie, S. 2008b. Migration, Work and Citizenship in the Enlarged European Union. Farnham: Ashgate.

Currie, S. 2009. Regular Migrants in the Irregular Workplace: Central and Eastern European Women in the UK after EU Enlargement, in *Gender and Migration in 21st Century Europe*, edited by H. Stalford, S. Currie and S. Velluti. Farnham: Ashgate.

Danzelman P. 2009 *British citizenship statistics, United Kingdom, 2008*. Home Office Statistical Bulletin, Home Office, Research, Development and Statistics Directorate (RDS).

Datta, A. 2009. This is Special Humour: Visual Narratives of Polish Masculinities on London's Building Sites, in *Polish Migration to the UK in the 'New' European Union. After 2004*, edited by K. Burrell. Farnham: Ashgate.

Davies, M. 2005. The Ethos of Pluralism. *Sydney Law Review*, 27(1), 87–112.

Davies, N. 2005. *God's Playground. A History of Poland.* Vol. 1 and Vol. 2, Oxford: Oxford University Press.

Demos. 2007. Recruitment 2020: How Recruitment is Changing and Why it Matters. London: Demos.

De Genova, N. 2004. The Legal Production of Mexican/Migrant 'Illegality'. *Latino Studies*, 2(2), 160–85.

De Genova, N., Peutz N. (2010) The Deportation Regime: Sovereignty, Space, and the Freedom of Movement, Durham: Duke University Press

Dench, S., Hurstfield, J., Hill, D., and Akroyd, K.2006. Employers' Use of Migrant Labour. Main Report. *Home Office Online Report 04/06*. Available at: http://www.northamptonshireobservatory.org.uk/docs/docrdsolr0406060818113351.pdf (date accessed 3 January 2012).

Deux, K. 2006. To Be an Immigrant: Psychological Design and Social Fabric. New York: Russell Sage.

Dopierala, K. 2003–2005. Encyklopedia Polskiej Emigracji I Polonii [The Encyclopaedia of Polish Emigration and Polish Diaspora]. Torun: Oficyna Wydawnicza Kucharski.

Dougan, M. 2004. A Spectre is Haunting Europe. Free Movement of Persons and the Eastern Enlargement, in *EU Enlargement: A Legal Approach*, edited by C. Hillion. Oxford: Hart Publishing.

Dougan, M. and Spaventa, E. 2003. Educating Rudy and the Non English Patient: A Double Bill on Residency Rights under Article 18 EC. *European Law Review*, 28(5), 699–712.

Drinkwater, S., Eade J., Garapich, M.2007. Poles Apart? EU Enlargement and the Labour Market Outcomes of Immigrants in the UK. *IZA Discussion Papers*. Available at: http://ideas.repec.org/p/iza/izadps/dp2410.html (date accessed 3 January 2012).

Dunn, E. 1999. Slick Salesman and Simple People. Negotiated Capitalism in a Privatised Polish Firm, in *Uncertain Transition: Ethnographies of Change in the Postsocialist World*, edited by M. Burawoy and K. Verdery. Lanham, MD: Rownam & Littlefield.

Dustmann, C., Frattini, T and Halls, C. 2009. *Assessing the Fiscal Costs and Benefits of A8 Migration to the UK*. CReAM Discussion Paper Series 0918, Centre for Research and Analysis of Migration (CReAM), Department of Economics, University College London. Available at: http://www.cream-migration.org/publ_uploads/CDP_18_09.pdf (date accessed: 5 January 2011).

DWP. 2007. *National Insurance Number Allocations to Overseas Nationals Entering the UK 2007*. Available at: www.dwp.gov.uk (date accessed 3 January 2012).

Dziennik Polski. 1947. *Do Not Borrow*. 31 March 1947: Dziennik Polski, in *The Formation of the Polish Community in Great Britain 1939–1950*. Sword, K., Davies, N., and Ciechanowski, J.. 1989. London: School of Slavonic and East European Studies.

Duvell, F. 2008. Clandestine migration in Europe. *Social Science Information*, 47(4), 479–97.

Ehrlich, E. 1912. Das Lebende Recht Der Voelker Der Bukowina. *Recht und Wirtschaft*, 1(273), 40–52.

Elster, J,, Offe, C., and Preuss, U. K.1998. Institutional Design in Post-Communist Societies. Rebuilding the Ship at Sea. Cambridge: Cambridge University Press.

EMAR (Employment Markets Analysis Research). 2008. *Agency Working in the UK: A Review of Evidence*. London: Department for Business, Enterprise and Regulatory Reform (BERR). Available at: http://www.bis.gov.uk/files/file48720.pdf (date accessed: 12 February 2012).

Emirbayer, M. and Mische, A. 1998. What is Agency? *American Journal of Sociology*, 103(4), 962–1023.

Encyclopaedia Britannica. 2007. Casimir I. Available at: Encyclopaedia Britannica Online: http://www.britannica.com/eb/article–9020621 (date accessed 3 January 2012).

EURES 2009. The European Job Mobility Portal. Available at: http://ec.europa.eu/eures/main.jsp?acro=lw&lang=en&catId=490&parentId=0 (date accessed: 3 September 2007).

European Commission. 2009. The European Job Mobility Portal: Information on the Transitional Rules Governing the Free Movement of Workers from, to and between the New Member States. Available at: http://ec.europa.eu/eures/main.jsp?acro=free&lang=en&countryId=UK&accessing=0&content=1&restrictions=1&step=1 (date accessed 3 January 2012).

Ewick, P. and Silbey, S. 1998. *The Common Place of Law. Stories from Everyday Life.* Chicago: University of Chicago Press.

Ewick, P. and Silbey, S. 2002. The Structure of Legality: The Cultural Contradictions of Social Institutions, in *Legality and Community. On the Intellectual Legacy of Philip Selznick*, edited by P. Selznick, R. A. Kagan, M. Krygier and K. I. Winston. Lanham, MD: Rowman & Littlefield.

Eyal, G., Szelenyi, I., and Townsley, E. 1998. Making Capitalism without Capitalists: The New Ruling Elites in Eastern Europe. London: Verso.

Feist, T. 2000. Transnationalization in International Migration: Implications for the Study. *Ethnic and Racial Studies*, 23(2), 189–222.

Feldman, E. 2001. Blood Justice, Courts, Conflict and Compensation in Japan, France and the United States. *Law and Society Review*, 34(3), 651–701.

Festinger, L. 1957. *A Theory of Cognitive Dissonance.* Evanston, IL: Row & Peterson.

Firlit, E. and Chłopecki, J. 1992. When Theft is Not Theft, in *The Unplanned Society: Poland During and after Communism*, edited by J. Wedel. New York: Columbia University Press.

Fisher, H. D. 2002. *The German Legal System and Legal Language.* London: Cavendish Publishing.

Fitzgerald, I. 2007 Working in the UK: Polish Migrant Worker Routes into Employment in the North East and North West Construction and Food Processing Sectors, London: Trades Union Congress

Foner, N. 1996. The Immigrant Family: Cultural Legacies and Cultural Changes. *International Migration Review*, 31(4), 961–74.

Freeman, T. 2006. Peoples Flows in Globalization. *Journal of Economic Perspectives*, 20(2), 145–70.

Friedman, L. M. 1975. *The Legal System: A Social Science Perspective.* New York: Russell Sage Foundation.

Friedman, L. M. 1977. *Law and Society: An Introduction.* Englewood Cliffs, NJ: Prentice Hall.

Friedman, L. M. 1990. *Republic of Choice.* Cambridge, MA: Harvard University Press.

Friedman, L. M. 2001. Some Comments on Cotterell and Legal Transplants, in *Adapting Legal Cultures*, edited by D. Nelken and J. Feest. Oxford: Hart Publishing.

Furnham, A. and Bochner, S. 1986. Culture Shock: Psychological Reactions to Unfamiliar Environments. London: Methuen.

Gadowska, K., and Majcherkiewicz T. 2005. 'Political Clientelism in Public Administration. A Case Study of Institutional Changes in the Post-Communist

State of Poland' in *Democratic Governance for the XXI Century: Challenges and Responses in CEE Countries* (conference proceedings) 19–21 May 2005 Moscow. Available at: http://unpan1.un.org/intradoc/groups/public/documents/nispacee/unpan023770.pdf (date accessed 12 February 2012).

Galasinska, A. and Kozłowska, O. 2009. Discourses of Normal Life among Post-Accession Migrants from Poland to Britain, in *Polish Migration to the UK in the 'New' European Union after 2004*, edited by K. Burrell. Farnham: Ashgate.

Galligan, D. J. 2007. *Law in Modern Society.* Oxford: Oxford University Press.

Garapich, M. 2008. The Migration Industry and Civil Society: Polish Immigrants in the United Kingdom before and after EU Enlargement. *Journal of Ethnic and Migration Studies*, 34(5), 735–52.

Gasiorowski, A. 1984. Rotation of the Elite of Power, in *The Polish Nobility in the Middle Ages. Anthologies*, edited by A. Gasiorowski. Wroclaw, Warsaw, Krakow, Gdansk and Lodz: Zaklad Narodowy im. Ossolinskich, Wydawnictwo Polskiej Akademii Nauk.

Geddes, A, Scott, S., and Nielsen, K2007. *Gangmaster Licensing Authority Evaluation Study: Baseline Report.* Nottingham: Gangmaster Licensing Authority.

Geertz, C. 1975. *Interpretations of Culture.* Oxford: Oxford University Press.

Geertz, C. 1983. Local Knowledge: Further Essays in Interpretive Anthropology. New York: Basic Books.

Gessner, V. 1994. Global Legal Interaction and Legal Cultures. *Ratio Juris*, 7(2), 132–45.

Gibson, J.L. and Caldeira, G.A. 1996. The Legal Cultures of Europe. *Law and Society Review*, 30(1), 55–86.

Giddens, A. 1984. *The Constitution of Society.* Cambridge: Polity Press.

Gilbert, N. G. and Mulkay, M. 1984. *Opening Pandora's Box: A Sociological Analysis of Scientists Discourse.* Cambridge: Cambridge University Press.

Glenn, H. P. 2000. *Legal Traditions of the World.* Oxford: Oxford University Press.

Glenn, H. P. 2004. Legal Cultures and Legal Traditions, in *Epistemology and Methodology of Comparative Law*, edited by M. V. Hoecke. Oxford: Hart Publishing.

Glick Schiller, N., Basch, L., and Szanton-Blanc, C. 1995. From Immigrant to Transmigrant: Theorizing Transnational Migration. *Anthropological Quarterly*, 68(1), 48–63.

Glick Schiller, N. 2007. Transnationality, in *A Companion to the Anthropology of Politics*, edited by D. Nugent and J. Vincent. London: Blackwell.

Gonzales, R. G. 2011. Learning to be illegal: Undocumented youth and shifting legal contexts in the transition to adulthood. *American Sociological Review* 76(4), 602–19.

Gordon, M. 1964. Assimilation in American Life: The Role of Race, Religion, and National Origins. New York: Oxford University Press.

Grabowska, I. 2005. Changes in the International Mobility of Labour: Job Migration of the Polish Nationals to Ireland. *Irish Journal of Sociology*, 14(1), 27–44.

Grillo, R., Ballard R., Ferrari A., Hoekema A.J., Maussen M. and Shah P. (eds) 2009. *Legal Practice and Cultural Diversity*. Aldershot: Ashgate

Grodziski, S. 2004. Z Dziejow Staropolskiej Kultury Prawnej [From the History of Polish Noble Legal Culture]. Krakow: Universitas.

Grzymała-Kazłowska A. (2001), Polscy nielegalni pracownicy w Belgii [Polish undocumented workers in Belgium], *CMR Working Papers*, No 41. Warsaw: Warsaw University.

Guild, E. and Carrera S. 2005. *No Constitutional Treaty? Implications for the Area of Freedom, Security and Justice* (CEPS Working Document No. 231). Available at: http://eudo-citizenship.eu/biblio/index.php?action=resourceView&id=12035&access=1 (date accessed: 12 March 2009).

Guiraudon, V. 2003. The Constitution of a European Immigration Policy Domain: A Political Sociology Approach. *Journal of European Public Policy*, 10(2), 263–82.

GUS. 2005. Praca Nierejestrowana. Unregistered Work in Poland. Analysis based on survey conducted in 2004. Warsaw: Main Statistical Office (GUS).

Hagan, J. M. 1994. *Deciding to Be Legal.* Philadelphia: Temple University Press.

Hamed, M. and Moore, J. I. 1999. Middle Easterners in American Courts, in *Immigrants in Courts*, edited by J. Moore. Seattle: University of Washington Press.

Hannerz, U. 1969. *Soulside: Inquiries into Ghetto Culture and Community.* Chicago: University of Chicago Press.

Hansen, R. 2000. Citizenship and Immigration in Post-War Britain: The Institutional Origins of a Multicultural Nation. Oxford: Oxford University Press.

Harding, A. 2001. Comparative Law and Legal Transplantation in South East Asia, in *Adapting Legal Cultures*, edited by D. Nelken and J. Feest. Oxford: Hart Publishing.

Harmon-Jones, E. and Harmon-Jones, C. 2002. Testing the Action-Based Model of Cognitive Dissonance: The Effect of Action Orientation on Post-decisional Attitudes. *Personality and Social Psychology Bulletin*, 28(6), 711–23.

He, X. 2005. Why Do They Not Comply with the Law? Illegality and Semi-Legality among Rural–Urban Migrant Entrepreneurs in Beijing, *Law and Society Review*, 39(3), 527–62.

Hein, J. and Berger, R. R. 2001a. Immigrants Culture and American Courts: A Typology of Legal Strategies and Issues in Cases Involving Vietnamese and Hmong Litigants. *Criminal Justice Review*, 26(1), 38–61.

Hein, J. and Berger, R. R. 2001b. Legal Adaptation among Vietnamese Refugees in the United States. *International Migration Review*, 35(1), 420–48.

Hill, R. J. 1981. Attitudes and Behaviour, in *Social Psychology: Sociological Perspectives*, edited by M. Rosenberg and R.H. Turner. New York: Basic Books.

HM Government. 2009a. *Direct Gov – Agency Workers – An Introduction.* Available at: http://www.direct.gov.uk (date accessed 3 January 2012).

HM Government. 2009b. *Employment Contracts.* Available at: http://www.direct.gov.uk (date accessed 3 January 2012).

Hoffmann, E. A. 2003. Legal Consciousness and Dispute Resolution: Different Disputing Behavior at Two Similar Taxicab Companies. *Law and Social Enquiry*, 28(3), 691–716.

Hofinger, C. 1997. *An Index to Measure Legal Integration.* Strasbourg: Council of Europe Directorate of Social and Economic Affairs.

Holden, L. 2011 (ed) Cultural Expertise and Litigation. Patterns Conflicts, Narratives, Abingdon: Routledge

Home Office. 2005. Illegal Working Taskforce Regulatory Impact Assessment from Immigration, Asylum and Nationality Bill. London: Home Office.

Home Office. 2011. Control of Immigration: Quarterly Statistical Summary, January–March 2011, London: Home Office

Hondagneu-Sotelo, P. 1994. *Gendered Transitions: Mexican Experiences of Immigration.* Berkeley, CA: University of California Press.

Horsley, W. 2004. *An Irish Welcome for EU Newcomers.* Available at: http://news.bbc.co.uk/1/hi/world/europe/3677257.stm (date accessed 3 January 2012).

House of Lords (2008) *Zalewska v Department for Social Development (NI)* Session 2007–8 [2008] UKHL 67, on appeal from [2007] NICA 17 2008 WL 4820337. Official transcript.

Huddleston, T. (2008) 'From Principles to Policies: Creating an Evidence Base for a European Approach to Migration Management', paper published at Heinrich Boel Stiftungwebsite. Available at: http://www.migration-boell.de/web/migration/46_1819.asp, (date accessed: 3 February 2011).

Hull, K. E. 2003. The Cultural Power of Law and the Cultural Enactment of Legality: The Case of Same-Sex Marriage. *Law and Social Enquiry*, 28(3), 629–57.

Hurtado, A., Gurin, P., and Peng, T.1994. Social Identities – A Framework for Studying the Adaptations of Immigrants and Ethnics: The Adaptations of Mexicans in the United States. *Social Problems*, 41(4), 129–51.

Iglicka, K. 2007. A Note on Rebirth of Migration Research in Poland after 1989, in *State of the Art of the Migration Research in Poland*, edited by A. Kicinger and A. Weinar. IMISCOE Working Paper, pp. 13–18. Available at: http://dare.uva.nl/document/96877 (date accessed 11 January 2011).

Inglis, K. 2004. The Accession Treaty and its Transitional Arrangements: A Twilight Zone for the New Members of the Union, in *EU Enlargement: A Legal Approach*, edited by C. Hillion. Oxford: Hart Publishing.

Jasienica, P. 1988. *Polska Anarchia* [*Polish Anarchy*]. Krakow: Wydawnictwo Literackie.

Jasinski, T. 2001. Tytulatura Boleslawa Chrobrego Na Zjezdzie Gnieznienskim [The Official Titles of Boleslaw Chrobry at Gniezno Union], in *Memoriae Amici Et Magistri: Studia Historyczne Poswiecone Pamieci Prof Wacława*

Korty 1919–1999, [In Memory of Friend and Master: Historical Studies Devoted to the Memory of Prof. Wacław Korta 1919–1999]edited by W. Korta, M. Derwich, W. Mrozowicz and R. C. Żerelik. Wroclaw: Instytut Historyczny Uniwersytetu Wrocławskiego.

Jayaweera, H. and Anderson, B. 2008. Migrant Workers and Vulnerable Employment: A Review of Existing Data. Report for TUC Commission on Vulnerable Employment. Oxford: Trades Union Congress and COMPAS.

Jazwinska, E., Fihel A., Praszalowicz D., Weinar A., Kaczmarczyk, P. 2007 Studies of mechanisms of emigration from Poland after 1989 in *State of the Art of the Migration Research in Poland*, edited by A. Kicinger and A. Weinar. IMISCOE Working Paper, pp. 13–18.

Jedruch, J. 1982. Constitutions, Elections and Legislatures of Poland, 1493–1977. A Guide to Their History. Pittsburgh: University Press of America.

Jettinghoff, A. 2001. State Formation and Legal Change: On the Impact of International Politics, in *Adapting Legal Cultures*, edited by D. Nelken and J. Feest, Oxford: Hart Publishing.

Johnson, D. 2002. *The Japanese Way of Justice: Prosecuting Crime in Japan.* Oxford: Oxford University Press.

Johnson, D. J. and Rusbult, C. E. 1987. Resisting Temptation: Devaluation of Alternative Partners as a Means of Maintaining Commitment in Close Relationships. *Journal of Personality and Social Psychology*, 57(6), 967–80.

Joppke, C. and Morawska, E. 2003. Toward Assimilation and Citizenship Immigrants in Liberal Nation-States. Basingstoke: Palgrave Macmillan.

Jordan, B. and Duvell, F. 2002 Irregular Migration: The Dilemmas of Transnational Mobility. Cheltenham: Edward Elgar.

Kallin, W. 2003. Human Rights and the Integration of Migrants, in *Migration and International Legal Norms*, edited by T. A. Aleinikoff and V. Chetail. The Hague: TMC Asser Press.

Kaminski, A. S. 1994. *Republic versus Autocracy, Poland-Lithuania and Russia, 1686–1697.* Cambridge, MA: Harvard University Press.

Kaminski, A. S. 2000. Historia Rzeczypospolitej Wielu Narodow, 1505–1795 [The History of Polish Multinational Republic 1505–1795]. Lublin: Instytut Europy Srodkowo-Wschodniej.

Kelman, H. C. 1974. Attitudes are Alive and Well and Gainfully Employed in the Sphere of Action. *American Psychologist*, 29(5), 310–24.

Kibria, N. 1993. Family Tightrope: The Changing Lives of Vietnamese Americans. Princeton, NJ: Princeton University Press.

Kicinger, A., Weinar A. 2007 (eds) *State of the Art of the Migration. Research in Poland,* IMISCOE Working Paper. Available at: http://dare.uva.nl/document/96877 (date accessed 11 January 2011).

Kochanowicz, J. 2004. Trust, Confidence, and Social Capital in Poland: A Historical Perspective. *Proceedings of the British Academy*, 123, 63–83.

Kojder, A. 1995. *Godnosc I Sila Prawa* [*Dignity and Power of Law*]. Warsaw: Oficyna Naukowa PWN.

Korkeakivi, A. and Zolotukhina, M. 1999. The Russian Federation, in *Immigrants in Courts*, edited by J. I. Moore. Seattle: University of Washington Press.

Kornai, J. 1980. *The Economics of Shortage.* Amsterdam: North Holland.

Kostiner, I. 2003. Evaluating Legality: Toward a Cultural Approach to the Study of Law and Social Change. *Law and Society Review*, 37(2), 323–68.

Krygier, M. 1990. Marxism and the Rule of Law: Reflections after the Collapse of Communism. *Law and Social Inquiry*, 15(4), 633–63.

Kubal, A. 2009. Why Semi-Legal? Polish Post-2004 EU Enlargement Migrants in the United Kingdom. *Journal of Immigration, Asylum and Nationality Law*, 23(2), 148–64.

Kubiak, H. 1975. O Koncepcję Badań Polonijnych W Kraju [Towards a Concept of Polish Diaspora Research in the Country]. *Przeglad Polonijny*, 1(1), pp. 15–27.

Kubiak, H., Kusielewicz, E., and Gromada, T.1988. Polonia Amerykanska. Przeszlosc I Wspolczesnosc [American Polish Diaspora. The Past and the Presence]. Wroclaw: Komitet Badania Polonii PAN.

Kuhn, T. 1962. *The Structure of Scientific Revolutions.* Chicago: University of Chicago Press.

Kula, Z. 2006. Zycie Codzienne W Komunizmie [Everyday Life in Communism], in Socjalizm W Zyciu Powszednim.Dyktatura a Spoleczenstwo W Nrd I Prl [Socialism in Everyday Life. Dictature and Society in DDR and PPL], edited by S. Kott, M. Kula and T. Lindenberg. Warsaw, Potsdam: Wydawnictwo TRIO and Zentrum fur Zeithistorische Forschung.

Kurczewski, J. 2007. Either Rightly or Like a Crook: Legal Culture of Polish Society after Communism. *Studia Socjologiczne* [*Sociological Studies*], 185(2), 33–60.

Kurkchiyan M. (2003) The Illegitimacy of Law in Post-Soviet Societies, in *Law and Informal Practices: The Post-Communist Experience,* edited by R. Kurkchiyan and D. J. Galligan. Oxford: Oxford University Press.

Kurkchiyan, M. 2005. Researching Russian Legal Culture, in *Theory and Method in Socio-Legal Research*, edited by R. Banakar and M. Travers. Oxford: Hart Publishing.

Kurkchiyan, M. 2010. Perceptions of Law and Social Order: A Cross-National Comparison of Collective Legal Consciousness. *Wisconsin International Law Journal*, 28(4), 146–68.

Kusters, J. 2009. Criminalizing Romani Culture through Law, in *Multicultural Jurisprudence: Comparative Perspectives on the Cultural Defense*, edited by A. D. Renteln and M.-C. Foblets. Oxford: Hart Publishing.

Kutrzeba, S. 1910. *Ordo Coronandi Regis Poloniae*. Kraków: Archiwum Komisji Historycznej.

Kuzma, E. 2004. Migracje Do Belgii: O Mozliwosciach i Barierach Wychodzenia Z Nielegalnosci [Migrations to Belgium: On Possibilities and Constraints of Escaping Irregularity], in *Polscy pracownicy na rynku Unii Europejskiej* [*Polish*

Workers on the European Union Labour Market], edited by P. Kaczmarczyk and W. Lukowski, Warsaw: Scholar.

Laciak, B. 2005. Obyczajowosc Polska Czasu Transformacji [Polish Habitualness in the Times of Transformation]. Warsaw: Trio.

Lahav, G. and Guiraudon, V. 2000. A Reappraisal of the State Sovereignty Debate: The Case of Migration Control. *Comparative Political Studies*, 33(2), 163–95.

Lane, C. and Bachmann, R. 1996. The Social Constitution of Trust: Supplier Relations in Britain and Germany. *Organization Studies*, 17(3), 365–95.

Latour, B. 2005, Reassembling the social: an introduction to Actor-network theory, Oxford ; New York, Oxford: University Press.

Legrand, P. 1999. *Fragments on Law-as-Culture.* Schoordijk Institute, W. E. J. Tjeenk Willink: Deventer.

Legrand, P. 2001. What Legal Transplants?, in *Adapting Legal Cultures*, edited by D. Nelken and J. Feest. Oxford: Hart Publishing.

Leighton, P. 2009. Temporary Agency Working and the European Employment Strategy, in *The European Social Model and Transitional Labour Markets*, edited by R. Rogowski. Farnham: Ashgate.

Lewitter, L. R. 1984. Conrad, Dostoyevsky, and the Russo-Polish Antagonism. *Modern Language Review*, 79(3), 653–63.

Liao, T. F. and Halas, E. 2007. Editors' Introduction: Cultural Becoming and Cultural Sciences. *Polish Sociological Review*, 158(2), 1–21.

Lim, S.-L. and Wieling, E. 2004. Immigrant Chinese American Women: Negotiating Values and Perceptions of Self in the Cultural Borderlands of East and West: A Qualitative Study. *Family Journal*, 12(2), 148–58.

Linz, J. and Stephan, A. 1996. *Problems of Democratic Transition and Consolidation.* Baltimore, MD: Johns Hopkins University Press.

Lockwood, D. 1964. Social Integration and System Integration, in *Explorations in Social Change*, edited by G. K. Zollschan and W. Hirsch. London: Routledge & Kegan Paul.

Long, N. 2001. Development Sociology. Actor Perspectives. London: Routledge.

Łozinski, W. 1960. *Prawem I Lewem.* [*Either Rightly or Like a Crook*]. Krakow: Wydawnictwo Literackie.

Lucassen, L,, Feldman, D., and Oltmer, J. 2006. *Paths of Integration: Migrants in Western Europe.* Amsterdam: Amsterdam University Press.

Ma, V. 1995. Cultural Defense: Limited Admissibility for New Immigrants. *San Diego Justice Journal*, 3(2), 461–84.

Maas, W. 2005. Citizenship, Free Movement, and EU Enlargement. *Jean Monnet/Robert Schuman Paper Series*, 5(34). Available at: http://aei.pitt.edu/8163/1/Maasfinal.pdf (date accessed 3 January 2012).

Machonin, P. 1997. *Social Strucure of Communist Societies 'Apres La Lutte'.* Social Structures in Transformation. Patterns and Paths. ESF Scientific Network, Institute of Sociology Academy of Sciences of the Czech Republic, Prague, 29 April.

Mahler, S. J. 1995. *American Dreaming: Immigrant Life on the Margins.* Princeton, NJ: Princeton University Press.

Markova, E. and Black, R. 2007. *East European Immigration and Community Cohesion.* York: Joseph Rowntree Foundation.

Marody, M. 1987. Antynomie Zbiorowej Podswiadomosci [Antinomies of Collective Subconsciousness]. *Studia Socjologiczne*, 2, 89–99.

Marody, M. 2000. Miedzy Rynkiem a Etatem. Spoleczne Negocjonowanie Polskiej Rzeczywistosci. [Between the Market and the Labour Contract. Social Negotiation of Polish Reality]. Warsaw: Scholar.

Marshall, A.-M. 2003. Injustice Frames, Legality, and the Everyday Construction of Sexual Harassment. *Law and Social Enquiry*, 28(3), 659–89.

Matejko, E. 2004. Migracja Sezonowa Jako Strategia Dzialania W Kontekscie Sytuacji Na Polskim I Hiszpanskim Rynku Pracy [Seasonal Migration as a Strategy in the Context of Situation on the Polish and Spanish Labour Market], in *Polscy pracownicy na rynku Unii Europejskiej* [*Polish Workers on the European Union Labour Market*], edited by P. Kaczmarczyk and W. Lukowski, Warsaw: Scholar.

Mazierska, E. 2009. In Search of Freedom, Bread and Self–Fulfilment: A Short History of Polish Emigrants in Fictional Film. *Polish Migration to the UK in the 'New' European Union after 2004*, edited by K. Burrell, Farnham: Ashgate.

McKay, S. 2009. Employer Use of Migrant Labour – Motivations, Experiences and HR Responses. London: Working Lives Research Institute and ACAS.

McKay, S. and Markova, E. 2008. *Understanding the Operation and Management of Employment Agencies in the UK Labour Market.* London: Working Lives Research Institute and London Metropolitan University.

Mead, G. H. 1964. Suggestions toward a Theory of the Philosophical Disciplines, in *Selected Writings of George Herbert Mead*, edited by A. Reck. Indianapolis: Bobbs-Merrill.

Menjivar, C. 2000. *Fragmented Ties: Salvadoran Immigrant Networks in America.* Berkeley, CA: University of California Press.

Menjivar, C. 2006. Liminal Legality: Salvadoran and Guatemalan Immigrants' Lives in the United States. *American Journal of Sociology*, 111(4), 999–1037.

Menski, W. 1988. English Law and Ethnic Minority Customs by S. Poulter – Review. *International and Comparative Law Quarterly*, 37, 218–21.

Menski, W. 1993. Asians in Britain and the Question of Adaptation to a New Legal Order: Asian Laws in Britain?, in *Ethnicity, Identity, Migration: The South Asian Context*, edited by M. Israel and N. Wagle. Toronto: University of Toronto Press.

Menski, W. 2006. Rethinking Legal Theory in the Light of South–North Migration, in *Migration, Diasporas and Legal Systems in Europe*, edited by P. Shah and W. Menski. London: Routledge-Cavendish.

Menski, W. 2007 'Immigration and Multiculturalism in Britain: New Issues in Research and Policy', London: School of Oriental and African Studies SOAS.

Menski, W. 2008. Angrezi Shariat: Glocalised Plural Arrangements by Migrants in Britain. *Law Vision*, 10, 10–12.

Merry, S. 1992. Anthropology, Law and Transnational Processes. *Annual Review of Anthropology*, 21, 357–79.

Merry, S. E. 1990. Getting Justice and Getting Even. Legal Consciousness among Working-Class Americans. Chicago: University of Chicago Press.

Mezey, N. 2001. Out of the Ordinary: Law, Power, Culture, and the Commonplace. *Law and Social Inquiry*, 26(1), 145–67.

Michalowski, R. 2005. Christianisation of Political Culture in Poland in the 10th and Early 11th Century, in *Political Culture in Central Europe (10th–20th Century) Part I, Middle Ages and Early Modern Era*, edited by H. Manikowska, J. Pánek and M. Holý. Warsaw and Prague: Institute of History, Academy of Sciences of the Czech Republic; Institute of History, Polish Academy of Sciences.

Michie, J. and Sheehan, M. 2003. Labour Market Deregulation, 'Flexibility' and Innovation. *Cambridge Journal of Economics*, 23(1), 123–43.

Migrants' Rights Network. 2011. Frequently Asked Questions About the Rights of EEA Nationals to Access Benefits and the Changes for A8 Nationals from 1 May 2011. London: AIRE Centre.

Miszalska, A. 1996. Homo Sovieticus W Swiecie Kapitalizmu [Homo Sovieticus in the Capitalist World]. *Kultura i Spoleczenstwo*, 44(4), 28–49.

Miszalska, A. 1998. Reakcje Spoleczne Na Przemiany Ustrojowe. Social Reactions toward the Transformation. Lodz: Wydawnictwo Uniwersytetu Lodzkiego.

Morawska, E. 2001. Structuring Migration: The Case of Polish Income-Seeking Travelers to the West. *Theory and Society*, 30, 47–80.

Morawska, E. 2004. Exploring Diversity in Immigrant Assimilation and Transnationalism: Poles and Russian Jews in Philadelphia. *International Migration Review*, 38(4), 1372–412.

Morawska, E. 2011. *A Sociology of Immigration. (Re)Making Multifaceted America*, Basingstone: Palgrave

Morawski, W. 2000. Zmiana Instytucjonalna. [Institutional Change.] Warsaw: PWN.

Morzol, I. and Ogórek, M. 1992. Shadow Justice, in *The Unplanned Society: Poland during and after Communism*, edited by J. Wedel. New York: Columbia University Press.

Nader, L. 1990. Harmony Ideology: Justice and Control in a Zapotec Mountain Village. Stanford, CA: Stanford University Press.

Neil, A. 2003 The Evolution of the Labour Law 1992–2003. Country Study: United Kingdom. Brussels: European Commission

Nelken, D. 1995a. Disclosing/Invoking Legal Culture: An Introduction. *Social & Legal Studies*, 4(4), 435.

Nelken, D. (ed.) 1995b. *Comparing Legal Cultures*. Aldershot: Ashgate.

Nelken, D. 2001. Beyond the Methaphor of Legal Transplants? Some Consequences of Autopoiesis Theory for the Study of Cross Cultural Legal Adaptation, in

Law's New Boundaries: The Consequences of Legal Autopoiesis (Applied Legal Philosophy), edited by D. Nelken. Aldershot: Ashgate.

Nelken, D. 2004a. Comparing Legal Cultures, in *The Blackwell Companion to Law and Society*, edited by A. Sarat. London: Blackwell.

Nelken, D. 2004b. Using the Concept of Legal Culture. *Australian Journal of Legal Philosophy*, 29(1), 1–26.

Nelken, D. 2007. Culture, Legal, in *Encyclopedia of Law and Society: American and Global Perspectives*, edited by D. S. Clark. London: Sage.

Nelken, D. and Feest, J. 2001. *Adapting Legal Cultures.* Oxford: Hart Publishing.

Ngai, M. M. 2004. *Impossible Subjects: Illegal Aliens and the Making of Modern America*, Princeton: Princeton University Press.

North, D. 1990. Institutions, Institutional Change and Economic Performance. Cambridge: Cambridge University Press.

Nowicka, E. 2000. Polacy Czy Cudzoziemcy? Polacy Za Wschodnia Granica [Poles or Foreigners? Poles Behind the East Border]. Krakow: Nomos.

Office for National Statistics. 2011. Polish People in the UK. Half a Million Polish Residents 2001–2010. London: Home Office.

Ojito, M. 1997. Culture Clash: Foreign Parents, American Child Rearing. *New York Times*, p. 14.

Okolski, M. 2007. Poland's Migration in the European Context, in *State of the Art of the Migration Research in Poland*, edited by A. Kicinger and A. Weinar. IMISCOE Working Paper, pp. 9–13. Available at: http://dare.uva.nl/document/96877 (date accessed 11 January 2010).

Okolski, M. and Jazwinska, E. e. 2001. Ludzie Na Hustawce. Migracje Miedzy Peryferiami Polski I Zachodu [People on a See-Saw. Migrations between the Peripheries of Poland and the West]. Warsaw: Scholar.

Opalinski, E. 1983. 'Postawa Szlachty Polskiej Wobec Osoby Krolewskiej Jako Instytucji W Latach 1587–1648: Proba Postawienia Problematyki.' ['The Attitude of Polish Nobility Towards the Monarch as an Institution, During the Years 1587 - 1648: Posing the Question', *Kwartalnik Historyczny* [*Historical Quarterly*] XC(4).

Opalinski, E. 2005. Civic Culture of the Polish Nobility in the 16th and Early 17th Century, in *Political Culture in Central Europe (10th–20th Century) Part I, Middle Ages and Early Modern Era*, edited by H. Manikowska, J. Pánek and M. Holý. Warsaw and Prague: Institute of History, Academy of Sciences of the Czech Republic, Institute of History; Polish Academy of Sciences.

Park, R. and Burgess, E. 1921. *Introduction to the Science of Sociology.* Chicago: University of Chicago Press.

Penninx, R. 2005. Integration of Migrants: Economic, Social, Cultural and Political Dimensions, in *The New Demographic Regime. Population Challenges and Policy Responses*, edited by M. Macura, A. L. MacDonald and W. Haug. New York and Geneva: United Nations, Economic Commission for Europe, United Nations Population Fund.

Petrażycki, L. 1955. *Law and Morality.* Cambridge, MA: Harvard University Press.

Pilch, A. 1984. Emigracja Z Ziem Polskich W Czasach Nowozytnych I Najnowszych (Xviii–Xx W.) [Emigration from Polish Territories in Modern and Contemporary Times (18th–20th Centuries)]. Warsaw: PWN.

Pirie, F. 2006. Legal Autonomy as Political Engagement: The Ladakhi Village in the Wider World. *Law and Society Review*, 40(1), 77–103.

Podgóecki, A. 1994. *The Polish Society.* London: Praeger.

Pollard, N., Latorre, M., and Sriskandarajah, D. 2008. Floodgates or Turnstiles? Post-EU Enlargement Migration Flows to (and from) the UK. London: Institute for Public Policy Research (IPPR).

Portes, A. 1996. *Global Villagers: The Rise of Transnational Communities.* Available at: http://prospect.org/cs/articles?article=global_villagers (date accessed 3 January 2012).

Portes, A. and Bach, R. 1985. *Latin Journey: Cuban and Mexican Immigrants in the United States.* Berkeley, CA: University of California Press.

Portes, A. and Rumbaut, R. 1990. *Immigrant America: A Portrait.* Berkeley, CA: University of California Press.

Portes, A. and Zhou, M. 1993. *The New Second Generation: Segmented Assimilation and its Variants.* Berkeley, CA: University of California Press.

Portes, J. and French, S. 2005. The Impact of Free Movement of Workers from Central and Eastern Europe: Early Evidence, *Working Paper No. 18*, London: Department of Work and Pensions, Available at: http://research.dwp.gov.uk/asd/asd5/WP18.pdf (date accessed 13 February 2009).

Portet, S. 2007. Elastycznosc Zatrudnienia W Polsce, Czyli O Odkrywaniu Rzeczy Zakrytych. [Uncovering the Flexibility of Polish Labour Market], in *Wymiary Zycia Spolecznego. Polska Na Przelomie Xx I Xxi Wieku* [*Dimensions of Social Life. Poland at the Turn of the 21st Century*], edited by M. Marody. Warsaw: Scholar.

Potter, P. B. 1999. Law and Legal Culture in China, in *Immigrants in Courts*, edited by J. I. Moore. Seattle: University of Washington Press.

Poulter, S. 1986. *English Law and Ethnic Minority Customs.* London: Butterworths.

Poulter, S. 1988. African Customs in an English Setting: Legal and Policy Aspects of Recognition. *Journal of African Law*, 31(1–2), 207–25.

Poulter, S. 1998. Ethnicity, Law and Human Rights: The English Experience. Oxford: Clarendon Press.

Pound, R. 1910. Law in Books and Law in Action. *American Law Review*, 44, 12–36.

Price, C. 1969. The Study of Assimilation, in *Migration*, edited by C. Price. Cambridge: Cambridge University Press.

Putnam, R. 2000. Bowling Alone: The Collapse and Revival of American Community. New York: Simon & Schuster.

Rabikowska, M. and Burrell, K. 2009. The Material Worlds of Recent Polish Migrants: Transnationalism, Food, Shops and Home, in *Polish Migration to the*

UK in the 'New' European Union after 2004, edited by K. Burrell. Farnham: Ashgate.

Read, J. G. 2004. Family, Religion, and Work among Arab American Women. *Journal of Marriage and Family*, 66(4), 1042–50.

REC. 2006. Annual Industry Turnover and Key Volumes Survey 2005/06. London: Ernst & Young and REC.

Redfield, R., Linton, R., and Herskovits, MJ. 1936. Memorandum for the Study of Acculturation. *American Anthropologist*, 38(1), 149–52.

Reich, M,G., David M, and Edwards, R.C.1973. Dual Labour Markets: A Theory of Labour Market Segmentation. *Digital Commons at University of Nebraska*. Available at: http://digitalcommons.unl.edu/econfacpub/3 (date accessed 3 January 2012).

Renteln, A. D. 2004. *The Cultural Defense*. New York: Oxford University Press.

Renteln, A. D. 2009. The Use and Abuse of Cultural Defense, in *Multicultural Jurisprudence: Comparative Perspectives on the Cultural Defense*, edited by A. D. Renteln and M.-C. Foblets. Oxford: Hart Publishing.

Rigo, E. 2011 'Citizens despite borders: Challenges to the Territorial Order of Europe' in *The Contested Politics of Mobility: Borderzones and Irregularity* edited by V. Squire, London: Routledge

Rogers, N. and Scannell, R. 2005. *Free Movement of Persons in the Enlarged European Union*. London: Sweet & Maxwell.

Romaniszyn, K. 1996. The Invisible Community: Undocumented Polish Workers in Athens. *New Community*, 22(2), 321–33.

Rosińska-Kordasiewicz A. (2005), Praca pomocy domowej. Doświadczenie polskich migrantek w Neapolu [Work of a domestic servant. Experience of Polish migrants in Naples], *CMR Working Papers*, No 4(62), Warsaw: Warsaw University.

Rosset, E. 1975. *Demografia Polski* [*Demography of Poland*]. Warsaw: PWN.

Ruhs, M. 2006. Greasing the Wheels of the Flexible Labour Market: East European Labour Immigration in the UK. *COMPAS Working Paper Series WP–06–38*. Available at: http://www.compas.ox.ac.uk/publications/working–papers/wp–06–38/ (date accessed 3 January 2012).

Ruhs, M. 2008. 'Changing Status, Changing Lives? The Influence of Change of Status on CEE Migrants' Wages'. Paper presented at the *Centre for Migration, Policy and Society Seminar Series*

COMPAS: University of Oxford, 24 February 2008.

Ruhs, M. 2011. Openness, Skills and Rights: An Empirical Analysis of Labour Immigration Programmes in 46 High- and Middle-Income Countries. *COMPAS Working Paper Series*. Available at: http://www.compas.ox.ac.uk/fileadmin/files/Publications/working_papers/WP_2011/WP1188%20Ruhs_Paper%20and%20Appendises.pdf (date accessed 3 January 2012).

Ryan, B. 2005. The Evolving Legal Regime on Unauthorized Work by Migrants in Britain. *Comparative Labor Law and Policy Journal*, 27, 43–5.

Ryan, B. 2008. The Accession (Immigration and Worker Authorisation) Regulations 2006. *Industrial Law Journal*, 37(1), 75–88.

Ryan, L., Sales, R., and Tilki, M. 2009. Recent Polish Migrants in London: Accessing and Participating in Social Networks across Borders, in *Polish Migration to the UK in the 'New' European Union. After 2004*, edited by K. Burrell. Farnham: Ashgate.

Rytter, M. 2011. Semi-legal family life: Pakistani couples in the borderlands of Denmark and Sweden, *Global Networks* 12(1), 91–108.

Saguy, A. C. and Stuart, F. 2008. Culture and Law: Beyond a Paradigm of Cause and Effect. *Annals of the American Academy*, 619, 149–64.

Sakson B. (2005), Po drugiej stronie Oceanu. Nowi emigranci z Polski w metropolii Chicagowskiej [On the other side of the Pond. New Polish emigrants in the Chicago Metropolis], *CMR Working Papers*, No 5(63). Warsaw: Warsaw University.

Salt, J. and Rees, P. 2006. Globalisation, Population Mobility and Impact of Migration on Population. Swindon: ESRC.

Sarat, A. 1977. Studying American Legal Culture. *Law and Society Review*, 11, 427–88.

Sarat, A. 1990. The Law is All Over: Power, Resistance and the Legal Consciousness of the Welfare Poor. *Yale Journal of Law and Humanities*, 3(434), 343–80.

Sarat, A. and Felstiner, W. 1995. Divorce Lawyers and their Clients: Power and Meaning in the Legal Process. Oxford: Oxford University Press.

Schneider, J. and Crul, M. 2010. New Insights into Assimilation and Integration Theory: Introduction to the Special Issue. *Journal of Ethnic and Racial Studies*, 33(7), 1143–8.Schuck, P. 1998. *Citizens, strangers, and in-betweens: essays on immigration and citizenship,* Oxford: Westview Press

Schuck, P. 2007. Law and the Study of Migration, in *Migration Theory. Talking across Disciplines*, edited by C. Brettell and J. F. Hollifield. London: Routledge.

Scott, S. 2009. Temporary Migrant Workers and the UK's Flexible Labour Market: Shifting Policy Narratives and Regulatory Rebalancing. Available at: http://www.pol.ed.ac.uk/__data/assets/pdf_file/0018/9126/Scott.pdf (date accessed 3 January 2012).

Sellin, T. 1938. Culture, Conflict and Crime. *American Journal of Sociology*, 44(1): 97–103

Serejski, M. H. 1970. Europa a Rozbiory Polski, Studium Historiograficzne [Europe and Polish Partitions, a Historical Study]. Warsaw: Panstwowe Wydawnictwo Naukowe.

Sewell, W. 1992. A Theory of Structure: Duality, Agency and Transformation. *American Journal of Sociology*, 98(1), 1–29.

Shah, P. 2007. *Law and Ethnic Plurality: Socio-Legal Perspectives.* Leiden: Martinus Nijhoff.

Shah, P. 2008. Coping with Super-Diversity in Law: Thoughts on the British Scene, in *Law and Religion in Multicultural Societies*, edited by R. Mehdi,

H. Petersen, E. Reenberg Sand, and G. R. Woodman . Copenhagen: DJOF Publishing.

Shah, P. 2009. Transnational Hindu Law Adoptions: Recognition and Treatment in Britain. *International Journal of Law in Context*, 5(2), 107–30.

Shah, P. 2011. When South Asians Marry Trans-Jurisdictionally: Some Reflections on Immigration Cases by an 'Expert', in *Cultural Expertise and Litigation, Patterns, Conflicts, Narratives*, edited by L. Holden. Abingdon: Routledge.

Siara, B. 2009. UK Poles and the Negotiation of Gender and Ethnic Identity in Cyberspace, in *Polish Migration to the UK in the 'New' European Union. After 2004*, edited by K. Burrell. Farnham: Ashgate.

Silbey, S. 2005. Everyday Life and the Constitution of Legality, in *The Blackwell Companion to the Sociology of Culture*, edited by M. D. Jacobs and N. W. Hanrahan. Oxford: Oxford University Press.

Skapska, G. 2002. Law and Society in a Natural Laboratory: The Case of Poland in the Broader Context of East-Central Europe. *Knowledge Base: Social Sciences in Eastern Europe*. Available at: http://www.gesis.org/knowledgebase/archive/legalstudies/poland/article1.html (date accessed 3 January 2012).

Slany, K. 2002. Imigracja Polska W Kanadzie W Dekadzie Lat Dziewiecdziesiatych [Polish Immigration in Canada in the 1990s], in *Emigracja Z Polski Po 1989 Roku* [*Emigration from Poland after 1989*], edited by B. Klimaszewski. Krakow: Grell.

Smith, J. R. and Hogg, M. A. 2008. Social Identity and Attitudes, in *Attitudes and Attitude Change*, edited by W. D. Crano and R. Prislin. New York: Psychology Press.

Smith, M. P. and Guarnizo, L. 1998. *Transnationalism from Below.* Piscataway, NJ: Transaction Publishers.

Smith, S. 2004. Immigration Hysteria: What They Said About – Immigration and the EU – Tabloids Threaten 'Flood' of Gypsies. *The Guardian*, 21 January. Available at: http://www.guardian.co.uk/world/2004/jan/21/eu.immigration (date accessed 3 January 2012).

Sojka-Zielinska, K. 2000. Drogi I Bezdroza Prawa. Szkice Z Dziejow Kultury Prawnej Europy [The Ways and the Whereabouts of Law. Essays on the History of Legal Culture in Europe.]. Wroclaw: Zaklad Narodowy im. Ossolinskich.

Song, J. H.-L. 1992. Attitudes of Chinese Immigrants and Vietnamese Refugees toward Law Enforcement in the United States. *Justice Quarterly*, 9(4), 703–20.

Spaventa, E. 2007. Free Movement of Persons in the European Union. Barriers to Movement in their Constitutional Context. The Hague: Kluwer Law International.

Spencer, S., Ruhs, M., Anderson, B., and Rogaly, B.2007. Migrants' Lives Beyond the Workplace. The Experiences of Central and East Europeans in the UK. York: Joseph Rowntree Foundation.

Staniszkis, J. 1984. *Poland's Self-Limiting Revolution.* Princeton, NJ: Princeton University Press.

Starnawski, J. 1972. Stanislaw Orzechowski – Wybor Pism [Stanislaw Orzechowski – A Collection of Essays]. Wroclaw, Warsaw, Krakow and Gdansk: PWN.

Starr, J. and Collier, J. 1989. *History and Power in the Study of Law.* Ithaca, NY: Cornell University Press.

Staskiewicz, W. 2007. Prawo Jako Narzedzie Polityki Panstwa Okresu Przemian (Przeszlosc Wobec Przyszlosci) [Law as the Instrument of the State During the Period of Changes (Past Versus Future)]. Prawo a polityka. Materialy z konferencji Wydzialu Prawa i Administracji [Law and Politics: Conference Proceedings, Law and Administration Department], Warsaw, 24 February.

Stawecki, T. 2000. Instrumentalne Traktowanie Prawa – Rozne Perspektywy, in Prawo I Lad Spoleczny. Ksiega Jubileuszowa Dedykowana Prof. Annie Turskiej [Law and Social Order. Volume Dedicated to Prof. Anna Turska], edited by A. Turska. Warsaw: PWN.

Stawecki, T. 2003. Obejscie Prawa. Szkic Na Temat Granic Prawa I Zasad Jego Wykladni [By-Passing the Law. A Comment on the Limits of Law and the Principles of Its Interpretation]. Naduzycie prawa: konferencja Wydzialu Prawa i Administracji [Abuse of Law: Conference of the Department of Law and Administration], Department of Law and Administration, University of Warsaw, 1 March.

Stawecki, T., Staskiewicz, W., and Winczorek, J.2008. Miedzy Policentrycznoscia a Fragmentaryzacja Wplyw Trybunalu Konstytucyjnego Na Polski Porzadek Prawny [Between Polycentricism and Fragmentarism. The Influence of Polish Constitutional Tribunal on Polish Legal Order]. Warsaw: Ernst and Young.

Stemplowski, R. 2009. *Transformation from State-Socialism into a Democratic State Ruled by Law*. Legacies and Prospects. Poland 1989: 20 Years On, St Anthony's College University of Oxford, 8 June.

Stone, J. 1999. What Exactly Have I Done? The Role of Self-Attribute Accessibility in Dissonance, in *Cognitive Dissonance: Progress on a Pivotal Theory in Social Psychology*, edited by E. Harmon-Jones and J. Mills. Washington DC: American Psychological Association.

Stone, J. and Fernandez, N. C. 2008. How Behaviour Shapes Attitudes: Cognitive Dissonance Processes, in *Attitudes and Attitude Change*, edited by W. D. Crano and R. Prislin. New York: Psychology Press.

Suarez-Orozco, M. and Suarez-Orozco, C. 2002. *New Immigration: An Interdisciplinary Reader.* New York: Routledge.

Sumption, M. and Somerville, W. 2009. *The UK's New Europeans. Progress and Challenges Five Years after Accession.* London: Migration Policy Institute: Equality and Human Rights Commission.

Swidler, A. 1986. Culture in Action: Symbols and Strategies. *American Sociological Review*, 51(2), 273–86.

Swidler, A. 2001 *Talk of Love. How Culture Matters.* Chicago and London: University of Chicago Press.

Sword, K., Davies, N., and Ciechanowski, J. 1989. *The Formation of the Polish Community in Great Britain 1939–1950.* London: School of Slavonic and East European Studies.

Ta, T. V. 1999. Vietnamese Immigrants in American Courts, in *Immigrants in Courts*, edited by J. I. Moore. Seattle: University of Washington Press.

Tajfel, H. 1981. Human Groups and Social Categories: Studies in Social Psychology. Cambridge: Cambridge University Press.

Tarkowska, E. and Tarkowski, J. 1988. Amoralny Familizm Czyli O Deezintegracji Spolecznej W Polsce Lat Osemdziesiatych [Amoral Familism or on the Social Disintegration in Poland], in *Grupy I Wiezi Spoleczne W Systemie Monocentrycznym* [*Social Groups and Social Ties in the Mono-Centric System*], edited by E. Wnuk-Lipinski. Warsaw: IFIS PAN.

Terry, D. J. and Hogg, M. A. 2000. *Attitudes, Behaviour and Social Context. The Role of Norms and Group Membership.* London: Lawrence Erlbaum.

Thomas, W. I. and Znaniecki, F. 1974. *The Polish Peasant in Europe and America.* New York: Octagon Books.

Trades Union Congress. 2007. *Migrant Agency Workers in the UK.* London: Equality and Employment Rights Department.

Triandafyllidou, A. 2006 (ed) Contemporary Polish Migration in Europe: Complex Patterns of Movement and Settlement, Washington DC: The Edwin Mellen Press.

Tubergen, F. V. 2006. *Immigrant Integration: A Cross-National Study.* Amsterdam: LFB Scholarly.

TUC Commission on Vulnerable Employment. 2008. *Hard Work, Hidden Lives: The Short Report of the Commission on Vulnerable Employment.* London: TUC Commission on Vulnerable Employment.

Turner, V. 1969. Liminality and Communitas, in *The Ritual Process: Structure and Anti-Structure*, edited by V. W. Turner. Chicago: Aldine Publishing.

UK Border Agency. 2004. *Worker Registration Scheme.* Available at: http://webarchive.nationalarchives.gov.uk/20090120164411/http://www.ukba.homeoffice.gov.uk/workingintheuk/eea/wrs/ (date accessed 3 January 2012).

UK Border Agency, DWP, HMRC and Department for Communities and Local Government. 2009. *Accession Monitoring Report, May 2004–March 2009.* London: Department for Work and Pensions; HMRC; Office of the Deputy Prime Minister.

UK Border Agency. 2010. *Government Keeps Work Restrictions for Eastern Europeans*, Press Release. Available at http://webarchive.nationalarchives.gov.uk/20100407072001/http://www.ukba.homeoffice.gov.uk/sitecontent/newsarticles/Government-keeps-work-restrict (date accessed 9 April 2010).

United Nations Development Programme. 2004. *Human Development Report Poland 2004 – Working Out Employment.* Available at: http://www.undp.org.pl/nhdr/nhdr2004.php (date accessed 3 January 2012).

Van Hook, J. and Bean, F. D. 2009. Explaining Mexican-Immigrant Welfare Behaviors: The Importance of Employment-Related Cultural Repertoires. *American Sociological Review*, 74(3), 423–44.

Van Niekierk, M. 2004. Afro-Caribbeans and Indo-Caribbeans in the Netherlands: Premigration Legacies and Social Mobility. *International Migration Review*, 38(1), 158–83.

Vertovec, S. 2006. The Emergence of Super-Diversity in Britain. *COMPAS Working Paper Series*. Available at: http://www.compas.ox.ac.uk/publications/working–papers/wp–06–25/ (date accessed 3 January 2012).

Vertovec, S. 2007. New Directions in the Anthropology of Migration and Multiculturalism. *Ethnic and Racial Studies*, 30(6), 961–78.

Vinogradoff, P. 1913. *Common-Sense in Law.* London: Thornton Butterworth Ltd.

Wakil, P., Siddique, C., and Wakil, F. 1981. Between Two Cultures: A Study in Socialization of Children of Immigrants. *Journal of Marriage and the Family*, 43(4), 929–40.

Walaszek, A. 2001. *Polska Diaspora* [*The Polish Diaspora*]. Krakow: Wydawnictwo Literackie.

Walster, E. 1964. The Temporal Sequence of Post–Decision Dissonance, in *Conflict, Decision, and Dissonance*, edited by L. Festinger. Stanford, CA: Stanford University Press.

Wandycz, P. 1974. *The Lands of Partitioned Poland.* Seattle: University of Washington Press.

Wandycz, P. 1980. *The United States and Poland.* Cambridge, MA: Harvard University Press.

Ward, C. and Kennedy, A. 1994. Acculturation Strategies, Psychological Adjustment and Sociocultural Competence During Cross-Cultural Transitions. *International Journal of Inter-cultural Relations*, 18(3), 329–43.

Wedel, J. 1986. The Private Poland: An Anthropologist's Look at Everyday Life. New York: Facts on File.

Wedel, J. 1992. The Unplanned Society: Poland During and after Communism. New York: Columbia University Press.

Weiss, F. and Wooldridge, F. 2002. *Free Movement of Persons within the European Community.* The Hague: Kluwer Law International.

Wenzel, M. 2009. *Introduction. Research Report: Nepotism. Bs/68/2009.* Warsaw: Centre for Public Opinion Research (CBOS).

Whitefield, S. 2005. *Political Culture and Post-Communism.* Basingstoke: Palgrave.

Włodarczak K. (2005), Proces adaptacji współczesnych emigrantów polskich do życia w Australii [Adaptation of the contemporary Polish emigrants to life in Australia], *CMR Working Papers,* No 3(61). Warsaw: Warsaw University.

Wnuk-Lipinski, E. 1991. Polish Society after the Communist Experiment, in *Poland into the 1990s. Economy and Society in Transition*, edited by G. Blazyca and R. Rapacki. London: Printer Publishers.

Yamamoto, R. 2007. Crossing Boundaries: Legality and the Power of the State in Unauthorized Migration. *Sociology Compass*, 1(1), 95–110.

Yanagisako, S. J. 1985a. Transforming Orientalism: Gender, Nationality, and Class in Asian American Studies, in *Naturalizing Power: Essays in Feminist Cultural Analysis*, edited by S. J. Yanagisako. New York: Routledge.

Yanagisako, S. J. 1985b. Transforming the Past: Tradition and Kinship among Japanese Americans. Stanford, CA: Stanford University Press.

Yngvesson, B. 1993. Virtuous Citizens, Disruptive Subjects: Order and Complaint in a New England Court. New York: Routledge.

Zirk-Sadowski, M. 2006. Transformation and Integration of Legal Cultures and Discourses – Poland, in Spreading Democracy and the Rule of Law?: The Impact of EU Enlargement on the Rule of Law, Democracy and Constitutionalism in Post-Communist Legal Orders, edited by W. Sadurski. London: Springer.

Index

For Product Safety Concerns and Information please contact our EU representative GPSR@taylorandfrancis.com
Taylor & Francis Verlag GmbH, Kaufingerstraße 24, 80331 München, Germany

www.ingramcontent.com/pod-product-compliance
Ingram Content Group UK Ltd.
Pitfield, Milton Keynes, MK11 3LW, UK
UKHW011000180926
475701UK00004B/482
9781138271616